Praise for Andy Caponigro's Work

"Breath master Andy Caponigro offers a full measure of wisdom and insight in *The Miracle of the Breath,* reliably presenting a sheaf of usable and useful techniques that ground, strengthen, and balance, thus enabling us to master fear, to heal, and to develop spiritually. Straightforward, well organized, and lucid, *The Miracle of the Breath* is destined to become the definitive text on breathwork and all its mysterious potencies for Western practitioners."

— Deborah Belle Forman, executive director, Swedenborg Foundation and transformational breath facilitator

"Simple, yet comprehensive in its approach, *The Miracle of the Breath* is a profound work that explores the mystery of breath and its implications for our health and spiritual advancement. Read the book, practice the exercises, and discover for yourself the secret link between mortality and immortality — your breath!

— Russill Paul, author of *The Yoga of Sound: Healing and Enlightenment through the Sacred Practice of Mantra*

"Andy Caponigro's breath work is so basic and powerful, it has the power to completely transform the way we approach health care."

— Joyce Perkins, RN, PhD, psychiatric nurse

The MIRACLE
of the
BREATH

The MIRACLE of the BREATH

Mastering Fear, Healing Illness, and Experiencing the Divine

Andy Caponigro

New World Library
Novato, California

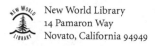
New World Library
14 Pamaron Way
Novato, California 94949

Interior design and typesetting by Tona Pearce Myers
Illustrations on pages 139 and 141 by Yuliya Rotar
Illustrations on pages 30 and 31 by Bill Mifsud

Library of Congress Cataloging-in-Publication Data
Caponigro, Andrew.
   The miracle of the breath : mastering fear, healing illness, and experiencing the divine / by Andy Caponigro.— 1st ed.
      p.   cm.
Includes bibliographical references and index.
ISBN 978-1-57731-478-3 (pbk. : alk. paper)
1. Breathing exercises. 2. Respiration—Religious aspects. 3. Meditation. 4. Healing. 5. Fear. I. Title.
RA782.C28 2005
615.8'36—dc22   2004021301

First printing, January 2005
ISBN 978-1-57731-478-3

New World Library is proud to be a Gold Certified Environmentally Responsible Publisher. Publisher certification awarded by Green Press Initiative.
www.greenpressinitiative.org

10 9 8 7

Dedicated
to

the healing of
the Human Family

May the knowledge of breath contained in this book
bring greater health and inner peace
to everyone who reads it.

May the spiritual knowledge this book offers bring greater
respect and understanding among the people
of all nations and all religious traditions.

CONTENTS

Introduction   xi

How to Use This Book   xv

PART ONE
The Miracle of the Breath

Chapter 1   The Breath of Life   3

Chapter 2   The Science of Breath   15

Chapter 3   Meditation on the Breath   27

Chapter 4   Breathing Blocks and Illness   41

Chapter 5   Breathing-Release Techniques   55

PART TWO
Mastering Fear

Chapter 6   Making Friends with Fear   73

Chapter 7   Grounding and Strengthening Techniques   83

Chapter 8   Breath-Balancing Techniques   97

Chapter 9   The Shield of Detachment   115

Chapter 10   Learning to Trust Your Breath   129

PART THREE
Healing Illness

Chapter 11   The Invisible Man   135
Chapter 12   The Healing Triangle   151
Chapter 13   Healing Respiratory Problems   159
Chapter 14   Fear and Emotional Illness   177
Chapter 15   Fear and Emotional Healing   189
Chapter 16   Pranic Energy Healing   207

PART FOUR
Experiencing the Divine

Chapter 17   The Breath of Creation   221
Chapter 18   Samadhi: The Breathless State   231
Chapter 19   Breath-Retention Techniques   245
Chapter 20   The Gateway to Creation   257
Chapter 21   The Sacredness of the Breath   269
Chapter 22   The Path of the Breath   281

Notes   287
Bibliography   293
Recommended Reading   297
Acknowledgments   301
Index   303
About the Author   315

INTRODUCTION

Thousands of years ago, great Hindu yogis and Chinese sages developed powerful systems of breath control, which they used for mastering fear, healing illness, and attaining enlightenment. These ancient sciences of breath possess remarkable powers because they tap into the Breath of Life — the spiritual life-force that gives our breath its life-sustaining powers.

The spiritual life-force that dwells in our breath is not the same as the physical process of breathing or the air we take into our lungs. Our breath is merely the vehicle through which the life-force manifests out here in the physical world. The Hindus call this life-force *Prana;* the Chinese named it *Chi.* The Hebrews call it the Breath of Life; Christians call it the Holy Spirit.

Because our breath is so intimately linked with the life-force, it controls every mental and physical process that takes place within our being. For example, all experiences of pain and fear are directly controlled by the breath. Eastern martial artists have known this fact for thousands of years. They used this knowledge to develop highly sophisticated systems of breath control for cultivating the virtues of strength, courage, and one-pointedness of mind so essential to being a warrior.

Our breath not only controls all experiences of pain and fear, it also contains some of the most powerful healing energies in the universe. By mastering the forces that dwell in our breath, we can gain some unique and remarkable powers for healing ourselves in body, mind, and spirit. The Eastern scriptures and yogic texts contain numerous references to the healing powers of the breath. However, they provide little practical information on how to develop these skills because the innermost secrets of breath control have traditionally been considered esoteric knowledge to be withheld from the uninitiated.

This book not only reveals those secrets, it also provides an integral system of breathing techniques that will enable you to immediately put this ancient knowledge to work. For example, the basic techniques taught in Parts 1 and 2 of this book are easy to learn and simple to use. Some of the techniques help us feel calm and solid; others help us feel more refreshed and energized; still others help reduce pain and fear and alleviate symptoms of illness. You can begin by practicing these techniques in the privacy of your home. As soon as you've got the hang of them, you can use them with great effectiveness in your daily life while functioning out in the marketplace.

Buddha once said to his son, "Always practice mindfulness of breathing, for when that is maintained it brings great fruits and many blessings." The fruits and blessings you personally gain from working with these techniques will depend mostly on the strength of your commitment and the amount of quality time you spend in making this knowledge your own.

HOW
to
USE THIS BOOK

THE MIRACLE OF THE BREATH is a complete and self-contained instruction manual for learning to master the science of breath. It is also a medical and sociological treatise that introduces some new and very practical concepts about the nature of fear and its critical role in the realms of psychology, religion, and healing.

Part 1, "The Miracle of the Breath," describes the spiritual basis and historical origins of the science of breath. It also provides specific meditation and breathing techniques that will immediately set you on the path to self-healing and spiritual growth.

Part 2, "Mastering Fear," provides some simple techniques for making friends with your fear and using its energies as your ally. These techniques can also be used to heal mental and physical illnesses by cleansing the layers of subconscious fear that are trapped in your mind and body.

Part 3, "Healing Illness," provides a set of advanced techniques that will enable you to use your breath for healing a broad spectrum of physical and emotional disorders, ranging from headaches, respiratory problems, and intestinal difficulties to anxiety attacks, insomnia, and conflicting emotions.

Part 4, "Experiencing the Divine," describes the transitions our consciousness undergoes as we enter the inner dimensions of Spirit. This part of the book also provides special meditation and breathing techniques for cultivating the state of enlightenment and entering into communion with God.

Read this book from beginning to end, as you would any other book. On your first time through, simply read the chapters that describe the breathing techniques without trying to practice them. The object is to treat your practice of breathing techniques as a project separate from reading the book.

For example, as soon as you've read chapter 3 ("Meditation on the Breath"), you can set up a regular practice schedule as described in that chapter and begin working with its meditation techniques on a daily basis. No matter how little or how much you practice each day, continue reading the rest of the book to gain an overview of the entire process involved in learning to master the science of breath.

As soon as you've become reasonably proficient with the

meditation techniques taught in chapter 3, you can begin to work with the breathing techniques described in the subsequent chapters. Each of the technical chapters will not only describe how to practice its techniques, it will also advise you on how and when to include those techniques as part of your daily practice.

Some Helpful Suggestions

- Study the breathing techniques in the same order in which they appear in this book. If you jump ahead of yourself or work in a random fashion, you'll spread your abilities much too thin.

- As you practice, remember that a few techniques mastered well are far more effective than many techniques learned superficially, so never try to hurry your progress by working with more kinds of breathing techniques than you can comfortably assimilate during the course of a single practice session.

Learning a subject by reading a book can never replace the experience of studying under the direct guidance of an accomplished teacher. With this in mind, I've taken special care to present these techniques much as I do in my workshops to make them as easy as possible to learn by yourself.

Note

THE BREATHING TECHNIQUES described in this book are not intended to replace conventional forms of medical treatment.

If you are under the care of a doctor, you should continue to follow your doctor's advice. These techniques can be used to enhance the healing effects of almost any kind of conventional medical treatment. However, they should not be used to replace prescribed medications or as a substitute for any prescribed form of medical treatment without consulting your doctor.

The statements I make about the relationship between breathing blocks and illness are based on thirty years of experience as a teacher and practitioner of breathwork. Since some of my findings do not agree with current medical thinking, I encourage you to seek a balanced perspective on any illness you may have by consulting with your doctor.

PART ONE

THE MIRACLE
of the
BREATH

CHAPTER ONE

THE BREATH
of
LIFE

God breathed the breath of life into man's nostrils,
and man became a living soul.

— GENESIS 2:7 (AV)

LEO TOLSTOY, THE GREAT RUSSIAN AUTHOR, once wrote a story about a beggar who lived in a hut by the side of a road, living off the few coins and scraps of food that travelers put into his begging bowl. When the old man died, the villagers buried him in a pauper's grave and burned his squalid hut to the ground. While raking through the ashes afterward, they struck something hard and metallic just beneath the earthen floor — and dug out an old treasure chest filled with silver, gold, and precious gems. The unfortunate man had struggled with poverty all his life while sitting just a few inches above a splendid fortune.

Like that beggar, most of us are living in a relative state of ignorance and poverty, unaware of incredible treasures that are closer to us than our breath. The key to unlocking these treasures is the Breath of Life — the spiritual life-force that dwells in our breath. By learning the secrets of breath control, we can master fear, heal diseases, and even become one with God.

The Breath of Life is the greatest of natural wonders. Even more, it is the greatest of all miracles. When I speak about the Breath of Life, I'm referring to the spiritual energy that gives our breath its life-sustaining powers. Our breath carries the life-force much like a car carries its driver. People never confuse a car with its driver, but even those who've studied the powers of the breath tend to confuse the physical breath (or the air they breathe) with the life-force that flows within it.

The spiritual life-force is a ray of pure Divine Consciousness that emanates directly from the Godhead — the formless dimension of reality that is the source of all creation. From the point of view of our spiritual self, this Divine ray is our soul's imperishable link with its Creator. From the point of view of our physical self, it is our direct link with the cosmic energies that give birth to the universe.

The Breath behind the Breath

THE HINDU SAGES RECOGNIZED THE DIVINE nature of the life-force thousands of years ago. They called it *Prana*. Since they also used the word *prana* to designate breath, wind, and air, they sometimes referred to the Pranic life-force as "the Breath behind the breath" to distinguish it from the physical process of breathing or the air we breathe into our lungs.

Because our breath is so closely linked with the life-force, the ancient Hindu masters called the human soul the *anu*, which means "the one who breathes." They measured the span of a person's life, not in terms of how many years they live, but in terms of the number of breaths they take from the moment they're born until the moment they die. They had observed that when we're born our first action is to breathe in — and that when we die our last action is to breathe out. Did you know that everyone dies on the out-breath?

Because our breath is so intimately linked with the pranic life-force, the Hindu masters teach that God is closer to us than our very own breath. Kabir, one of India's great poet-saints, wrote this humorous and down-to-earth verse to remind his followers that, if they want to know where God is, they needn't look any farther than their breath:

> *Are you looking for me? I am in the next seat.*
> *My shoulder is against yours.*
> *You will not find me in Indian shrine rooms,*
> *not in synagogues, not cathedrals,*
> *not in masses, nor sacred songs.*
> *Not in legs winding around your own neck,*
> *nor in eating nothing but vegetables.*
> *When you really look for me, you will see me instantly.*
> *You will find me in the tiniest house of time.*
> *Kabir says: "Student, tell me, what is God?"*
> *He is the Breath inside the breath.*[1]

In the Hindu tradition, God, Prana, and Divine Consciousness are considered to be one and the same. This is why the Hindu sages also call Prana "the Breath of God." They go on to say that God creates the universe with his own breath because the pranic life-force (or Breath of God) is the same as Divine Consciousness in its creative (or moving) aspect.

The Taoist sages of ancient China also recognized the Divine nature of the spiritual life-force that dwells in the breath. They called it *Chi*. One Taoist text, entitled *The Utmost Secrets of the Methods of Breathing*, tells us that "[Chi] is the functioning of the Spirits."[2] The Chinese considered this Divine energy to be so indispensable to life that their pictographic symbol for Chi is the same as that for rice — the staff of life in China. To avoid confusing Chi with the physical breath, the Chinese masters sometimes called it the "inner breath" that motivates the "outer breath." This is such a vitally important distinction that one Taoist master warned his disciples:

> People confuse the external breath with the internal breath. Those who do breathing exercises ought to be careful... it is atrocious to mistake one breath for the other.[3]

The Taoists masters rarely use the concept of God to explain the creation of the universe. Nevertheless, like their Hindu counterparts, they teach that the universe is created by a Divine cosmic breath. For example, in the *Tao Te Ching* the Chinese sage Lao Tzu says: "Tao is the breath that never dies. It is the mother of all creation."[4]

The Spirit of Life

THE INTIMATE BOND THAT EXISTS between the spirit of life and the physical breath was also recognized by the ancient Greeks and Romans. For example, the Greeks called the life-force *Pneuma*. *Pneuma* has the same range of meanings as *prana*, and more. It not only refers to breath, air, wind, and the spiritual life-force, it also means "spirit" and "soul." However, its essential meaning was the concept of "Spirit in union with breath." *Pneuma* is the root of many modern-day English words, such as *pneumonia* and *pneumatic,* which refer to the physical breath or the compression of air. These days, however, we've lost track of the fact that the ancient word *pneuma* primarily referred to the mystical union of spirit, soul, and breath.

The Romans were also aware of the direct connection between spirit, soul, and breath. For example, the Latin word *spiritus* not only has the same range of meanings as *pneuma* (breath, wind, spirit, soul, and life-force), it also means "God within the breath." The Romans paid tribute to the link between spirit and breath by coining the Latin word *respire,* which means "to breathe."

Respire is composed of the prefix *re-* (which means "return") and the root *spiritus* (which means "spirit"). This remarkable word literally describes how the spirit of life leaves our body — and then returns — with every cycle of breathing. Our English word *respiration* is derived from the Latin *respire.* Here too, however, we've lost the essential meaning of the original Latin word. We've forgotten about the *spirit* in *respiration,* and we merely use this word in a mechanical sense to designate the movement of air in and out of our lungs.

The Latin verb *expire* is another ancient word that describes the intimate bond between the physical breath and the life-force. *Expire* is composed of the prefix *ex-* (which means "out of") and the root *spiritus* (or "spirit"). It not only means "to breathe out," it also means "to die." Literally translated, *expire* means "the exiting of the spirit." This is a perfect description of what happens at the moment of death, when the spiritual life-force leaves a person's body along with the last out-breath.

Have you ever wondered why people say, "God bless you!" when someone sneezes? This custom dates back to medieval times, when people believed that the force of a sneeze temporarily separated the breath (and the spirit of life) from a person's body. Our ancestors would quickly bless the sneezer to prevent evil spirits from entering and possessing the vacated body until the owner's spirit (or soul) returned on the next in-breath.

The link between breath and spirit is recognized in the languages of ancient and modern cultures throughout the world. In Hawaii, for example, the word *Ha* means both "God" and "breath." Everyone has heard the traditional Hawaiian greeting *"aloha,"* which means "may God be with you." However, few people are familiar with the rest of the Hawaiian greeting ritual: a hug and a few gentle breaths on the cheek of the other person, meaning "I honor the spirit of God within you."

Nowadays, traditional blessings such as these are considered to be quaintly superstitious customs, but the people of ancient cultures took the term *Breath of Life* in its most literal sense. To this day, Brahmin priests in India chant divine mantras and perform sacred fire rituals to install the Breath of Life (or Prana) into newly made statues of saints or gods. To confirm the success of their devotions, they hold a mirror close to the statue's nose. When the mirror fogs up, they know that the spirit of the sacred personage has taken up residence within the statue.

The ancient Egyptians held strikingly similar beliefs about the link between spirit and breath. Whenever they conquered a new country, they would systematically break the nose off the statues of all the previous gods and rulers. This wasn't done merely to dishonor their enemies; their intention was to kill the statue's spirit so that the conquered gods could never rise from defeat to challenge them again. The way the ancient Egyptians figured it, the best way to kill any spirit was to stop it from breathing once and for all!

The Breath of the God of Israel

THE LINK BETWEEN SPIRIT AND BREATH is mentioned throughout the Bible, yet most modern-day Jews and Christians are unaware of this relationship. For example, the ancient Hebrew word *ruah* not only meant "spirit," "breath," and "wind"; it was also used in essentially the same ways as the Greeks, Hindus, and Romans used the words *pneuma, prana,* and *spiritus*. The ancient Hebrew scribes often linked the word *ruah* with *Yahweh* (the name of the God of Israel). Thus, the term *ruah Yahweh,* which appears often in the Old Testament, can be translated to mean "the spirit of God," "the breath of God," or "the wind of God" (God's breath manifested as wind).

The meaning of many biblical passages can be significantly altered by choosing one meaning of *ruah Yahweh* over another. For example, one translation of the second verse in Genesis says:

In the beginning... the earth was without form and void, and darkness was upon the face of the deep. And the spirit of God moved upon the face of the waters.[5]

According to a different translation, "a mighty wind" swept over the waters. At first sight, these translations appear to be contradictory. But they're actually saying the same thing, because "the mighty wind" and "the spirit of God" are simply different names for ruah Yahweh — the breath of Almighty God. Notice, too, how closely this biblical passage resembles the Hindu teaching that says, "God created the universe with his own breath."

Ruah Yahweh is also mentioned in relation to the creation of Adam, the first man. Genesis 2:7 (AV) says: "God breathed the breath of life into man's nostrils, and man became a living soul." In this passage, *ruah Yahweh* is translated as "the breath of life" rather than "the breath of God." The image of God infusing his spirit into man's body by way of the breath is more than a poetic metaphor; it's a physical matter of fact.

During the Israelites' flight from Egypt, Moses invoked the help of ruah Yahweh as the wind of God to part the waters of the Red Sea:

> *Then Moses stretched his hand out over the sea, and the Lord swept the sea with a strong east wind throughout the night and turned sea into dry land.*[6]

Once his people had safely crossed to the other side, Moses commanded God's wind to change direction, whereupon the waters returned to normal and drowned the Egyptian army. After their deliverance, the Israelites sang these words of praise to Yahweh:

> *At the breath of your anger, the waters piled up and stood like a mound in the midst of the sea. The enemy boasted, "I will pursue and overtake them," [but] when your wind blew, the sea covered them.*[7]

The Old Testament contains many more references to ruah Yahweh, which are variously translated to mean "God's spirit," "God's wind," or "God's breath." In the second Book of Kings, for example, God's breath appears as the great whirlwind that carries Elijah up to heaven in a flaming chariot. Later, in the Book of Job, the prophet Elisha says:

> *The spirit of God hath made me, and the breath of the Almighty hath given me life.*[8]

The Breath in the New Testament

IN THE NEW TESTAMENT, all references to God's spirit, breath, or wind appear as the word *pneuma*, instead of *ruah*, because the Gospels were originally written in Greek. In John 3:8 (AV), for example, Jesus appears to be speaking in riddles when he says to the bewildered Nicodemus:

> *The wind [pneuma] blows where it wills, and you can hear the sound it makes, but you do not know where it comes from or where it goes. So it is with everyone who is born of spirit [pneuma].*

The early Christian fathers also used the term *Hagios Pneuma*, which means "Holy Spirit" or "Holy Ghost" in Greek. The Holy Ghost's link with the physical breath is mentioned in the passage from Luke that recounts the poignant moment in which Jesus takes his last earthly breath and expires on the cross:

> *And Jesus said, "Father, into Thy hands I commend my spirit," and having said thus, he gave up the [holy] ghost.*[9]

When the Roman Catholic Church came into dominance hundreds of years after Jesus died on the cross, the Greek term *Hagios Pneuma* was replaced by *Spiritus Sanctus,* which means "Holy Spirit" in Latin. The most unmistakable reference to the Holy Spirit's link with the breath is found in John's description of the events following the Resurrection, when Jesus mysteriously appears in a locked room where the apostles are hiding:

> Jesus said to them, "Peace be with you. As my father has sent me, so I send you." And when he said this, he breathed upon them and said, "Receive ye the Holy Spirit. Whose sins ye forgive are forgiven them."[10]

Was Jesus' act of breathing upon the apostles merely a symbolic gesture? In 553 A.D., the members of the Second Council of Constantinople decreed that Jesus had literally used his breath to transmit the powers of the Holy Spirit directly into the apostles. They compared this action to the moment in which God breathed the breath of life into Adam's nostrils (Genesis 2:7 AV).

How Did We Ever Lose Track?

TODAY'S WESTERN LANGUAGES CONTAIN few words that honor the divine connection between the spirit of God and our physical breath. Even worse, we've stripped ancient root words, such as *pneuma* and *respire,* of their spiritual resonance and retained only their designations of material things, such as air, breath, and the physical process of breathing. To the best of my knowledge, the French philosopher Henri Bergson is the only modern Western thinker who tried to explain the miracle of life by postulating the existence of a spiritual force, which he called the *elan vital,* or "vital spirit." *Elan vital* is the only modern Western term that embodies the same concept of "spirit in breath" as do the ancient words *prana, chi, pneuma, ruah,* and *spiritus.*

Hebrew scholars and Christian theologians still use the words *ruah* and *pneuma* in their original sense of "spirit" and "soul." Unlike the ancient Hebrews and early Christian fathers, however, today's theologians and scholars have completely forgotten that the Holy Spirit literally dwells in our breath. At the end of one of my seminars, a senior Catholic priest came over to tell me how impressed he was by what I'd said about the link between the Holy Spirit and our physical breath. However, there was one thing he couldn't quite understand: "How did we ever lose track of something so obvious and important?"

Western theologians aren't the only ones who've lost track. Most Western scientists and philosophers have also forgotten about the vital link between spirit and breath. This is one of the most unfortunate blind spots in Western thinking, because we've been completely overlooking a spiritual Rosetta stone that can help us decipher some of the deepest mysteries of human existence and provide us with a master key for unlocking the secrets of creation. The Eastern masters discovered this key thousands of years ago and used it to develop powerful systems of breath control for mastering fear, healing illness, and attaining the state of enlightenment.

Buddha is the most famous Eastern master who became enlightened by meditating on his breathing and tracing the spiritual life-force back to its source. Meditation on the breath was the chief spiritual discipline he practiced to attain his state of enlightenment. It was also the chief spiritual practice he later passed on to his followers. Two weeks before he died, the Buddha summoned his monks to a great gathering and informed them that he would soon be leaving their midst. If they had any last questions to ask him, this was the time to do it.

One of the youngest monks respectfully raised his hand for permission to speak:

"Please tell me, Master, what have you gained from meditating on your breath for all these years?"

Buddha replied, "I have gained nothing from meditating on my breath."

Upon hearing these words, many of the monks at the assembly became visibly upset. One of the senior monks rose to his feet and protested:

"But Master! If you have gained nothing from meditating on your breath, why have you been telling me to practice breath-meditation these past twenty-five years?"

The Buddha replied: "What I said is true. I have gained nothing from meditating on my breath; but let me tell you what I have lost. I have lost my fear of sickness, I have lost my fear of old age, and I have lost my fear of death."

If you earnestly work with the meditation and breathing techniques described in the following chapters, you will have plenty of opportunities to experience the truth of the Buddha's words for yourself.

CHAPTER TWO

THE SCIENCE
of
BREATH

Master of breath is master of life.

— HINDU APHORISM

THOUSANDS OF YEARS AGO, the Eastern masters used the intimate link between the breath and the spiritual life-force to develop powerful systems of breath control. These sciences of breath were used to cultivate a wide range of extraordinary powers, from healing illnesses and performing miracles to entering into communion with God. The Hindu masters called their system "Prana Yoga," which in Sanskrit means "the path of the breath." The Taoist masters of China gave their science of breath several names, including Primordial Breathing, Original

Breathing, and Embryonic Breathing. Hundreds of years after Buddha died, the Tibetan Buddhists developed an exceptionally powerful system of breath control known as *Dumo* — a cross-cultural offspring of the earlier systems developed by the Hindu, Buddhist, and Taoist masters.

Over the centuries, humans worldwide have developed countless systems of breath control to harness the breath's remarkable powers. For example, the Eastern martial artists discovered that all experiences of pain and fear are directly controlled by the breath. They used this knowledge to develop special systems of breath control for cultivating extraordinary degrees of strength, courage, and calmness of mind. Although there are no such formal systems here in the West, many of our finest athletes — particularly runners, swimmers, and boxers — have intuitively developed their own special ways to control their breath and tap its amazing powers.

The state of our physical, mental, and spiritual health completely depends on the health of our breath. In other words, whatever is happening with our breathing is also happening at all other levels of our being because the breath controls every mental, physical, and spiritual process that takes place within our system. When our breathing is calm and peaceful, our mind and body are peaceful, too. When our breathing is agitated or disturbed for any reason, our mind and body feel correspondingly scattered and disturbed. These relationships are so irrevocably fixed in nature that breath, mind, and body can coexist in no other way.

Whenever we hold our breath to block feelings of pain or fear, we unwittingly create blocks in our breathing that impede the movements of the life-force as it flows through our system.

With time, the blocks in our breathing become deep-rooted habits that erode our feelings of wholeness and breed a host of mental and physical problems.

The following quotes, taken from the writings of several Taoist masters, provide an excellent thumbnail sketch of how the health of our body, mind, and spirit is inseparably linked with the health of our breath:

If man's breath is prosperous, then the body is prosperous... man's bodily decline is always due to the decline of the breath.... If the breath is congested or isolated it leads to illness. When man's breath is exhausted, then the body is destroyed.[1]

Breath is ruled by the mind. If the mind is unruly, then the breath is unruly. If the mind is proper, then the breath is proper.[2]

If one refines the breath and the mind at the same time... one's spirits and emotions will not be disturbed and one will be increasingly clear and peaceful.[3]

The breath is the mother of the soul. Soul and breath follow each other just as form and shadow do.[4]

When the breath is smooth and calm, one can look internally at the spiritual palaces.[5]

If the breath is interrupted, the soul gives up. If the soul is extinguished then the body dies.[6]

The Five Stages of Perfecting the Breath

EVER SINCE EARLY CHILDHOOD, most people have interfered with the flow of their breath to block their feelings of pain and fear. As a result, most adults have developed breathing patterns that are relatively weak and imbalanced. It doesn't matter why we wish to practice breathing techniques — to master our fear, heal ourselves, or experience Divine communion — the first and most important task is to improve the vigor, strength, and flow of our breath by bringing its movements into healthier states of balance.

To develop its highest potentials, our breath must undergo five stages of development, which I call "the five stages of perfecting the breath." Each stage of development requires special techniques for improving our patterns of breathing in the ways described below. As you read the following descriptions, bear in mind that it is virtually impossible to understand the effects each technique produces until you've practiced them and experienced their results. Also note that I have indicated the chapter in which you will learn more about each stage.

1. **Meditation on the Breath** (chapter 3)

   Meditation on the breath is the first and most important technique to learn when studying any system of breath control. Meditation quiets the mind and guides it into a fearless, calm, detached state known as "witness consciousness" (see chapter 21). The effectiveness of all other breathing techniques ultimately depends on the depth and quality of our meditations because meditation is the only state in which we can perceive the blocks in our breathing and consciously help them change.

It is also the only state in which we can access the healing energies of prana and direct them to specific parts of our mind and body that are most in need of help.

2. **Breathing-Release Techniques** (chapter 5)

Once we've learned how to meditate, the next step is to move our breath out of its habitual ruts by working with breathing-release techniques. Releasing techniques expand and invigorate the flow of our breath by dispersing the fear-ridden blocks in our breathing. As our breath begins moving more freely, the increased flow of prana produces considerable amounts of spontaneous healing throughout our mind and body.

3. **Grounding and Strengthening Techniques** (chapter 7)

Grounding and strengthening techniques deepen and strengthen the flow of our breath. As their names imply, they help us to feel solid and grounded in both our mind and body. The deeper and stronger our breathing becomes, the stronger our healing abilities also become.

Grounding and strengthening techniques (called "solidifying" techniques by some of the Taoist masters) enable us to stay remarkably calm and steady during times of crisis. This class of techniques is often used by Eastern warriors and martial artists to cultivate extraordinary degrees of stamina, strength, and courage.

4. **Breath-Balancing Techniques** (chapter 8)

Once we've learned to expand and deepen the flow of our breath, the next step is to improve the balance of tensions between our in- and out-breaths. All feelings of anxiety and self-conflict are created by throwing the tensions of our in- and out-breaths out of synch with each other. Breath-balancing techniques help improve our breathing patterns by balancing the tensions of our in- and out-breaths. Furthermore, as our in- and out-breaths become more evenly matched, our feelings of anxiety, self-conflict, and self-doubt spontaneously begin to fade and disappear.

5. **Breath-Retention Techniques** (chapter 19)

Once our breathing patterns have become freer, stronger, and more evenly balanced, we're ready to work with retention techniques. Retention techniques enable us to suspend the movements of our breath for extended periods of time. Eastern yogis and martial artists sometimes use this class of techniques for accumulating great inner reserves of spiritual strength and power. The main purpose of retention techniques, however, is to prepare our mind and our breath for entering the state of samadhi — the deepest level of meditative consciousness our mind can possibly enter.

Samadhi is the highest goal of all spiritual practices, for it is from within this state that our most profound experiences of Divine communion and spiritual liberation take place. The Hindus call it "the breathless state" because when we enter into samadhi our breath completely stops moving for minutes (even hours) at a time without harm to our body. While we're in this state, tremendous spontaneous healing takes place throughout our mind and body because our consciousness has merged with the healing energies of Prana in their purest and most powerful form. (For more on samadhi, see chapter 18.)

Fully Developed Sciences of Breath

A FULLY DEVELOPED SYSTEM OF BREATH CONTROL includes all five kinds of techniques, each practiced at appropriate times and in mutually enhancing ways. Of the countless systems of breath control human beings have ever created, only a handful meet these criteria. The sacred breath traditions of India, China, and Tibet are perhaps the finest examples of fully developed sciences of breath. These ancient systems of breath control were developed and gradually refined over thousands of years by successive generations of Eastern sages and masters.

Over the past forty years, increasing numbers of Westerners have also begun working with various kinds of breathing techniques that reduce pain and stress, promote mental and physical healing, and trigger altered states of consciousness. In comparison to the Eastern systems of breath control, however, most of the recently developed systems are partial and incomplete.

Working with breathing techniques is somewhat like playing the game of golf. To play a round of eighteen holes, we need a full set of clubs to deal with the ever-changing lie of the ball. A fully developed system of breath control similarly provides us with the full range of techniques we'll need to guide our breath through its various stages of healing and transformation. In comparison, working with an incomplete system of breathing techniques is somewhat like playing a game of miniature golf or hitting a bucket of balls at a driving range. Although both are related to the game of golf, neither can be compared with playing on an eighteen-hole golf course using a full set of clubs.

In some cases, working with an incomplete set of breathing techniques can produce uncomfortable and even dangerous physical and emotional side effects. For example, some of the newer systems of breath control rely heavily on the use of releasing techniques to disperse the blocks in a person's breathing, but they provide no grounding, strengthening, or balancing techniques to counteract the dangers of "over-releasing."

The main function of releasing techniques is to disperse the fear-ridden blocks in our breathing. However, our breath can only do so much "letting go" during a given period of time. If we continually work with releasing techniques without counterbalancing their dispersive effects by working with grounding, strengthening, and balancing techniques, we run the risk of incurring classic symptoms of over-release, such as hyperventilation, dizziness, shortness of breath, panicky feelings, muscle spasms, and arrhythmia (irregular heartbeat).

Most of the time, these unpleasant side effects will gradually subside on their own after the practices are discontinued — but this isn't always the case. Over the years, I've helped several people who were suffering from chronic feelings of anxiety, which they incurred by working with lopsided systems of breath control. One woman did so much over-releasing in a "new age" breathing workshop that she became emotionally unstable and was unable to work for nearly two years. At one of my "Miracle of the Breath" healing retreats, she learned how to ground herself and bring her anxiety under control by restabilizing her breathing patterns. Within a few weeks, she was able to return to work.

When working with any system of breath control, always

remember that breathing techniques release powerful forces that profoundly affect the mind and the body. Although most techniques are relatively safe and easy to use, they should always be practiced in meditation, and with sensitivity and moderation to ensure that you neither overtax your system nor create debilitating side effects that will put your health at risk. This advice holds doubly true when it comes to working with intense and forceful breathing techniques, such as the ancient Hindu practices of *bastrikha* and *kapalabhati*. The prolonged, insensitive, or lopsided practice of such forceful techniques can cause feelings of panic and stress, even in highly disciplined yogis.

The breathing techniques set forth in this book constitute a fully developed and well-balanced system of breath control. They have been thoroughly tested in workshops and private sessions for at least twenty-five years and have proven to be safe and effective tools for spiritual growth and self-healing for thousands of people. As long as you follow the instructions provided with each technique, there will be no danger of creating unpleasant or harmful side effects.

Healing with the Breath

BREATHING TECHNIQUES CAN BE USED for almost as many different purposes as there are people who want to use them. This book focuses on using the breath's powers to master fear, heal illness, and experience the Divine within. These three goals are essentially one and the same because each is inseparably linked with how well (or how badly) we handle our feelings of fear.

Over the years, I've studied as many of the ancient scriptures and Eastern texts on healing with the breath as I could find translated into English. Most of these writings affirm the healing powers contained in the breath. However, they provide little practical information on how to actually develop these skills because healing with the breath has traditionally been considered a sacred and esoteric kind of knowledge to be withheld from the uninitiated. As one Taoist master cautioned his readers:

Those who by chance get this secret must be careful not to teach or demonstrate it lightly.7

I've been able to reconstruct many of the teachings set down by the ancient masters, even some that were veiled in symbolism and metaphor. However, most of the techniques I personally use and teach are based on what I've learned by studying my own breath and "listening" to what it tells me is needed. After years of studying, practicing, and teaching these skills, I've found that healing with the breath is an inborn talent in everyone. It is also one of the simplest, most natural and powerful healing modalities ever developed by human beings. With dedicated practice and reliable guidelines to follow, almost anyone can tap the powerful gifts of healing that lie dormant within the breath.

THE BASIC AND ADVANCED TECHNIQUES

The healing techniques described in this book fall into two groups. The first includes the basic techniques taught in chapters 3, 5, 7, and 8. The second group includes the advanced healing techniques taught in Part 3.

The basic techniques are used to improve the health of our breath by strengthening and balancing its movements. In the process, they trigger various kinds of spontaneous healing throughout our mind and body. The advanced techniques

enable us to heal or alleviate more difficult, deep-rooted problems by consciously directing healing prana to specific parts of
our mind and body that are most in need of help.

A Few Helpful Suggestions

- When you're ready to learn the basic techniques, be
  sure to study them in the order in which they appear
  in this book. If you jump too far ahead of yourself or
  try to skip over certain techniques, you'll spread
  your abilities too thin.

- Every advanced technique in this book is either a
  variation of one of the basic techniques or a combination of two or more basic techniques. So don't try
  to work with the advanced techniques until you've
  mastered the basic techniques taught in chapters 3,
  5, 7, and 8.

- You don't have to learn every technique in this book
  in order to use your breath for healing yourself. You
  may learn as many or as few techniques as you wish.
  It all depends on what you'd like to accomplish.

- As you build your repertoire, remember that a few
  basic techniques well mastered are far more effective
  and powerful than many techniques superficially
  learned.

- To speed up the learning process, you can send for
  some of the CDs and audiotapes I've produced to
  augment the teaching materials contained in this
  book. Information about purchasing tapes or at-
  tending one of my workshops can be found at my
  website, www.miracleofthebreath.com.

As you work to master the techniques described in the following chapters, bear in mind that full and perfect mastery of the breath is a long-term process that takes many years to complete, so make it a special point to never hurry your progress. An ancient Chinese proverb says, "A thousand-mile journey begins with the first step." In this case, the first step you'll take on your journey toward self-healing and self-mastery is to learn how to meditate on your breath.

CHAPTER THREE

MEDITATION
on the
BREATH

Meditation is the quieting of the mind.

— SWAMI MUKTANANDA

MEDITATION IS ONE OF THE MOST ANCIENT and powerful healing modalities ever developed by human beings. The word *meditation* comes from the Latin words *mederi* (which means "to heal" or "to look after") and *medicus* (which means "healer"). This is no mere coincidence; meditation quiets our mind and brings our consciousness into contact with the most powerful healing energies in the universe. Here in the West, medical researchers have repeatedly confirmed ancient claims about the healing powers of meditation. These days, increasing numbers of therapists and mainstream doctors prescribe various meditation techniques for a broad spectrum of problems, ranging from headaches, chronic pain, and cardiac disorders to anxiety, insomnia, and depression.

Just what is meditation? A great twentieth-century master of meditation named Swami Muktananda used to define meditation as "the quieting of the mind." At the very least, meditation can help us feel more calm, rested, and reenergized. At best, it can be used as a path for attaining enlightenment or for entering into communion with God.

There are hundreds of valid techniques that can guide our mind into the realms of meditative consciousness. Some involve the repetition of divine names or sacred sounds called "mantras." Others employ the technique of visualizing in our mind's eye such things as colors, geometric shapes, or peaceful scenes from nature. Still others involve focusing our attention on an external object, such as a candle flame or an image of one's chosen deity.

It doesn't matter which techniques a person might prefer, because they all bring us into the same state of meditative consciousness. This is something like saying that sleep is sleep, no matter how we manage to enter that state. Some people might drink a cup of warm tea; others might count sheep or read until their eyes get tired. In the end, however, everyone enters the same state of sleeping consciousness.

Of the many techniques that can quiet our mind and bring us into the meditative state of consciousness, meditation on the breath is one of the simplest, most ancient, and most powerful of all. This is the form of meditation we'll be using throughout this book.

Finding a Comfortable Posture

BEFORE YOU BEGIN TO MEDITATE, it's important to find a comfortable and well-supported posture to sit in. Some people like to sit on the floor with their legs crossed; others prefer to sit in a chair. Either position is fine. No matter which posture you prefer, it is important to sit with your back reasonably straight. If you slump or sit carelessly, the flow of your breath — and therefore the flow of prana — will be greatly reduced.

To get a firsthand experience of why sitting up straight is so important, take a few moments right now to try this simple exercise:

1. Sit in your chair with your spine reasonably erect, and become aware of your breathing. As you inhale and exhale, notice the volume of air that enters and leaves your lungs.

2. Next, slump over then notice the change in the volume of air that enters and leaves your lungs.

As you can see, whenever you slump, the "size" of your breath becomes drastically reduced. So whenever you sit to meditate, sit up as straight as you can without forcing or straining to keep your spine erect. If you make your body too rigid or tense, it will interfere with your ability to meditate.

If you choose to meditate sitting on the floor, use a firm pillow or a folded blanket to support your buttocks. This will raise your hips above your knees and make it easier to keep your spine erect (see Figure 3.1). If you prefer to sit on a chair, choose one with a perfectly straight back and a seat that is parallel to the floor. If the back of the chair is slanted, place a pillow or a

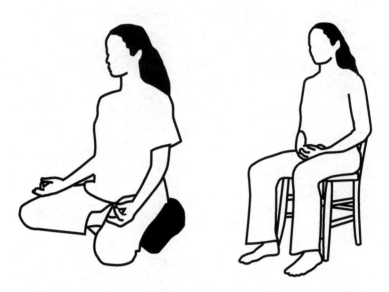

Figure 3.1: Two seated positions for exercises

folded blanket between yourself and the back of the chair to help keep your spine erect.

Now set this book aside for a few minutes and experiment with finding a comfortable posture that enables you to sit with your back reasonably straight, without effort or strain.

The Position of Your Hands

The position in which we hold our hands also affects the flow of our breath and the amount of prana that moves through our

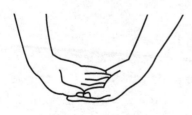

Figure 3.2: Concentration pose

system. My favorite hand position is known as the "concentration pose": rest both hands in your lap, one hand nestled inside the other, with the tips of your thumbs touching (as shown in Figure

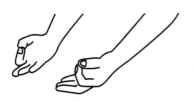

Figure 3.3: Chin mudra

3.2). Statues and paintings of Buddha usually depict him meditating with his hands in this position.

Another option is the *chin mudra* (a Sanskrit term unrelated to the chin on your face). This is done by touching the tips of your thumbs to the tips of your index fingers, then resting your hands on your thighs (as shown in Figure 3.3). Your palms may face up toward the ceiling or down toward your thighs, whichever feels most comfortable.

MEDITATION ON THE BREATH

THE FOLLOWING INSTRUCTIONS WILL TEACH you how to meditate on your breath. Read them two or three times to fix their message in your mind, then set this book aside and meditate on your breath for ten or fifteen minutes without interruption.

1. Sit in a comfortable posture, then close your eyes and focus your mind on your breathing in any way that feels easy. For example, you might notice your chest rising and falling as the air enters and leaves your body, or you might feel the cool air coming in and the warm air going out.

2. It really doesn't matter how you keep track of your breathing. Just follow its movements as closely and trustingly as a baby duck follows its mother. Feel the air come into your body; feel the air going out.

3. No matter what the state of your breathing, don't try to change its movement. If your breathing seems too

shallow, slow, or erratic, don't try to breathe more deeply or control your breath in any way. You'll learn how to correct these and other problems later on. For the moment, give your mind a much-needed vacation. Just keep watching your breath and let it do whatever it pleases.

4. Don't consciously try to calm your mind or relax your body. Just keep watching your breath; let the meditative process do all the work of helping your system relax. As your mind becomes absorbed in your breathing, accumulated layers of tension and stress will spontaneously begin to "lift" from your system. Your body will slowly begin to relax and your mind will gradually become more peaceful.

5. The spiritual life-force that dwells in your breath is infinitely wise. It continually nurtures you and breathes for you twenty-four hours a day, with no conscious effort on your part. So the more absorbed your mind becomes in the movements of your breath, the easier it will be for the spirit of life to take care of you.

6. If your mind sometimes wanders off to another subject and you forget to watch your breath, don't worry. It's the mind's nature to wander, so you haven't done anything wrong. As soon as you realize that your mind has been wandering, just bring it back to watching your breath.

7. When you're ready to end the session, open your eyes very gradually and gently to avoid disturbing your state. When you finally stand up and begin to

move around the room, hold on to that state for as long as you can. Move slowly and gracefully in accordance with your newfound feelings of peace.

What to Watch For

Most people find meditation to be an easy and pleasant experience right from the start. By the end of their first session, they usually feel more calm, clear, and refreshed. Some beginners even find that long-standing problems, such as chronic headaches or feelings of pain, improve or completely clear up.

If you don't notice any immediate or dramatic changes when you first begin to meditate, that doesn't mean you're doing something wrong. It usually takes five to ten minutes before even experienced meditators begin to experience significant changes in their mental and physical tensions. As long as you keep your mind focused on your breathing, you can be sure that the meditative process is working, even if you're not aware of it.

In later chapters, you'll be learning how to access the healing energies contained in your breath and guide them to specific parts of your mind and body for healing. During these early stages, however, just stay in touch with your breathing and let the meditative process do the work of relaxing any symptoms of tension or stress you may feel in your mind or body.

Meditative Consciousness

MEDITATION MIGHT SEEM TO BE A MYSTERIOUS PROCESS when you're first learning to do it. However, once you discover that the meditative state of consciousness is closely related to the sleeping state, much of the mystery disappears. For example, everyone is familiar with the experience of sleeping lightly versus being deeply asleep. When our state of sleep is shallow, the slightest sound can wake us up. When we're deeply asleep, however, even the siren of a passing fire engine won't disturb our sleep. The same things are true for meditation. When our meditative state is relatively shallow, distracting influences such as sounds in the outside world or feelings of discomfort in our body can easily interfere with our ability to meditate. The deeper our meditation becomes, however, the easier it is to stay in the meditative state despite distracting influences.

At the deepest level of meditative consciousness (which is called "samadhi"), our attention is turned so completely inward that distractions in the outside world can't reach our mind at all. However, meditators rarely enter the state of samadhi before gaining a certain amount of experience and accumulating considerable reserves of meditative energy by practicing on a regular basis. (See "The Four Stages of Samadhi" in chapter 18.)

Moving beyond Distractions

In my workshops, I teach a simple technique for moving beyond the most common distractions that interfere with meditation. I call this technique "staying balanced in your canoe." When you're sitting in a canoe, the most important thing to remember is to always keep your balance. For example, you might want to reach for a sandwich, cast for a fish, or lean over the side to pick a water lily. But whatever you want to do, you must first and foremost stay balanced in your canoe to keep it from tipping over. Learning to meditate on your breath is very much like learning to keep your balance when sitting in a canoe.

Whenever you sit to meditate, think of your mind as a

person and your breath as a canoe. No matter what kinds of thoughts or feelings show up in your mind or body, always remember to stay balanced in your canoe. This means that, no matter what impressions enter your mind, always keep watching your breath. If you keep your mind focused on your breathing, most unwanted thoughts and feelings will fade away by themselves.

Learning how to stay balanced in your canoe will strengthen your meditative skills and provide a solid foundation for working with the breathing techniques described in subsequent chapters. In Part 3 of this book, you'll learn how to send healing prana to painful or distressed areas of your mind and body. However, your ability to target specific disturbances and send them "booster shots" of healing prana will depend on how well you've learned to stay balanced in your canoe, meaning how well you've learned to keep watching your breath no matter what kinds of distractions show up in your mind or body.

The following instructions will help you overcome distracting thoughts and feelings by staying balanced in your canoe. Read the instructions two or three times to fix them in your mind, then "get into your canoe" and spend the next fifteen minutes meditating on your breath.

1. Sit in a comfortable posture, then close your eyes and begin to meditate on your breath. As you meditate, if your mind becomes filled with distracting thoughts, don't let them come between you and your breath. Just stay balanced in your canoe — which means, no matter what kinds of thoughts might enter your mind, don't let them distract you from staying in touch with your breath.

2. Don't "talk back" to your thoughts, and don't try to force them out of your mind. The more attention you give them, the stronger they'll become. If you keep watching your breath, even the most nagging and persistent thoughts will eventually lose their strength and fade away.

3. The same is true for most feelings of discomfort that show up in your body. If you stay balanced in your canoe — which means, if you keep watching your breath and learn to ignore the symptoms of discomfort — most of these feelings will tend to improve or disappear on their own.

4. This isn't an exercise in "yogic self-denial," so it's perfectly fine to scratch an itch or to readjust your posture — but only if you really need to. You'll soon discover that most feelings of discomfort will resolve themselves simply because you're meditating on your breath. The harder you work to stay with your breath despite distracting thoughts or feelings, the deeper your meditation will become and the stronger your feelings of peace will be.

5. When you're ready to end the session, carefully hold on to your peaceful feelings so as not to lose them. As you return to the surface of your consciousness, think of yourself as a deep-sea diver who's found a sunken treasure chest; the peace we find in meditation is the most precious stuff in the world. When you begin to move about the room again, move slowly and gracefully in accordance with your new-found feelings of peace.

SETTING UP A PRACTICE SCHEDULE

NOW THAT YOU'VE LEARNED how to meditate on your breath, the next step is to deepen and strengthen your meditative abilities by practicing on a regular basis. I recommend that most people begin by practicing thirty to forty-five minutes a day, eventually building up to a full hour. Generally speaking, the longer you meditate without interruption, the deeper your state will become and the more prana will flow through your system. For example, one sitting of forty consecutive minutes will usually produce more transformation and healing than several brief sittings that add up to the same amount of time.

However, if you find it difficult to meditate for forty consecutive minutes, you can meditate for several shorter periods of time. The healing effects of these shorter sittings won't usually be quite as powerful as the longer ones, but they're still wonderfully beneficial and helpful. These days, many people lead such busy lives that it's difficult for them to set aside a large block of time for meditation. If this is the story of your life, too, you'll find the following suggestions very helpful for making the best use of your time:

- One of the best times to meditate is immediately after waking up. So start your day by meditating for fifteen or twenty minutes before you eat breakfast and go off to work. You might have to wake up fifteen minutes earlier to do this, but it will be worth the effort. You'll be surprised at how much sharper and clearer your mind will be for the rest of the day.

- Take brief meditation breaks throughout the day. Meditation is so good for reducing anxiety and stress that even a two- or three-minute meditation break can effectively clear your circuits and keep your workday tensions from building up. If you plan your lunch break carefully, you can create an extra five or ten minutes to meditate just before you return to work.

- Another way to log more meditation time is by meditating on your breath while performing routine tasks, such as sealing envelopes, eating lunch, or driving a car (with your eyes open, of course). This practice can be wonderfully productive, and it's surprisingly easy to do.

- When you get home from work, slip into comfortable clothing and freshen up a bit, then sit quietly and meditate on your breath for five or ten minutes before eating your dinner or doing your usual evening activities.

- Bedtime is an especially fruitful time to meditate. If you meditate on your breath for a few minutes before you fall asleep, the meditative state will persist during your sleep, making it much more restful and healing.

- To sum up, if you start the day with fifteen minutes of meditation, and take brief meditation breaks here and there throughout the day, you can easily accumulate forty-five minutes to an hour of meditation time every day.

What to Watch For

The depth and strength of your meditations will greatly depend on the discipline and regularity with which you practice. The deeper and stronger your meditations become, the greater the healing benefits you'll derive from each session. If you practice regularly, these benefits will accumulate from session to session and gradually transform the overall state of your health. You should also bear in mind that, in order for your meditation breaks to be effective out in the world, you must first learn to master these techniques in the privacy of your home.

Meditation is usually practiced with closed eyes. This makes it easier to turn within by eliminating many distracting influences. You might be surprised to learn, however, that you can also meditate with your eyes open. As I pointed out earlier, you can watch your breath while performing routine tasks such as driving a car or waiting in line at the bank.

Generally speaking, meditating with your eyes open isn't quite as powerful as meditating with your eyes closed. Nevertheless, it can still be a very effective practice. Once you've learned how to meditate at home with closed eyes, you'll find it remarkably easy to meditate on the movements of your breath when your eyes are open.

CHAPTER FOUR

BREATHING BLOCKS
and
ILLNESS

Man's bodily decline is always due to the decline of the breath.
If the breath is congested and isolated, it leads to illness.
— THE RECOVERY OF THE GENUINE BREATH

PRANA DOES MORE THAN IGNITE THE SPARK OF LIFE; it is also the intelligent force known as Mother Nature — the inner wisdom that knows how to grow our hair, digest our food, and heal our wounds without anyone telling it how. Because our breath is so intimately linked with the life-force, it is the command post for every mental and physical process that takes place in our system. This means that whatever is happening with our breathing is also happening throughout our mind and body. For example, when our breathing is calm and peaceful, our mind and body are peaceful too. When our breathing is disturbed, our mind and body feel correspondingly scattered and disturbed. These relationships are so irrevocably fixed in nature that breath, mind, and body can coexist in no other way.

The Hindu and Chinese masters have always taught that breathing blocks are a major cause of illness because they disrupt the flow of prana (or chi) to the various parts of our system. In the words of the Taoist masters:

> *Where there is any blockage or stagnation [of breath], there will be disease.*[1]

> *If the breath is congested and isolated, it leads to illness.*[2]

In his book *Man's Eternal Quest*, Swami Yogananda similarly states:

> *The two basic causes of illness are underactivity and overactivity of the life-energy, prana.*[3]

My own experience in healing with the breath has repeatedly confirmed the truth of these ancient teachings. Over the past twenty-five years, I've seen firsthand how breathing blocks can create a host of physical and mental problems, ranging from asthma and gastrointestinal disorders to depression and psychotic breaks. However, the connection between breathing blocks and illness by no means ends there. The healing techniques I've developed clearly reveal that all diseases of the mind and body are inseparably linked with the blocks in our breathing. These include physical disorders that are ostensibly due to "external" factors, such as accidents, infections, and congenital diseases.

Breath, Fear, and Illness

FEAR IS THE LINK THAT CONNECTS our breathing blocks with all forms of illness. Where there is injury or disease, there is always pain and fear, and all experiences of pain or fear are completely controlled by the breath. Although most of us are unaware of this fact, we instinctively use our breath's powers to block our unwanted feelings. For example, whenever we feel scared or hurt, we automatically hold our breath to block our feelings of fear and sensations of pain in our body. Whenever we do this, however, we invariably create stressful tensions throughout our mind and body.

In most people, these tensions appear as a vague sense of worry in their minds and as minor feelings of tension or stress in their bodies. As our breathing blocks grow stronger with time, these ill-defined feelings of discomfort can gradually worsen and take the form of recognizable medical disorders. For example, our once-vague feelings of mental unease can eventually develop into serious emotional disorders, such as chronic anxiety, depression, paranoia, or obsessive-compulsive behavior.

The corresponding state of anxious tension reflected in the body's tissues is the cause of many more "physical" problems than most doctors currently suspect. For example, I've found that most breathing disorders, such as asthma, emphysema, sleep apnea, and COPD (chronic obstructive pulmonary disorder), are caused primarily by the fear-ridden blocks in one's breathing. Although factors such as allergies, environmental pollutants, and cigarette smoking often play a significant role in the development of breathing disorders, they're usually not the original cause but merely contributing factors.

Respiratory disorders are by no means the only kinds of physical problems we create by blocking our breath in fear. The meditation and healing techniques I've developed clearly reveal that many mysterious neural diseases, such as Bell's palsy and trigeminal neuralgia are actually psychosomatic illnesses that people create by tensing up in their breathing to control their feelings of anger, fear, and timidity (see chapter 16).

Ironically, holding our breath to block feelings of fear does nothing to reduce the amount of fear in our system; it only reduces our awareness of the fear. The fear isn't gone; it's only been pushed deeper inside, where it turns into anxiety and becomes part of our so-called subconscious mind (see chapter 14). The layers of fear that stay trapped in our system exacerbate all symptoms of illness. In some cases, they can even create entirely new symptoms that have nothing to do with the original illness or injury. The good news, however, is that this blocking process can be reversed. Most symptoms of illness can be significantly reduced, and often completely healed, by using the breath to clear out the layers of subconscious fear that are trapped in a sick person's system.

Pranic Energy Healing

OVER THE YEARS, I've developed a unique mind/body therapy that I call "pranic energy healing" because it is based on using the pranic life-force within the breath to promote mental and physical healing (see chapter 16). Pranic energy healing employs a combination of meditation, breathwork, and gentle bodywork techniques that enable me to release the fear-ridden blocks in a person's mind and body and transmit booster shots of healing prana to diseased or injured parts of their system. This combination of techniques also enables me to read my client's emotional state with such remarkable accuracy that I can even discern the repressed emotions that are linked with specific physical problems.

One of the most powerful aspects of pranic energy healing is that it enables me to use my breath to "vacuum" pain, fear, and tension from another person's system (more about this in chapter 16). As I work with my clients, they can actually feel long-held tensions and waves of anxious energy gradually leaving their system. Most people experience immediate improvement in, and often full release from, chronic symptoms that have plagued them for many years. Over the past twenty-five years, I've repeatedly seen seemingly miraculous healings of chronic conditions that couldn't be helped by conventional treatment, just by using the breath to cleanse layers of subconscious fear from a person's system.

One particularly dramatic example occurred several years ago at one of my seminars on pranic energy healing. I was working with Karen, a volunteer from the audience, who'd been in constant pain for thirty-five years after her leg was crushed in a childhood accident. As usual, the first thing I did was teach her how to meditate on her breathing. Then I set to work with my hands and breath to draw some pain and fear from her leg.

Within minutes, Karen began to relive the day of the accident. She remembered how scared she'd been in the emergency room, and how both her father and the doctor had sternly ordered her to stifle her tears. She also realized, for the first time in her life, that she'd been repressing those feelings of terror ever since. That evening the pain in Karen's leg disappeared, and we'd only worked together for twenty-five minutes. When we spoke on the phone two weeks later, she told me the pain was still gone.

Teresa's story provides another striking example of how the fear that stays trapped in one's system can seriously retard or complicate the healing of any disease or injury. Teresa was a Brazilian woman who came for treatment of a bee sting she'd gotten about four weeks earlier. The back of her hand, where she'd been stung, was still painful; it was swollen and showed little or no signs of healing. The moment I touched Teresa's hand to examine it, I could see that she was abnormally scared of her injury.

After teaching Teresa how to meditate on her breath, I began working with my own breath to remove some pain and fear from her hand. Within two or three minutes, Teresa began to recall a long-forgotten incident. As a child, she'd been bitten by a Brazilian insect that lays its egg under the victim's skin, where it gestates for six weeks until it hatches. Since the wound can't heal until the larva matures, young Teresa endured six weeks of pain and anxious concern before the larva finally emerged from the wound.

It became clear that Teresa's bee sting was healing so slowly because of the subconscious fear she was still harboring from her childhood experience. As I kneaded the swollen tissue and used my breath to remove some of the pain and fear, Teresa's anxiety began to subside, her pain disappeared, and within fifteen minutes of when we'd started, most of the swelling was gone. By the next day, Teresa's hand was completely normal.

Self-Conflict and Infectious Diseases

BREATHING BLOCKS ARE THE RESISTANCE we create against our own feelings. These attempts to block our unwanted feelings by interfering with the movements of our breath are the source of every bit of self-conflict and self-doubt we experience in life. Self-conflict is like a civil war that depletes our inner resources and weakens the integrity of our system. Whenever we hold our breath to block fearful emotions or feelings of pain, we create contradictions in our mind and body that weaken our defenses and make us more susceptible to catching infectious diseases. For example, self-conflict is the real cause of the "depression" in "clinical depression" and the "fatigue" in "chronic fatigue syndrome." It is also the reason why women who feel conflicted about having a female body tend to have difficult menstrual periods and are often highly susceptible to yeast infections.

When Louis Pasteur first discovered that microscopic organisms are linked with certain diseases, a great debate arose among the medical experts of his time. On one side of the controversy were Pasteur and his followers, who believed that microorganisms were the cause of infectious diseases. Among those who challenged this idea was a brilliant and equally well-known physiologist named Claude Bernard. Bernard's research had convinced him that the human body possesses remarkable powers to resist invasion by microorganisms.

Bernard likened microorganisms to seeds that can produce various diseases, and the human body to the soil in which the seeds of illness sprout and grow. His theory was that microorganisms can only flourish within a person's body when the "soil" is fertile enough — which means, only if the person's biological defenses have become weak enough for the microorganisms to "take root" in his system.[4] While lying on his deathbed, Pasteur himself agreed with Bernard's conclusions, saying, "Bernard was right. The germ is nothing; the soil is everything."

My own experience has taught me that the truth lies somewhere between these points of view. It takes both the "seed" and the "soil" to cause infectious disease. Many factors can weaken our ability to resist infections, ranging from toxic substances in our environment to our own emotional conflicts. For example, the candida organism is present in everyone's body, but it never appears as an illness until one's system becomes seriously imbalanced. We only contract the "disease" of candida when we become badly run down from pushing our system too hard, or after taking antibiotics that destroy the intestinal flora that keep the candida yeast in check.

Of the many factors that can weaken our immune system, self-conflict is by far the most common and debilitating of all. I've found that people who are emotionally well balanced tend to be more resistant to infectious diseases than people who are emotionally at odds with themselves. I believe that this is one of the main reasons why some people who are infected with HIV never develop a full-blown case of AIDS. Recent medical research has similarly shown that psychotic people (the most self-conflicted of all human beings) are much more likely to contract life-threatening diseases than people who are more emotionally stable and healthy.

Allergies and Autoimmunity

SELF-CONFLICT CAN ALSO CREATE biochemical imbalances and conditions of systemic stress that make us hypersensitive to certain foods and substances that simply wouldn't affect us if our system weren't so out of balance. I've worked with dozens of people whose hypersensitive reactions to foods and airborne pollutants significantly decreased or completely cleared up after

I'd helped them reduce their levels of self-conflict by cleansing subconscious fear from their system. One of these people was an allergy therapist whose own allergies were so severe that they kept him from working for three months. After a single session together, he returned to his practice in less than a week.

Some people's levels of self-conflict are so intense they develop an extreme form of allergic response known as "environmental illness." People who suffer from this disease are abnormally sensitive to environmental substances that would usually cause no adverse effects in most other people. Of the three cases of environmental illness I've worked with, two people learned how to use their breath to weaken their hypersensitive reactions, while the third became totally free of her symptoms.

Autoimmunity is another disease that is rooted in a person's conflicting emotions. I've found that people with autoimmune diseases suffer from physiological contradictions in their body that reflect the psychological conflicts they hold in their minds. In a manner of speaking, these people have become allergic to their own body. Over the years, I've worked with eight or nine women who suffered from lupus and its close relative, malignant rheumatoid arthritis. In every case, I found that their major symptoms (poor circulation, chronic fatigue, aches and pains in their muscles and joints) were directly linked with their emotional conflicts — especially with feelings of anger toward their own body.

Lupus gets its name from the Latin word *lupus,* which means "wolf." One of the most striking symptoms of this disease is a wolf-like mask — a pattern of redness around the person's eyes and nose that resembles the markings on a wolf's face. I've found that these rosaceous flushes are caused by the deeply repressed feelings of anger that are seeking release or expression in any way possible. In most cases, I was able to help these people reduce the severity of their symptoms by cleansing some layers of fear from their system. Although the symptoms weren't completely gone, they had become considerably weaker and were much easier to live with. Once these women reduced their levels of subconscious fear, they also became correspondingly less angry toward their own body.

"She Pushed Me!"

SELF-CONFLICT NOT ONLY WEAKENS THE INTEGRITY of our system and makes us more susceptible to infectious diseases, it can also cause harm to our body by making us accident-prone. When Ann called to schedule a healing session, she told me that she had fallen and fractured some bones in her ankle two years earlier. Despite her doctors' best efforts, the ankle had stubbornly refused to heal. By the time she called me, Ann's ankle had developed an infection known as tuberculosis of the bone, and she was scheduled for surgery in three weeks. Her doctors were going to scrape the bones in an effort to stop the infection — but they weren't very hopeful about the outcome. If the procedure proved unsuccessful, they would have to amputate.

During our first session, I learned that Ann harbored intense fear and anger toward her injured ankle but stubbornly ignored those feelings. Her determination to push away her fear and pain was so incredibly strong that it seemed as if, psychically speaking, she'd already cut off her foot at the ankle. As I worked to lift some of the fear and tension that had accumulated in Ann's ankle over the past two years, the pain, swelling, and discoloration gradually began to subside. By the end of our first session, Ann was able to walk much more comfortably. She was also less afraid to put weight on her ankle and was feeling less resentful toward her injury.

By the end of our second session one week later, Ann's ankle showed even greater signs of improvement. Our third session was scheduled just four days before Ann was to undergo surgery. That morning, she arrived at my office with the wonderful news that her doctor had canceled the operation because her ankle was healing normally. "I don't know what you're doing that's different," he had said, "but whatever it is, just keep doing it." Ann didn't have the nerve to tell her doctor about the unconventional work we'd been doing, but she knew that it had made the critical difference.

When I thought that Ann was ready to hear my full diagnosis, I asked her, "Can you see that it was only your fear and anger that kept your ankle from healing?"

"Yes," she answered.

"Well, here's something else for you to think about. I'll bet you were feeling angry and scared at the moment when you broke your ankle. In fact, it was your anger and fear that really caused that accident."

Ann's eyes flashed at the memory. "You're right," she snapped angrily. "It happened while I was moving furniture from my dead mother's apartment. I didn't want to be there, and I was feeling so mad at her that I swear she pushed me!"

The Breath Holds the Key to All Healing

THERE IS AN OLD ADAGE that says, "The doctor sets the bone, but Mother Nature does the healing." The intelligent force known as Mother Nature is simply another name for prana, the spiritual life-force that dwells in our breath. Prana not only bestows the spark of life, it is also the inner wisdom that heals our diseases and regulates all of our bodily functions for as long as we're alive. In fact, the pranic life-force is the only force in the world that can heal.

The spirit of life that dwells in our breath spontaneously heals most illnesses and injuries without the aid of doctors, medicines, or outside help of any kind. However, there are no physicians, medicines, or healing techniques that can cure even the slightest health problem without the presence of prana. At their best, all healing techniques and medicines serve in the same capacity as a splint does for a broken bone; although they can facilitate the healing process, in and of themselves they can produce no actual healing. No one can heal a wound on a corpse, simply because: No breath = no life-force = no healing.

Thousands of years ago, Chinese acupuncturists discovered that a patient who breathes more fully and easily always heals more rapidly. To this day, traditional Chinese acupuncture sessions routinely include "the respiratory technique," which increases the flow of Chi by opening up the patient's breathing. The effectiveness of all healing modalities can be similarly enhanced by improving the flow of a patient's breath.

For example, Dr. Wilhelm Reich developed special techniques for healing repressed emotions by releasing the blocks in his patients' breathing. These days, many psychotherapists and most bodywork therapists use similar breathing techniques to enhance the effectiveness of their work. Even mainstream doctors appreciate the fact that full and open breathing stimulates all of the body's vital functions. Like healers of every time and place, when a doctor walks into a recovery room and finds the patient breathing restfully and deeply, the doctor knows that the healing process is working.

The techniques presented in the following chapters will teach you how to promote mental and physical healing by releasing the blocks in your breathing. These techniques will enable you to alleviate — if not completely heal — symptoms of pain and illness by using your breath to cleanse hidden layers of subconscious fear that are trapped in your mind and body. This kind of healing is extremely effective and remarkably simple. However, it can only be done from within the meditative state of consciousness.

Meditation quiets our everyday mind and guides it into a fearless, calm, detached state known as "witness consciousness" (see chapter 21). It is only from within this detached state of mind that we can return to the feelings of pain and fear that we originally blocked with our everyday mind and give them the special attention they need. Although our breathing blocks affect every thought, emotion, and cell in our body, we can't detect them in our everyday state of consciousness because they've become second nature. Meditation on the breath induces a state of meditative sensitivity and inner self-awareness that enables us to perceive these normally hidden blocks and study them in minute detail.

When we're in meditation, the first things we notice are the surface distortions in our breathing patterns. These take the form of various tensions, slackness, erratic rhythms, and brief cessations in the movements of our breath. At deeper levels of meditative consciousness, we can actually perceive the underground streams of anxiety that we create by suppressing our breath in fear. The same techniques that enable us to detect and release the blocks in our breathing also enable us to "dry up" the subconscious streams of anxiety that feed into our symptoms of illness, and enhance the flow of prana to areas of our mind and body that were formerly blocked and deprived.

Now that you've learned how to meditate and have learned some basic facts about breathing blocks and their relation to fear and illness, you're ready to begin guiding your breath back to wholeness and even beyond. As described in chapter 2, the process of healing your breath begins with breathing-release techniques to disperse the habitual blocks in your breathing. Once your breath begins moving more freely, you'll be ready to work with the grounding, strengthening, and balancing techniques (described in Part 2) to strengthen your breath and develop its healing powers to their fullest potential.

CHAPTER FIVE

BREATHING-RELEASE TECHNIQUES

Those who are good at circulating the breath energy are able to get rid of all diseases.

— TAOIST MASTER

THE PURPOSE OF BREATHING-RELEASE TECHNIQUES is to disperse the blocks in our breathing and move our breath out of its usual ruts. As these techniques release and expand our breathing, they cleanse layers of subconscious fear from our mind and body and increase the flow of prana to all parts of our system. At my workshops, I usually tell the following story to illustrate the vital role of releasing techniques in restoring the health of our breath:

Back in my days as a professional musician, I used to pal around with a brilliant young guitarist named Chuck Miller. Chuck lived in a small apartment in Boston with his dog Andres, a remarkably intelligent and playful cocker spaniel. Since he lived in the middle of the city, Chuck had to keep Andres on a leash whenever they went for a walk. In those days, I owned a beautiful piece of land in Maine where I loved to go camping with family and friends. One day, Chuck and I packed up our guitars and drove there to spend a few days in the woods. We also brought Andres, who'd never been out of the city.

As we were setting up the tent, Chuck and I looked admiringly at the thousands of wooded acres that surrounded our campsite. "What a great place for Andres to be," we said. "Now he can run around as free as he pleases, and do whatever he wants!" But for some reason, Andres would never venture into the woods by himself. Instead, he was always under our feet.

Every time I turned around to do something, I'd find myself stumbling over Andres, until I finally lost my patience and began to scold him. "For God's sake, Andres! Will you please go chase a squirrel or something?" But he always stayed close to our heels.

It took me two days to realize that Andres was restricting his movements to an area that was approximately the size of Chuck's apartment. Although he was off his leash in the midst of thousands of acres of wooded land, in his mind, Andres was still in his Boston apartment. It was all he'd ever known.

Meditating on our breath is something like taking our breath off its leash and giving it permission to move freely.

When we first learn how to meditate, however, our breath tends to behave the way Andres did at the campsite. For years, we've restricted its movements in order to block our unwanted feelings, so it's little wonder that our breath continues to hold itself back even though we've given it permission to move freely.

Whenever we sit to meditate, our breath usually relaxes and begins to flow with more ease — but only to a certain degree. It can't take full advantage of the freedom that meditation offers because the blocks in our breathing have become deep-rooted habits. Unless we take special steps to get our breath moving out of its usual ruts, it will tend to stick to its old habits — just like Andres did at the campsite. This is the main reason for practicing breathing-release techniques.

The techniques you're about to learn — "Tarzan" and "gentle rapid breathing" — are more than just physical exercises; they're powerful mind-altering techniques that must be practiced in meditation. You can expand your breathing and invigorate your body by doing physical exercises like jogging and swimming, but exercise alone will never give you the power to release the blocks in your breathing or cleanse old layers of fear from your system. These powers are only available from within the meditative state of consciousness.

BREATHING-RELEASE TECHNIQUE #1: THE TARZAN TECHNIQUE

DO YOU REMEMBER HOW TARZAN used to yell at the top of his voice and beat on his chest with his fists? This isn't just a Hollywood cliché; he was imitating the battle cry of the African gorillas. This gesture does more than intimidate a gorilla's enemies; it also enables the gorillas to feel strong and centered in the face of danger. It brings feelings of strength and power because it keeps the pectoral muscles from locking up in fear and by promoting a strong outflow of breath (see the discussion of angina pectoris in chapter 6).

I've translated this gorilla behavior into a great breathing-release technique that I call "the Tarzan technique." It's one of the first techniques I teach my students because it has a remarkable ability to disperse breathing blocks and bring immediate feelings of strength and confidence. The following instructions will teach you how to do the Tarzan technique. When you're ready to include Tarzan in your daily meditation practice, read these instructions several times to fix them in your mind, then spend about five or ten minutes experimenting with this introduction to the Tarzan technique:

1. Sit in a comfortable posture and focus your attention on the movements of your breath as the air swings in and out of your body. Once your mind is attuned to these rhythms, on one of the inhalations take in a little more air than usual. As you exhale, make a strong, continuous "aaahhh" sound and beat on your chest with alternate fists, as gorillas do. Be sure to pummel your chest vigorously enough to make your voice crack (but not enough to hurt yourself), and let the sound arise from your chest, not your throat.

2. Continue playing Tarzan for five or ten seconds (always watching your breath), then discontinue the technique and give your breath a chance to assimilate the invigorating waves of energy it releases.

3. As your breath readjusts its movements, keep watching it and study the changes that are now taking place in your breathing. Notice how much faster your breath is moving. Notice how much freer and more open your breathing has become. Notice how much more alive you feel as the new waves of energy go coursing through your system.

4. Once your breath has restabilized its movements (this usually takes from thirty to forty-five seconds), you're ready to do another round of Tarzan.

What to Watch For

When you make the "aaahhh" sound, don't sing it like a note or "yodel" it at the top of your voice as Tarzan did in the movies. Just make a firm, vigorous, outgoing sound of "aaaahhhh" — but not so loud that it disturbs your next-door neighbors.

Each time you repeat this technique, do it a bit differently. For example, you might begin by beating your chest relatively slowly and gently, then a bit faster and stronger with each succeeding trial. You can also experiment with making the sound louder or softer. Whatever you do, be sure to pummel your chest vigorously enough to make your voice crack, and always remember to keep watching your breath.

Some people notice dramatic changes in their breathing after the first round; others don't see much difference until they've done two or three successive rounds. Don't worry if your breath seems to be responding slowly. Just do the technique a few more times, and you'll soon find yourself breathing more easily and feeling much more alive.

HEALING BENEFITS

Once your breath is moving more freely, the waves of prana released by the Tarzan technique will spontaneously begin to correct all sorts of physical problems and systemic imbalances. In the words of one Taoist master:

> *By exercising the breath, the joints will not be troublesome and the breath energy will not be stagnant in the veins and arteries.*[1]

Immediately after doing this technique, most people typically report that they feel less stress, more vitality, and a greater sense of physical ease.

The Tarzan technique also dispels anxiety from the mind and body and spontaneously promotes feelings of courage and determination. Gorillas are said to be extremely shy creatures who tend to withdraw from strangers. When they feel threatened, however, they instinctively roar and beat their chest, which transforms them into formidable and aggressive opponents. When people practice the Tarzan technique, they experience the same kind of transformation.

I've found that children love to play Tarzan — not only because they think it's fun, but because it immediately lifts their spirits and boosts their feelings of confidence. Over the years, I've taught at least ten youngsters how to use this technique to overcome their feelings of shyness or inadequacy. It works just as well for adults. You can always give yourself a quick boost in confidence by doing a few rounds of Tarzan any time you feel scared — for example, just before speaking in public or when you're about to ask your boss for a raise.

As long as you practice the Tarzan technique with sensitivity and discrimination, it's safe for almost anyone. People who suffer from hypertension, cardiac problems, breathing disorders, and panic attacks can benefit from this technique, but they should practice it very carefully and sensitively at first: a firm, unforced sound and a gentle tapping on the chest for no more than five or ten seconds at a time. Once they're breathing more easily, they can work a bit more vigorously, as long as it feels appropriate.

Those who suffer from severe anxiety attacks or feelings of suffocation should avoid using Tarzan and work, instead, with the gentle rapid breathing technique (taught later in this chapter). As soon as their symptoms of distress begin to ease, they can try working with Tarzan again.

PRACTICING TARZAN ON A DAILY BASIS

NOW THAT YOU KNOW how to do the Tarzan technique, you're ready to include it in your daily meditation practice. I recommend starting each meditation session by doing three rounds of Tarzan to wake up your breathing. Once your breath is moving more freely, you can return to meditating on the movements of your breath (as you learned in chapter 3).

Three consecutive rounds of the Tarzan technique, interspersed with assimilation periods, make one full cycle of Tarzan. During the course of a twenty-minute meditation session, you can do as many as four cycles (twelve rounds) of Tarzan to energize your breathing whenever it seems to be getting sluggish. To make the Tarzan technique part of your daily meditation sessions, just follow these steps:

1. As always, begin by sitting in a comfortable upright posture and meditating on the movement of your

breath. Once you're attuned to its rhythm, do the Tarzan technique for five or ten seconds to invigorate your breathing. Then stop and give your breath a chance to assimilate the new waves of energy that this technique releases.

2. As your breath is readjusting its tensions, keep on meditating and study the changes your breath undergoes as it adjusts to the stronger currents of energy that are now flowing through your system. Once your breath has restabilized its movements, you're ready to do another round of Tarzan.

3. After you've done three consecutive rounds (or one full cycle) of Tarzan, return to meditating on the movements of your breath until you feel the urge to do a few more rounds.

What to Watch For

During the early stages of expanding your breath, you may find that it opens up and begins to move more vigorously, only to soon slow down again. When this happens, it is usually an indication that your "holding patterns" (the habitual blocks in your breathing) are pulling your breath back into its old safety zones. The best way to overcome this tendency is to be vigilant. Once you've enlivened your breathing, keep watching your breath to be sure that it doesn't revert to its old defensive habits. When you see this beginning to happen, simply do another few rounds of Tarzan, then return to meditating on your breath as usual.

During these early stages of learning, don't be alarmed if your old habits continually reassert themselves. If you study the movements of your breath during the assimilation periods, you'll find that the resistances in your breathing are gradually becoming weaker and that your breath is slowly reclaiming its freedom of movement with every round of Tarzan. This is the way your breath used to move when you were a child, and it still wants to move that way. With time and regular practice, the habitual blocks in your breathing will become weaker with each passing day. Your breathing will eventually become so open and free that you'll rarely need the Tarzan technique to wake it up and get it moving again.

As you watch your breath to observe how its movements are changing during the assimilation periods, you're also cultivating an important skill, which the Buddha called "mindfulness of breathing." This practice will not only strengthen and deepen your meditative abilities, it will also help you develop an unerring sense for the best time to do another round of Tarzan. Mindfulness of breathing is essential to working with the more advanced healing techniques taught in the later chapters. With enough time and experience, this kind of meditational awareness will even reveal the inner laws that govern the breath.

BREATHING-RELEASE TECHNIQUE #2: GENTLE RAPID BREATHING

THIS NEXT RELEASING TECHNIQUE — gentle rapid breathing — is based on an ancient yogic technique called *bastrikha,* which means "bellows" in Sanskrit. Bastrikha is called "the bellows breath" because it is done by forcing air in and out of the lungs, as if pumping a set of blacksmith bellows. Some people call it "the breath of fire" because it is traditionally practiced with great force to "stoke" the purifying fires of yoga.

When bastrikha is practiced less forcefully, it becomes an

invaluable breathing-release technique that I call gentle rapid breathing. Like the Tarzan technique, gentle rapid breathing disperses blocks and enlivens our breathing. However, there are also some very important differences between them. Tarzan is a relatively forceful technique that is used to dislodge some of the grosser blocks in our breathing, while gentle rapid breathing is a much more refined tool that enables us to disperse subtle tensions and energy blocks that Tarzan simply can't reach.

Another difference between these techniques is that gentle rapid breathing can be used to direct healing prana to disturbed areas of our mind and body with pinpoint accuracy — something that can't be done with Tarzan. Later on (in chapter 12), you'll be learning to use gentle rapid breathing as a guided healing technique. At this time, however, you'll be using it to free up your breathing and smooth out some of its "wrinkles."

This technique produces healing effects similar to those of Tarzan: reduced stress, increased vitality, and an immediate sense of breathing more easily. Like Tarzan, it also strengthens our feelings of self-confidence. However, it does so in a different way. The Tarzan technique fosters outgoing feelings of strength, courage, and determination, whereas gentle rapid breathing fosters subtler feelings of inner calm and strength.

INTRODUCTORY EXERCISE

THE FOLLOWING INSTRUCTIONS will teach you how to do the gentle rapid breathing technique. When you're ready to make it part of your daily meditation practice, read these instructions carefully, then spend about ten minutes experimenting with this introductory exercise to familiarize yourself with how the technique is done:

1. Think of how a dog pants to cool itself on a hot day; then begin panting through your mouth like that dog. Pant gently, without forcing, and be sure that your in-breaths and out-breaths feel reasonably even and well matched.

2. Now do the same thing again, but this time close your mouth and "pant" through your nostrils instead. Once you've gotten the knack of panting through your nostrils, you can begin to work with this technique in a more structured way.

3. To do this, sit in a comfortable posture and begin to meditate on your breath. Once your mind is attuned to its movements, breathe gently and rapidly through your nostrils for five or ten seconds. When you discontinue the technique, keep watching your breath and study the changes it makes in your breathing.

4. When you perform the gentle rapid breathing technique correctly, it brings feelings of aliveness that are relatively calm and quiet compared to the more intense, vigorous feelings that Tarzan produces. Once your breath has readjusted its movements, you're ready to do another round.

5. Each time you repeat this technique, try changing the speed with which you breathe. For example, experiment with breathing a bit faster or a bit more slowly. You can also experiment with varying the force or intensity with which you breathe. In other words, try breathing a bit more forcefully (or a bit more gently) with each succeeding round.

What to Watch For

Whenever you increase the force or speed of your breathing, don't try to "help" by pushing with your head and shoulders. Let the breathing muscles in your ribcage do all the work without tensing any other part of your body. At the end of each round, keep watching your breath and carefully study how the different degrees of speed and force have affected the movement of your breath.

This technique is not a deep-breathing exercise, so don't try to force large quantities of air in and out of your lungs by "pushing" from your diaphragm. Gentle rapid breathing is a very sensitive technique that works best when your breath is delicately concentrated in the region of your sinuses, throat, and bronchial tubes.

Gentle rapid breathing should almost always be done through your nose and rarely through your mouth. Breathing in and out through the mouth can be (unconsciously) used as a way to disguise the blocks in your breathing. If your sinuses are badly congested, it's okay to practice by breathing through your mouth — but only until your sinuses begin to clear. In chapter 13, you'll be learning how to use this technique to reduce inflammation and congestion in the tissues of your upper respiratory system and to alleviate the symptoms of asthma.

REGULAR PRACTICE

ONCE YOU'VE LEARNED how to do this technique, you're ready to integrate it into your daily practice. This can be done in the same way as with the Tarzan technique. Read the following instructions carefully, then put them to work by meditating for fifteen to twenty minutes, including this technique as part of your practice.

1. Sit in a comfortable posture, then begin to meditate on your breath. Once your mind is attuned to its movements, do a round of gentle rapid breathing, while always watching your breath. Pant rapidly and gently through your nostrils for five or ten seconds with any degree of speed or force that feels appropriate. When you finally stop, keep watching your breath and notice the changes this technique has produced in its movements.

2. One of the first things you'll notice is that you're now breathing with a new sense of ease. Along with this feeling of breathing more easily, you'll also find that you feel a bit more calm and solid. By the time your breath has readjusted its movements, it will be "idling" much more smoothly — something like an automobile engine after its carburetor has been adjusted. As soon as your breath has resettled its movements, you can then do another round of the gentle rapid breathing technique.

3. Once you've done three consecutive rounds (interspersed with assimilation periods), return to meditating on your breath as usual until it feels like time to do another three rounds.

What to Watch For

As your breath readjusts its tensions, it may sometimes develop an erratic catch — a kind of sobbing effect reminiscent of the way a child breathes when she's been very scared and is just beginning to let go of her fear. This sobbing effect is actually a sign that some of the hidden layers of anxiety are being released from your system, so just allow it to happen.

There is no "right way" to do this technique — no ideal speed or degree of force. Sometimes it's best to breathe rapidly and vigorously; other times it's better to breathe more slowly and gently. As long as you stay mindful of what your breath is doing, it will always tell you what degree of speed or force is best to work with at any given time.

Integrating Tarzan and Gentle Rapid Breathing

YOU CAN DEEPEN YOUR MEDITATIONS and speed your breath's development by including both Tarzan and the gentle rapid breathing technique as part of your daily practice. I recommend beginning each meditation session with three rounds of Tarzan, followed by three rounds of gentle rapid breathing. Then return to simply watching your breath without trying to influence its movements.

As you meditate, if your breathing becomes sluggish or slows way down, do a few more rounds of gentle rapid breathing to wake it up again, then go back to meditating on your breath. As your breathing blocks grow weaker with time, it will require less and less coaxing from either Tarzan or the gentle rapid breathing technique to get your breath moving freely again.

Before long, these techniques will take on a life of their own. Every so often, you'll be pleasantly surprised to notice your breath spontaneously "kicking in" to support you when you least expect it to happen. A good example of this happened with Brett, a prominent Boston psychiatrist who attended one of my eight-week meditation courses. At the beginning of the fourth evening class, Brett shared this incident with the rest of the group:

> *On my way into work this morning, I got caught in some heavy traffic and found myself getting unbearably frustrated. Had I been late for my first appointment, the rest of my day would have been a disaster. Just when I thought I might scream out loud in frustration, I suddenly I found myself watching my breath and I spontaneously began doing the gentle rapid breathing technique. This breathing stuff really works! My breath not only calmed me down all by itself, I even got to work on time!*

Brett was ecstatic about the way his breath had spontaneously come to his rescue when he most needed its help. However, it was only able to do this because, despite his incredibly busy schedule, Brett had set aside some regular time to practice these techniques at home. Anyone who practices as faithfully as Brett did will soon begin having similar experiences.

PART TWO

MASTERING
FEAR

CHAPTER SIX

MAKING FRIENDS
with
FEAR

One who conquers others is strong; one who conquers himself is strongest.

— LAO TZU

MARK TWAIN ONCE QUIPPED, "Everyone talks about the weather, but no one does anything about it." As a healer, I've noticed that everyone talks about fear but no one does much about it — mostly because they know little or nothing about how it's created or what it actually is. Most people think of fear as an inner enemy that must always be kept under control. For example, during the depths of the Great Depression, President Roosevelt made the famous statement "There is nothing to fear but fear itself." In the science fiction novel *Dune*, Paul (the hero) kept his mind steady in a crisis by reminding himself that "fear is the mind-killer." However, fear is neither an enemy nor a mind-killer; it is one of the most powerful and beneficial allies we can have in times of danger.

I once read a remarkable newspaper story about a mother who "miraculously" saved a trapped child from certain death by lifting a truck. At the time, I was a college student living in Boston, and the story came from the Midwest, but it stuck with me all these years. The newspaper account described how a three-year-old girl had become pinned under an overturned truck. Her mother, a slightly built woman, had single-handedly raised the truck enough for bystanders to pull the child to safety. When an astonished newspaper reporter asked the woman what made her even think of trying to lift the truck, she replied, "I never stopped to think for a moment. I was much too scared for my baby!" How did she do it? This heroic woman had inadvertently discovered some of the incredible powers that fear can bestow in moments of crisis. In order to consciously tap into these powers, however, we must first understand the true nature of fear.

Danger Consciousness

FEAR IS THE EMOTION WE EXPERIENCE whenever we think we're in danger. Pure fear — fear uncontaminated by anxiety — usually comes upon us suddenly, triggering a series of physiological changes that prepare our body for unusually intense forms of action. For example, a sudden rush of adrenaline causes our breath to speed up and our heart to beat faster. As the energies of fear course through our body, they quicken our reflexes and infuse our muscles with new feelings of strength. Although these sudden changes initially feel disconcerting because they are so intense, we must allow the energies of fear to flow through our system without resisting them, because they are the source of power that can enable a scared mother to lift a truck off her child.

The changes that take place in our mental processes are even more striking. Immediately after the energies of fear begin preparing our body for action, our mind becomes profoundly still and the world suddenly appears in slow motion. The rhythms of our breath and heart begin to slow down to match our calm and unhurried state of mind. Our body begins to feel steady, strong, and delicately poised for action, like a powerful lioness carefully stalking her prey.

It takes but a few seconds for our mind and body to enter this profoundly calm and one-pointed state, which I call "danger consciousness." Once we're in it, seemingly impossible tasks can be accomplished with ease. An American soldier who slipped into this state during a fierce battle in Vietnam found that he could easily sidestep the fire of a sniper; the bullets seemed to be coming toward him in slow motion.

This type of slow-motion perception has been reported by great warriors and martial artists of all cultures. For example, Chief Crazy Horse, the great American Indian warrior, was said to be virtually invincible during battle because he could consciously induce this state by meditating just before entering the fray.

Morihei Ueshiba, the great founder of the gentle martial art of Aikido, seems to have been permanently established in danger consciousness. For example, eyewitnesses have testified that Master Ueshiba could dodge bullets that were fired at him point-blank. Although he had once been rejected by the Japanese army for being too small, Ueshiba could perform prodigious feats of strength, such as moving enormous boulders with

his bare hands or flattening a squad of attackers with a powerful shout (more about this in chapter 8).

Danger consciousness is a state of profound meditative
absorption in whatever task is at hand. It enables us to experience the peace and stillness of deep meditation even though
we're performing intense, dangerous physical actions in the
outside world (see chapter 18, "Samadhi"). Warriors who enter
this state become virtually invincible because this slow-motion
view of reality gives them an enormous advantage over any
adversary who is still functioning in "normal" time. Great martial artists can enter this state at will and dispatch a surrounding band of attackers as if they had eyes in the back of their
head. I've heard that some can even accomplish this feat while
wearing a blindfold.

Breath, Fear, and Anxiety

FEAR SENDS AN URGENT MESSAGE to the mind and body:
"Danger! Do something!" The way to tap into the extraordinary
powers that fear can supply is to concentrate on the "Do something!" part of the message. Then, like Master Ueshiba or that
heroic mother, we can move mountains. On the other hand,
if we concentrate on the "Danger!" part of the message and
become overly concerned with protecting ourselves, we tend
to resist the energies of fear as they move through our mind
and body in the mistaken belief that they're threatening our
strength and stability. When we resist the empowering energies
of fear, however, we transform them into the crippling energies of
anxiety.

Despite what we've so often heard, fear does not "clutch at
our heart." We do the clutching ourselves. When we get scared,

we tend to hold our breath and we instinctively tighten our chest muscles to block the intense feelings that fear triggers in the region of our heart. This attempt to "get a grip on oneself" is actually a form of self-conflict that throws the rhythms and tensions of our breathing muscles out of synch with those of our heart. When we clutch in our chest to block feelings of fear, it not only creates anxiety, with all of its characteristic feelings of agitation, confusion, and paralysis, but it is also the cause of angina pectoris, which literally means "anxiety in the pectoral muscles."

Many people think that our heroes and heroines are fearless, but this is simply not true. They get scared, too, but they handle their fear better than the rest of us do. Contrary to public opinion, our heroes and heroines are not fearless; they are courageous. When courageous people become afraid, they don't close down on the flow of their breath to block their feelings of fear. They keep their breath open and flowing no matter how scared they are. We call such people "lion-hearted" because they gracefully accept the intense feelings that fear triggers in the region of their chest and heart. This acceptance turns the energies of their fear into a powerful ally.

"Chicken-hearted" people, on the other hand, are afraid to experience the symptoms of fear that show up in their mind and body. When they get scared, they resist these symptoms and try to control them by suppressing the flow of their breath. This frightened reaction to their own feelings of fear creates an energetic backlash that scatters their thoughts and actions like a flock of scared chickens. Fear never makes us feel weak or confused. The act of suppressing our breath to block and control our feelings of fear is what scatters our thoughts and weakens our actions. Thus, during the Great Depression, President

Roosevelt might have more accurately said, "There is nothing to fear but *the fear of fear*." And Paul, the hero of *Dune*, could have reminded himself that "*anxiety* (not fear) is the mind-killer."

It makes no difference whether our sense of fear has been triggered by an oncoming truck, a painful injury, a difficult emotion, or a traumatic memory. Whenever we use our breath to block our feelings of fear, we invariably create feelings of anxiety that remain trapped in our system and become part of our so-called subconscious mind (see chapter 14). The sad truth is that what most of us usually call "fear" isn't true fear at all; it's anxiety. The even sadder truth is that most of us have scarcely experienced real fear since we were children. In those rare moments when we do feel real fear, it is quickly transformed into anxiety because our habit of clutching to suppress our fear has become so deep-rooted and automatic.

Breath, Strength, and Courage

WHENEVER WE SUPPRESS OUR BREATHING to block feelings of fear, we create anxiety. To control this anxiety, we suppress our breathing even more — which causes us to feel more anxious than ever. When this vicious cycle spirals out of control, it leads to feelings of outright panic. Warriors from all cultures instinctively counteract this tendency to panic by shouting fierce war cries as they charge into battle. The war cries are partly intended to frighten their enemies, but more important, they counteract any tendency toward suppressing their breath in fear.

All great athletes and warriors are at least subconsciously aware of the breath's power to control pain and fear. As the going gets tougher, they intuitively tap into deeper reserves of strength and courage by changing the intensity, rhythm, and speed of their breathing. The exhilarating experience that runners call "second wind" is an example of how keeping the breath open, balanced, and flowing enables us to tap into these hidden reserves of energy. The Eastern martial artists brought this intuitive understanding to such high levels of conscious awareness that they were able to develop sophisticated systems of breath control for cultivating the virtues of strength, courage, and stamina that are essential to being a warrior.

Greatness of Spirit

SUPPRESSING OUR BREATH TO BLOCK FEELINGS of fear not only creates anxiety, it also causes us to become discouraged — or "dis-spirited." Whenever we suppress our breathing to block feelings of fear, we weaken our connection with the spirit of life that strengthens and supports us. Greatness of spirit is the quality we most admire in our finest athletes and warriors. For example, great warriors are distinguished by the courage they display in the face of pain, fear, or even death. No matter how scared they get, they never lose touch with the spirit of life by suppressing their breath in fear.

By way of comparison, great saints and realized beings are distinguished not by their courageousness, but by their lack of fear, because they have completely transcended their fear of death. It takes courage to master our feelings of fear. It takes even greater amounts of courage to move beyond our sense of fear and lose our fear of death. Before we can become as fearless as our sages and saints, however, we must first have the courage of a warrior.

For example, Socrates was a famous warrior who became a great sage by graduating from the realms of sustained courageousness into the realms of fearlessness. As a young man, he was considered to be one of the most courageous and formidable soldiers ever to serve in the Athenian army. The turning point in his life occurred when he participated in an incredibly fierce battle that tested his strength and courage to their limits for three straight days and nights.

When the battle was over, Socrates climbed to the top of a nearby hill, leaned on his spear to support himself, then gazed across the battlefield in a trance-like state in which he stood motionless for twenty-four hours. By the time he turned to descend the hill, Socrates was no longer the courageous warrior who had fought in the recent battle. He had become transformed into the fearless sage who could remain calm and cheerful even while drinking a lethal cup of hemlock.

Mahatma Gandhi was a spiritual warrior who led his people to independence armed not with weapons of war, but with his sense of courage and his faith in God. Studying the career of this remarkable man is like retracing the footsteps of a saint in the making. Gandhi repeatedly jeopardized and eventually sacrificed his life to set his people free. By remaining courageous, no matter how much pain and fear he had to face to help his people, he became a saint-like being who transcended his fear of death.

Teresa of Avila was a "warrior-in-spirit" who became a saint by courageously surmounting incredible amounts of pain, fear, sickness, and self-doubt. Throughout her life, Teresa suffered from a relentless series of painful illnesses that tested her faith and courage beyond all limits of normal human endurance. Even her mystic experiences were often the cause of great personal torment. Teresa's inner experiences were so unique and beyond the ken of traditional Catholic doctrine, she sometimes feared they might be of the devil, or that she might be going mad. Even worse, if the Spanish Inquisitors had learned of her "unorthodox" experiences, they might have condemned her as a heretic. It was only Teresa's incredible sense of courage and faith in God that enabled this heroic soul to enter into rapturous states of Divine communion and transcend her fear of death.

Self-Mastery

IN THE SCIENCE FICTION MOVIE *The Empire Strikes Back,* Yoda tests Luke's courage and self-mastery by sending him into a dark, forbidding jungle swamp. When Luke inquires, "What is in there?" Yoda replies, "Only what you take with you." Within the swamp, Luke encounters his deepest fear in the form of a vision of Darth Vader — his greatest enemy. The lesson that Luke eventually learns is that self-mastery cannot be attained by confronting our fears and doing battle with them. This approach is destined to fail because we are the source of our feelings of fear. The harder we try to resist them, the weaker we'll get because we're fighting no one but our self.

This theme is also expressed in Swami Yogananda's book *Autobiography of a Yogi,* in which he tells of meeting the "Tiger Swami" — a Hindu monk who was famous throughout India for his ability to wrestle wild tigers and kill them with his bare hands. Repenting of his needless killing of tigers for the sake of riches and fame, the Tiger Swami eventually renounced his spectacular career to become a seeker of God. When the teenaged Yogananda praised the swami for being so brave as to wrestle wild tigers, the monk replied, "My son, fighting tigers is nothing compared to fighting the beasts of ignorance and fear that roam the jungles of the human mind."

These "beasts of ignorance" are nothing but the personal

demons of fear that lie hidden away in the dark recesses of our minds. It is impossible to get rid of them by trying to fight them. Paradoxical as it may seem, the only way to cast these "demons" out of our mind is by learning to accept our feelings of fear whenever they show up. The "secret" to accepting our feelings of fear is to be courageous enough to feel them, and the key to accomplishing this lies in trusting the innate wisdom of the breath. If we keep our breath open and flowing — instead of closing it down in fear — the Divine Spirit that gives us life will always be there to support us.

In times of crisis, great saints and enlightened beings not only keep their breath open and flowing, but their breathing always stays calm and peaceful because they live in a permanent state of union with the spirit of God that dwells in their breath. This ability to keep their breath "as soft and gentle as a newborn babe's"[1] (in Lao Tzu's words) gives them the full protection and guidance of the Holy Spirit during times of crisis. This is why the Bible says:

> *Though I walk through the valley of the shadow of death,*
> *I shall fear no evil, for Thou art with me.*[2]

Each of us has the same inner tools for cultivating the virtues of strength, courage, and fearlessness as the great warriors and saints because our breath derives its powers from the same Divine source. The techniques described in the following chapters will teach you how to use your breath to make friends with your fear and turn its energies into your ally. As they balance and strengthen your breathing, these techniques will also promote spontaneous healing throughout your mind and body by cleansing the hidden layers of anxiety that have become "trapped" within your being by supression of the breath in fear.

CHAPTER SEVEN

GROUNDING and STRENGTHENING TECHNIQUES

The wise man would strengthen his breathing to strengthen his chi.

— TAOIST APHORISM

THE BREATHING TECHNIQUES you've learned so far are an invaluable set of tools for working with fear. Each type of tool helps us to master feelings of fear in its own special way. For example, meditation on the breath quiets the mind and gently dissolves the hidden layers of anxiety that weaken our sense of confidence. Breathing-release techniques help us stay strong and centered in the face of fear by promoting a strong outflow of breath. They also reduce hidden layers of subconscious anxiety by dispersing the fear-ridden blocks in our breathing.

The grounding and strengthening techniques described in this chapter will provide you with yet another set of tools for mastering fear. As the words *grounding* and *strengthening* imply, these techniques help us feel more solid and strong in mind and body by deepening and strengthening our breathing. This class of breathing practices, which the Chinese masters call "solidifying techniques," is especially favored by Eastern martial artists, who use them to cultivate extraordinary degrees of strength, stamina, and courage.

GROUNDING TECHNIQUE #1: SOLIDIFYING THE BREATH

"SOLIDIFYING THE BREATH" is based on an ancient *mudra* (yogic hand position) that brings feelings of strength and groundedness throughout the mind and body by deepening and strengthening our breathing. This technique can produce such powerful results because it increases the compressive forces within our breath. Just as the power of an engine depends on the amount of compression it can build up in its cylinders, our feelings of strength and power similarly depend on the amount of compression with which we breathe — the depth and strength of our breathing.

The compressive forces within our breath should always match the amount of tension we have in our muscles. For example, when we're using our muscles to perform delicate tasks, our breathing should be equally gentle and delicate. The harder our muscles have to work, the deeper and stronger our breathing must be to support the needs of our muscles. The ability to increase the compressive forces within one's breath — to "concentrate one's chi," as the Taoist masters would say — is the secret to the legendary feats of strength performed by such great martial artists as Morihei Ueshiba. In chapter 6, for example, I mentioned that Master Ueshiba could move huge boulders with his bare hands or flatten a squad of attackers with a single shout.

This next technique — solidifying the breath — enables us to bring the compressive forces of our breathing into perfect synch with our muscular state. Whenever you feel anxious, scattered, or out of control, this technique can help you quickly collect and ground yourself.

In addition to its grounding and strengthening effects, it also reduces the negative effects of shallow (or blocked) breathing. People with chronic breathing disorders will find this technique particularly helpful because it instantly increases the volume of air that enters the lungs and disperses the feelings of anxiety that usually accompany shortness of breath. This is how solidifying the breath is done:

1. Sit in a comfortable posture and begin to meditate on your breath. As you meditate, pay attention to how relatively deep or shallow your breathing is, but don't try to change its movement.

2. Once you're in touch with the movements of your breath, make a fist with each of your hands by closing your fingers loosely over your thumbs. Then — still watching your breath — squeeze your thumbs firmly with one steady pressure and hold it for a minute or so.

3. As soon as you squeeze your thumbs, your breathing will become markedly deeper and stronger. If you study the changes that take place in your feelings, you'll discover that along with the new feelings of

strength in your breathing, you also feel more solid and grounded in both your mind and your body.

4. The harder you squeeze your thumbs, the deeper your breathing will become and the more solid and strong you'll feel at every level of being. Try this for yourself right now by squeezing your thumbs a bit harder, then hold the new pressure steadily for a minute or so and study the changes that take place in your mind and body.

5. As soon as you squeeze your thumbs a bit harder, notice how much deeper and stronger your breathing becomes. Notice how much calmer your mind is. Notice how much stronger and more solid you feel in both your mind and body.

6. Study these changes for another minute or so, then release your thumbs and allow your breathing to return to its original state. Once you've released the pressure on your thumbs, notice how relatively weak and shallow your "normal" way of breathing feels compared to the way it felt while you were squeezing your thumbs.

To Strengthen Your Everyday Breathing

You can gradually deepen and strengthen your everyday breathing — the way you normally breathe when you're not in meditation — by including the solidifying technique as part of your daily practice. When you practice this technique in conjunction with Tarzan or gentle rapid breathing, its strengthening effects become greatly multiplied.

This is how to do one full round of the solidifying technique:

1. Sit in a comfortable posture and begin to meditate on your breath. Once you're in touch with its movements, do a few rounds of Tarzan and/or the gentle rapid breathing technique to wake up your breathing. Once your breath is more open and flowing, pay attention to how relatively deep or shallow your breathing is, but don't try to change its movements.

2. Still watching your breath, squeeze your thumbs with one steady pressure, then study the increased feelings of strength and groundedness this higher state of compression brings to your mind and body. Notice how much deeper and stronger your breathing is. Notice how much calmer your mind is. Notice how much stronger and more solid you feel in your mind, your breath, and your body.

3. Next, squeeze your thumbs even harder and hold this new pressure steadily for another minute or two. While your breathing is learning to function at these higher levels of tension and compression, study the changes taking place in your mind and body.

4. Notice that each time you increase the pressure, it not only deepens and strengthens your breathing, it also brings increased feelings of strength and groundedness to both your mind and body.

5. You can increase the pressure on your thumbs three or four times in succession, with assimilation periods in between. You may also work with any amount of pressure that feels right at the time and hold it steady for as long as you wish.

6. When you're ready to end this practice, release the pressure on your thumbs very gradually and gently. If you do this properly, by the time you've released your thumbs, your mind, body, and breathing will feel nearly as solid and strong as they did when you were squeezing your thumbs.

7. Once you've finished doing a full round, simply return to your basic breath meditation until you're ready to end the session.

If it feels appropriate, you may do two or three rounds of the solidifying technique during the course of a single session. Over time, the feelings of increased strength and groundedness you cultivate during your daily practice will gradually become part of your everyday life.

A Few Helpful Suggestions

The traditional way of doing this technique is to squeeze your thumbs, as described earlier. However, I've developed an alternative method that offers much more control of your breath and is considerably easier on your thumbs. Buy a matched pair of sponge-rubber balls that are a bit smaller and softer than a tennis ball. Whenever you practice the solidifying technique, squeeze the balls instead of your thumbs.

The rubber balls will enable you to work with greater amounts of pressure and for longer periods of time, without hurting your thumbs. Working with a set of rubber balls will also give you much subtler degrees of control over the compressive forces within your breath. When you begin to work with the guided healing techniques in Part 3 of this book, these subtler degrees of control over the compressive forces within your breath will prove especially valuable. If you can't find a suitable pair of rubber balls at your local toy store, you can order a set at my website (www.miracleofthebreath.com).

GROUNDING TECHNIQUE #2: MEDITATION ON THE HEARTBEAT

THE RHYTHM OF YOUR HEARTBEAT and the rhythm of your breath can function independently, or they can work in perfect synch. Most of the time, their rhythms tend to be independent. When their rhythms become synchronized, however, your heart and breath both function at much higher levels of efficiency.

This next technique — meditation on the heartbeat — will teach you how to synchronize your heartbeat with the movements of your breath. This state of synchronicity strengthens every function of the heart and lungs. It enhances the flow of prana moving through your system and brings new feelings of strength, peace, and wholeness throughout the mind and body. People who suffer from panic attacks, shortness of breath, or heart-related problems, such as angina or arrhythmia (erratic heartbeat), will find this technique especially helpful for reducing their negative symptoms.

This is how meditation on the heartbeat is done:

1. As usual, close your eyes and begin to meditate on your breath. Once you're attuned to its movements, do a few rounds of Tarzan and/or the gentle rapid breathing technique to wake up your breathing. Once your breath is more open and flowing, focus your attention on your heartbeat without losing track of your breath.

2. As you meditate on your breathing and your heart-beat at the very same time, their rhythms will grad-ually come into synch. Don't try to bring their rhythms into alignment by consciously controlling their movements. Simply meditate on your breath and heartbeat simultaneously and their rhythms will synchronize themselves.

3. As the rhythms of your breath and heart come into synch, new feelings of peace, wholeness, and inner well-being will gradually permeate your mind and body. The longer you stay in this synchronized state, the deeper and stronger these feelings will become.

4. Your heartbeat is present in every artery, vein, and capillary in your body. By feeling your heart's pulsa-tion as fully as you can throughout your body, the beneficial effects of this technique will become greatly multiplied.

You may practice meditation on the heartbeat as often as you wish and for as long as it feels appropriate. The more often you work with this technique, the more your breathing and your heartbeat will tend to stay in synch even when you're not in meditation.

Your breath and your heartbeat are the most powerful uni-fying forces in your body. If you meditate on your breathing and your heartbeat as you drift off to sleep, your sleep will be far more healing and restorative than it would be in your normal state of consciousness. In the words of one Chinese master:

The heart controls the whole body. It is the king of the five viscera. If one contemplates on it both in action and quiescence, the [powers of Chi] will function.[1]

What to Watch For

Bringing your breathing and your heartbeat into synch does not mean that you will inhale, then exhale, with each and every heartbeat. It simply means that as the air enters and leaves your body, each inhalation and exhalation will commence on a heartbeat.

There are times when your inhalations and exhalations will be so evenly matched that they'll not only be in synch with the beat of your heart, they'll also last for equal numbers of heartbeats. When this occurs, it indicates that your heart, your breath, and your consciousness are in an especially high state of balance. Although this is a very desirable state, you should never force your heart or your breath to achieve it. It can only occur when your mind, heart, and breathing have entered a particularly delicate state of balance that cannot be forced.

Some people find it difficult to feel their heartbeat when they first work with this technique. If you have this problem, you can bring your heartbeat into clearer focus by gently restraining your breathing. If you keep your breath from moving for just a few moments (without forcing), you'll find it much easier to feel your heartbeat. Once you're in touch with the beat of your heart, allow your breath to move again, but do so very carefully to be sure that its movements don't overshadow your heartbeat, as they were doing before you gently restrained your breath.

GROUNDING TECHNIQUE #3: STRENGTHENING THE HEART

BRINGING THE RHYTHMS OF OUR HEART and breath into synch is only part of the process of attaining new levels of wholeness and strength. To reach our highest potential, the compressive forces within our breath should always match the compressive forces within our heart as it pumps the blood through our body.

Basically, the heart is simply a specialized muscle. The harder our muscles must work to accomplish their tasks, the harder our heart must also work to fulfill the needs of our muscles. And the harder our heart must work to pump blood through our body, the deeper and stronger our breathing must be to fully support its actions.

When their compressions and timings are evenly matched, our breath and heart begin to function at their highest levels of efficiency and power. For example, the sudden burst of energy that athletes experience when they get their "second wind" is due to the fact that the rhythms and compressions of their heart and breath are functioning at much higher levels of synchronicity than they usually do.

Most of the time, the compressive forces within our heart and those of our breath are poorly matched, and their rhythms are rarely in synch. These are two of the main reasons why some people are prone to have heart attacks while doing strenuous tasks like shoveling snow or climbing a flight of stairs. The strenuous actions performed by their heart are poorly supported by the compressive forces within their breath.

This next technique — strengthening the heart — uses a combination of the solidifying technique and meditation on the heartbeat to produce greater feelings of wholeness and strength than we could possibly get by practicing either technique by itself. I've named it "strengthening the heart" because it not only deepens and strengthens our breathing, it is also a great technique for strengthening and healing a weak or damaged heart. It begins in the same way as meditation on the heartbeat.

This is how it is done:

1. Sit in a comfortable meditation posture, then close your eyes and begin to meditate on your breath. Once you're attuned to its movement, meditate on the rhythms of your heartbeat and breath to bring them into synch.

2. Once the rhythms of your heart and breath have come into synch, squeeze your thumbs (or rubber balls) with one steady pressure to deepen and strengthen your breathing, and notice how this affects your heartbeat.

3. Notice that as soon as you squeeze your thumbs (or rubber balls), your heartbeat becomes a bit stronger right along with the increased strength of your breathing. This increase of strength in your heartbeat is an indication that your heart and breath are not only rhythmically synchronized, they're also working with equal degrees of compression.

4. The next step is to give your heart a chance to assimilate the new feelings of strength and support it is now receiving from your breath. To do this, keep squeezing your thumbs (or rubber balls) with the same pressure and hold it steady for a minute or two while your

heart accommodates its movements to the increased support it is now receiving from your breath.

5. You can make your heartbeat even stronger by squeezing your thumbs (or rubber balls) a bit harder. The harder you squeeze, the stronger your breathing and heartbeat will both become.

6. You can increase the pressure on your thumbs (or rubber balls) two or three times in succession, with assimilation periods in between. You may work with any amount of pressure that feels right at the time, and hold it steadily for as long as you wish.

7. When you're ready to stop practicing the technique, be sure to release the pressure on your thumbs (or rubber balls) very gradually and gently. If you do this properly, by the time you've completely released the pressure, your heartbeat and breathing will feel nearly as strong as they did while you were squeezing.

8. Once you've finished a full round of strengthening the heart, return to your basic breath meditation until you're ready to end the session.

If it feels appropriate, you may do two or three rounds of this technique during the course of a single session. Over time, the heart strengthening and deeper breathing that result from your daily practice will gradually become part of your everyday life.

What to Watch For

Before you undertake any form of physical exercise that is intended to strengthen your heart, bring the rhythms of your breath and heart into synch. This state of rhythmical synchronicity will help to ensure that your breath will be giving your heart all the support it needs to safely accomplish its tasks.

If you have a severe heart problem, begin by working with only moderate amounts of pressure on your thumbs (or rubber balls). As you become increasingly comfortable and familiar with this technique, you can gradually increase the pressures with which you work. As long as you keep the rhythms of your breath and your heartbeat in synch, there will be little danger of over taxing your heart. However, if this technique seems to aggravate your symptoms instead of helping you feel more solid and strong, simply stop practicing it.

CHAPTER EIGHT

BREATH-BALANCING TECHNIQUES

If one's inhalations and exhalations are not balanced, one loses the harmonious breath energy of heaven and earth. This is how diseases are produced.

— TAOIST TEXT

THERE ARE ONLY TWO WAYS TO BLOCK FEELINGS of pain and fear as they enter our mind and body. The first is to tense up to resist our unwanted feelings. The second is to "play possum" — to become passive and limp to avoid feeling our pain and fear. When we tense up in our mind, we also tense up in our body. When our mind becomes passively quiet, we become passive and limp in our body, too. Our mind and body are so closely linked that it is impossible to tense up or go slack in one without doing the same in the other.

Both ways of blocking — tensing up or going limp — are completely controlled by the breath. For example, whenever we block feelings of pain or fear, the first thing we do is tense up (or "clutch") on the in-breath to resist our unwanted feelings. Then we go slack (or "collapse") on the out-breath to avoid the feelings of anxiety and tension we created by clutching as we breathed in. At the end of the out-breath, we completely stop breathing for a moment or two in order to avoid the feelings of stress and conflict that we created by clutching and collapsing as we breathed in and out.

In deep meditation, we can directly perceive three related phenomena: how all feelings of anxiety are created by clutching on the in-breath; how all feelings of passivity (such as helplessness, discouragement, and dismay) are created by collapsing on the out-breath; and how all feelings of apathy, lethargy, and depression are created by pausing and lingering at the end of the out-breath before we breathe back in.

Every fear-ridden block in our mind and body is created by clutching, collapsing, and lingering in the pause at the end of the out-breath. These are universal responses to pain and fear, which everyone shares to varying degrees. Over time, the particular ways in which we clutch, collapse, and pause with every cycle of breathing become deep-rooted habits that lock us into characteristic patterns of emotional highs and lows. When the tensions of a person's in- and out-breaths become severely imbalanced, that person can begin to suffer from the crippling emotional disorder known as bipolar disorder or manic/depressive behavior.

The Emotional Roller Coaster

WHEN LOTTE CAME TO ONE OF MY WORKSHOPS, her in- and out-breaths were so terribly out of balance I was amazed at how well she could function in society without the aid of medication. While coaching her on how to work with some of the breathing techniques, I was struck by how closely her breathing patterns resembled those of two concentration-camp victims I'd helped in the past.

When I inquired into her background, Lotte told me that she had been born after World War II, but that both of her parents were survivors of the Nazi death camps. Although they never spoke of their experiences in her presence, as a child Lotte had internalized the unresolved feelings of terror that her parents still harbored in their minds. In the process, she had incorporated the same imbalance of tensions into her own breathing patterns. As a result, ever since early childhood, Lotte had been living on an emotional roller coaster that subjected her to sudden extreme mood swings, which ranged from intense anxiety to helplessness and depression.

Over the next two days, Lotte did such an extraordinary job of bringing her mood swings under control by learning to balance her in- and out-breaths, she seemed to become a new person. At the end of the workshop, several participants openly remarked on how much stronger and more composed she had become in only two days. They weren't the only ones to notice the positive changes in Lotte's demeanor. A few days later, when Lotte went for her weekly singing lesson, her teacher complimented her on the new feelings of strength and confidence that he could hear in her voice.

Breathing Disorders

THE HABIT OF CLUTCHING, collapsing, and pausing as we breathe in and out is the basic cause of many respiratory disorders, such as asthma, emphysema, and sleep apnea. Asthma provides one of the simplest examples of how our tendency to clutch, collapse, and pause as we breathe can seriously impair the health of our breath. People with asthma characteristically find it difficult to breathe air into their lungs while they're having an attack. This is primarily due to the fact that, when asthmatic people clutch on the in-breath, they tense up in such a way that their bronchial tubes become severely constricted in fear. The habit of clutching in fear on the in-breath is also the source of the intense feelings of anxiety that characterize asthma attacks (for more on this, see chapter 13, "Healing Respiratory Problems").

In the case of emphysema, people characteristically find it difficult to expel the air from their lungs when they try to exhale. According to conventional medical thinking, this happens because the alveoli (the tiny air sacs that branch off the bronchial tubes) have lost their elasticity. This loss of elasticity is usually attributed to external factors, such as cigarette smoking and repeated exposure to various toxins and air pollutants. However, my experience has been that although external factors such as these can contribute to the severity of emphysema, they're usually not its original cause. The real cause is the contradictory tensions that people create by suppressing their breath in fear.

When people with emphysema clutch on the in-breath, their alveoli become rigidly fixed in fear. When they collapse on the out-breath, the alveoli become too weak and flaccid to adequately squeeze the air from their lungs. From a medical point of view, the alveolic tissues seem to have lost their elasticity because they've suffered some sort of physical damage. It has been my experience, however, that the alveoli haven't lost their elasticity because they have been physically damaged; they have lost their ability to expand and contract as they normally should because they are simultaneously confused by — and deadlocked between — the fear-ridden contradictions that exist between the person's in- and out-breaths.

A Case of Emphysema

I once worked with a fifty-year-old woman named Diane whose breathing problems provided a vivid example of how emphysema is directly linked with the habit of clutching and collapsing as we breathe in and out to block our fearful thoughts and feelings. As I helped Diane release the blocks in her breathing, she began to experience intense grief over her husband, who had been killed in a late-night auto collision five years earlier.

Diane explained that the hospital had phoned her after midnight to tell her that her husband was dead. As she told me this, she suddenly remembered that her first emphysema attack had occurred at the very moment she learned of his death. She remembered how she'd caught her breath "to get a grip on herself." Ever since receiving the shocking news, she had been subconsciously holding her breath as if trying to hold on to her husband. To her distraught mind, letting go of her in-breath would be the same as admitting that he was dead.

It was easy to see why Diane found it difficult to let go of her husband. As a child, her parents had been disrespectful and abusive toward her — a pattern that had continued into many of her adult relationships. Her husband was the only person who had truly loved and respected her — and suddenly he was gone.

Ever since that midnight call, Diane had been holding on to her in-breath to stem the tide of anxiety and grief that continually threatened to overwhelm her. But the harder she clutched on the in-breath to control her fearful emotions, the more she collapsed on the out-breath to avoid the feelings of fear she tried to disguise by clutching as she breathed in. With time, her in-breath became so chronically tense and rigidly fixed — and her out-breath so feeble and disempowered — that she could scarcely muster the strength or willingness to expel the air from her lungs.

By the end of the session, Diane's breathing had greatly improved. I recommended that she come back for more work because the contradictions in the movements of her breath were too deeply entrenched to eliminate in a single session. I suggested that, in the meantime, she try to accept the fact that her husband was dead. Perhaps she could take some flowers to his grave and spend some time talking to his spirit.

Diane never returned to finish the healing process we started that day. Perhaps her breathing problems had improved more than I thought. My guess, however, is that she just wasn't ready to face the grief that would surely rise to the surface of her mind as her breathing returned to normal.

Breath-Balancing Techniques

THE PURPOSE OF BREATH-BALANCING TECHNIQUES is to bring the tensions of our in- and out-breaths into healthier states of balance by correcting our habits of clutching, collapsing, and pausing to block our feelings of fear. The more evenly matched our in- and out-breaths are, the calmer and more collected we'll feel in mind and body and the less anxiety, discouragement, and depression we'll experience in the course of everyday life. The techniques described in this chapter will not only help you control your mood swings, they will also increase the volume of air that enters your lungs and enhance the flow of prana to every part of your mind and body.

Whenever you're feeling overly tense and filled with stress, you'll find these techniques extremely useful for regaining your equilibrium and helping your system relax. When correctly practiced, people with chronic breathing disorders such as asthma, emphysema, sleep apnea, and COPD (chronic obstructive pulmonary disorder) will find them especially helpful in dispersing the blocks in their breathing and reducing the feelings of anxiety that invariably accompany shortness of breath.

BREATH-BALANCING TECHNIQUE #1: GENTLING THE IN-BREATH

THE FIRST STEP IN GUIDING THE TENSIONS of our in- and out-breaths into healthier states of balance is to "gentle" the in-breath, which means to weaken the habit of clutching in fear as we breathe in. This next technique, gentling the in-breath, not only enables us to weaken our habit of clutching on the in-breath, it also dissolves the feelings of tension and anxiety that result from catching our in-breath in fear.

If you practice this technique on a regular basis, your habit of clutching apprehensively as you breathe in will grow weaker with each passing day. Over time, you'll find yourself breathing more easily and performing the chores of your everyday life with increased freedom and ease. This is how to gentle your in-breath:

1. Sit in a comfortable posture and begin to meditate on your breath. Once you're in touch with its

movement, become aware of the volume of air that enters your lungs each time you breathe in.

2. Next, whenever you inhale, imagine that you are breathing the air into your body (as if) from between your legs. As soon as you do this, the amount of air that enters your body will noticeably increase.

3. This is a visualization technique, so don't actually breathe from between your legs. Simply imagine that the air is coming into your body *as if* from between your legs, and the column of air that enters your body will immediately become a bit deeper, longer, and more refined.

4. This increase in the volume of air is a sign that the tensions of your in-breath have begun to relax and your habit of clutching is already becoming weaker. As your in-breath relaxes its tensions, not only will the amount of air that enters your lungs increase of its own accord, you'll also begin to feel more calm and relaxed throughout your mind and body.

5. Once you've learned how to gentle your in-breath by breathing in (as if) from between your legs, keep watching your breath and continue to gentle each of your in-breaths for the remainder of the practice session.

BREATH-BALANCING TECHNIQUE #2:
CORRECTING THE PAUSE

THE NEXT STEP IN BALANCING THE TENSIONS of our in- and out-breaths is to correct the habit of lingering in the pause that occurs at the end of the out-breath. This "lingering" pause should not be confused with the natural pause that briefly occurs at the turnaround points in our breathing. When our breathing patterns are well balanced, the pauses that occur at the end of our in- and out-breaths are usually very brief (lasting no longer than a split second) and of equal duration.

You can distinguish the lingering pause from the natural pause by comparing the pause at the bottom of your out-breath with those that occur at the top of your in-breath. If the pauses at the end of your exhalations are noticeably longer (which is the case for most people), then you should definitely work with this next technique.

The lingering pause we are discussing here is a passive form of blocking. It is an emotional state of "limbo" to which our mind retreats to escape from its unwanted feelings. Correcting this "neurotic" pause is an extremely important phase of healing oneself in body, mind, and spirit because this is one of the most insidious, disruptive, and deceptive "places" our mind can possibly enter. If we study this pause in meditation, at first glance it appears to be a very restful and comforting place — a haven of safety and protection from any feelings of conflict or tension we might have in our mind and body. Unfortunately, these impressions are completely deceptive.

Lingering in the pause at the end of the out-breath not only brings illusory feelings of comfort and safety, it is dangerous to our mental health because it causes our emotional disturbances to accumulate and eventually become worse than ever. For example, lingering in the pause to escape feelings of anxiety sows the seeds of emotional disorders such as insomnia, depression, and panic attacks, which eventually sprout and blossom at a later date.

The pause at the end of the out-breath is not only where our mind goes to hide from unwanted thoughts and feelings, it is also the dimension of consciousness in which all forms of mental dissociation are born. For example, this is the place in which the mind can "leave" the body and seek relief from troubled feelings by indulging in daydreams and fantasies. The lingering pause at the end of the out-breath is also the dimension of consciousness in which all hallucinations take place.

Earlier in this chapter, I pointed out that all feelings of apathy, lethargy, and depression are created by lingering in the pause at the end of the out-breath. It is no coincidence that the word *apathy* refers to a listless state of consciousness in which the afflicted person is "without emotions," nor is it a coincidence that the word *lethargy* comes from the word *lethal*. Both words are remarkably appropriate because lingering at the end of the out-breath is a form of emotional suicide in which we are literally killing our consciousness to avoid our unwanted thoughts and feelings.

This next technique, "correcting the pause," will enable you to weaken the habit of pausing and lingering at the end of the out-breath. The weaker your habit of pausing becomes, the more clear, conscious, and present your mind will be in all circumstances of your daily life. This means that you'll not only stop "spacing out" to escape difficult thoughts and feelings, you'll also have fewer experiences of helplessness and depression in both your dreams and your everyday state of waking consciousness.

Correcting the pause begins the same way as gentling the in-breath. If you practice this technique on a regular basis, your habits of clutching and pausing as you breathe in and out will grow weaker with each passing day. This is how it's done:

1. Sit in a comfortable posture and begin to meditate on your breath. Once you're in touch with its movement, become aware of the volume of air that enters your body each time you breathe in.

2. Next, whenever you inhale, imagine that you are bringing the air into your body (as if) from between your legs. As soon as you do this, the tensions of your in-breath will begin to relax and the amount of air entering your body will noticeably increase.

3. The next step is to correct any tendency to linger in the pause at the end of your out-breath — and this is how it is done: When you exhale, don't allow your breath to linger before you breathe back in. When you reach the bottom of each exhalation, remind your breath to come right back into your body, breathing in (as if) from between your legs.

4. Once you've learned how to keep your breath from pausing at the end of the out-breath, be vigilant for the remainder of the practice session. At the end of each exhalation, don't allow your breath to pause and linger. Bring the air right back into your body as if breathing in from between your legs.

Combining Techniques
in Regular Practice

ONCE YOU'VE LEARNED HOW GENTLE YOUR IN-BREATH and correct the pause, you can include both techniques as part of your daily practice by using them in conjunction with the breathing-release and grounding techniques you learned in chapters 5 and 7. This is how it is done:

1. Sit in a comfortable posture and begin to meditate on your breath. Once you're in touch with its movements, do a few rounds of Tarzan and/or the gentle rapid breathing technique to invigorate your breathing. As soon as your breath is more open and flowing, begin gentling your in-breath and correcting the pause.

2. Each time you inhale, bring the air into your body as if breathing from between your legs. At the end of every out-breath, don't allow your breath to linger; bring the air right back into your body, as if breathing in from between your legs.

3. You can do as many rounds of Tarzan and/or gentle rapid breathing to enliven your breath as you wish. During the assimilation period at the end of each round, be sure to keep gentling your in-breath and correcting the pause.

4. Once you've finished working with the Tarzan and gentle rapid breathing techniques, you can work with the solidifying technique for the remainder of the session: Squeeze your thumbs (or rubber balls) with one steady pressure. As soon as you squeeze the rubber balls, not only will your breathing become deeper and stronger, the tensions of your in- and out-breaths will also become a bit more evenly matched.

5. Each time you increase the pressure on the balls, study the changes this makes in your breathing. Notice how the increased pressure brings increased feelings of strength, balance, and evenness to the movements of your breath.

6. You may do as many rounds of the solidifying technique as you like. You may work with any amount of pressure that feels right at the time, and hold it steadily for as long as you wish.

7. Each time you increase the pressure, remember to keep gentling your in-breath and correcting the pause while your breath readjusts its tensions. Each time you inhale, imagine that you are breathing the air into your body as if from between your legs. At the end of each exhalation, be careful not to pause and linger before you breathe back in.

8. When you're ready to discontinue practicing the solidifying technique, release the pressure on your · thumbs or the rubber balls very gently and gradually. If you do this properly, by the time you've released your grip, your in- and out-breaths will feel nearly as strong and evenly matched as they did while squeezing the balls.

Over time, the improvements you make in your breathing during the course of your daily practice sessions will tend to persist beyond the sessions and gradually become a normal part of your breathing.

BREATH-BALANCING TECHNIQUE #3: STRENGTHENING THE OUT-BREATH

THE OUT-BREATH REPRESENTS the "masculine" (or active) aspect of our being. It is sometimes called the "manifesting breath" because breathing out is the basis of every action we take in life.

It could also be called the "attack breath"; the intense shouts and battle cries that martial artists and warriors make vividly illustrate how feelings of strength and assertiveness are directly linked with the vigor and strength of the out-breath.

When our breathing patterns are well developed, the tensions of our in- and out-breaths are evenly matched. Western prize-fighters intuitively cultivate this equalized balance of tensions by learning to breathe in or out with exactly the same intensity. A well-trained boxer can instantly pivot between breathing in and breathing out with equal degrees of control, the better to "absorb" the force of a punch with his in-breath, then send it back to his opponent on the out-breath with even greater force.

This next technique, "strengthening the out-breath," will enable you to strengthen your exhalations and weaken the habit of collapsing as you breathe out. As your exhalations grow firmer and stronger, the tensions of your in- and out-breaths will become more evenly matched. You'll also begin to experience new feelings of strength and stability in both your mind and body.

Strengthening the out-breath is done at the end of the out-breath, just before breathing back in. This is the same point in your breathing cycle at which you would correct the pause by bringing the air right back into your body. This time, instead of correcting the pause at the end of the out-breath, you'll be learning to "push" the air out of your body by contracting your diaphragm with a short, sudden thrusting movement. As soon as you "thrust" from your diaphragm with moderate force, the air will immediately reenter your body with new feelings of firmness and strength.

Strengthening the out-breath begins in exactly the same way as gentling the in-breath. This is how it's done:

1. Sit in a comfortable posture and begin to meditate on your breath. Once you're in touch with its movement, become aware of the volume of air that enters your lungs each time you breathe in.

2. Next, whenever you inhale, imagine that you are breathing the air into your body as if from between your legs. As soon as you do, the amount of air that enters your body will noticeably increase.

3. At the end of the out-breath, instead of correcting the pause, contract your diaphragm with a moderate degree of force and thrust the air from your body with a short, sudden stroke. As soon as you do this, the air will come right back into your body with new feelings of firmness and strength.

4. While your breath is readjusting its tensions, study the changes this technique has produced in its movements. Notice that your breath is now moving more freely, your out-breaths have become a bit stronger, and the tensions of your in- and out-breaths have become a bit more evenly matched.

STRENGTHENING THE OUT-BREATH WITH BREATHING-RELEASE TECHNIQUES

Once you've learned how to strengthen the out-breath, you can make this technique part of your daily practice by using it in conjunction with the Tarzan and gentle rapid breathing techniques. This is how it's done:

1. Sit in a comfortable posture and begin to meditate on your breath. Once you're in touch with its movements,

do a few rounds of Tarzan and/or the gentle rapid breathing technique to invigorate the flow of your breath.

2. As soon as your breathing is more open and flowing, begin gentling your in-breath by breathing the air into your body as if from between your legs.

3. At the end of each exhalation, thrust the air from your body by contracting your diaphragm with a moderate degree of force. As soon as you thrust at the end of the out-breath, the air will come right back into your body with new feelings of vigor and strength.

4. As your breath readjusts its tensions, if you study the changes this technique has produced, you'll find that your breath is moving with greater freedom and ease and your out-breaths have become a bit stronger and the tensions of your in- and out-breaths have become a bit more evenly matched. Along with these changes in your breathing, you'll find that you're also feeling more calm and solid throughout your mind and body.

What to Watch For

You may use Tarzan or the gentle rapid breathing technique to enliven your breath as many times as you wish. Each time you use the thrusting technique, give your breath four or five cycles of breathing to readjust its tensions before doing another round of strengthening the out-breath. Over time, the improvements you make during the course of your daily practice sessions will become part of your everyday breathing.

Perfecting the Balance of Tensions

PERFECTING THE TENSIONS of our in- and out-breaths is not a straight-line process that can be completed in weeks, months, or even years of continuous practice. It is a gradual and long-term process that involves many emotional ups and downs because the tensions of our in- and out-breaths are continually changing with every shift in our emotions. More than a thousand years ago, a Taoist master wrote:

> *It is within the nature of the common man's breathing to have difficulty retaining the inhalation, while the exhalation is easily exhausted.*[1]

This ancient Chinese master meant that as long as we're not fully enlightened and still have our sense of fear, we will always create imbalances in the flow of our breath by clutching, collapsing, and pausing when our pain and fear seem too great to bear.

Every so often, the tensions of our in- and out-breaths will come into balance all by themselves for any number of reasons. This is especially true in the case of well-trained athletes or people who regularly practice spiritual disciplines. For the most part, however, these inadvertent states of balance and the feelings of strength, peace, and solidity that accompany them will be relatively short-lived.

The only people whose in- and out-breaths remain perfectly balanced at all times and under all circumstances are great saints and perfected spiritual masters. Unlike most ordinary people, they've become completely independent of life's ups and downs because their consciousness is permanently established in a Divine state of peace (see chapter 18, "Samadhi"). Until we attain that very same state, the tensions of our in- and out-breaths will continually shift and change with the ever-changing circumstances of daily life.

Breath-balancing techniques are some of the most empowering of all breathing practices because they enable us to control our most basic reactions to fear: the tendency to clutch, collapse, and pause to block our scariest thoughts and feelings. Bringing these basic reactions under control is the very essence of self-mastery, for as we change our way of relating to fear, we also change our relationship with everything else in life.

CHAPTER NINE

THE SHIELD
of
DETACHMENT

Detachment is the fruit of meditation.

— BUDDHA

IN ANCIENT CHINA, there once lived a cruel robber baron who took great pleasure in robbing and killing helpless villagers, then burning their homes to the ground. When people heard he was riding their way with his murderous band of thieves, the villagers would run to hide in the nearby hills. The chieftain was an arrogant man who considered himself to be an utterly fearless, invincible warrior. Nothing brought him greater satisfaction than to ride into a village and find it deserted. To his pride-filled mind, a hastily abandoned village was a tribute to his "greatness" — a sign of the terror the mere mention of his name could instill in others.

One day, when the peasants of a certain village learned that this robber baron was heading their way, they snatched up whatever possessions they could hold in their arms and hurried to hide in the hillside caves. The only person who stayed behind was an old Zen master who lived in a small temple at the edge of town. When the chieftain arrived with his band of raiders, he was enormously pleased to find the village empty — until he discovered the old master quietly hoeing the temple garden as if nothing unusual were going on. Livid with rage, he grabbed the old man by the front of his robe, pressed a dagger against his throat, and bellowed, "Don't you know who I am? I'm the one who can slit your throat without blinking an eyelash!"

The master calmly looked into the bandit's eyes and said, "And don't you know who I am? I'm the one who can let you slit my throat without blinking an eyelash." Upon hearing these words, the "fearless" bandit felt a cold chill of terror run down his spine for the first time in many years.

The Tides of Fear

FEAR IS A GIVEN IN LIFE. Except for those rare and fleeting moments in which we're having a mystical experience or sharing deep feelings of love and trust with another person, fear is as ever-present in our lives as the ocean waters are at the seashore. When our sense of fear is at "low tide," we feel relatively strong, secure, and happy. No matter how strong or confident we might feel at the time, however, our sense of fear is never completely gone. It will eventually return as surely as high tide at the beach.

Anyone who claims they never get scared is either a saint, a self-deluded fool, or a liar. The only people who've truly transcended their sense of fear are great saints and realized beings. Until we attain the same level of self-mastery as the Zen master in the preceding story, our feelings of strength and security will depend not on how well we manage to block or avoid our feelings of fear, but on how honestly we handle them whenever they show up. For example, the robber had deluded himself into thinking he was fearless by repressing his feelings of fear—then cruelly projecting them onto his victims. When the Zen master held a mirror of true fearlessness in front of the robber baron's eyes, the robber became filled with terror as the waves of fear he'd repressed for so many years rose to the surface of his consciousness.

Although there are thousands of things that can trigger our fears, we have only one *sense of fear* and one basic set of responses that spring into action the instant we get scared. It doesn't matter whether we become scared because we're about to lose a parking space in the middle of New York City or a close friend who is dying of cancer. In either case, we'll experience the same kinds of energies moving through our system. Although we'll experience much more fear at the thought of losing a friend than at the thought of losing a parking space, our physical and emotional responses will be essentially the same in both cases, differing only in their intensity.

Many people mistakenly believe that, in order to become fearless, we must confront each of our personal fears and overcome them one by one. But self-mastery isn't a matter of overcoming our fears one at a time; it's a matter of learning to handle the feeling of fear itself, no matter what initially triggers it.

Slaying the Medusa

THERE ARE TWO KINDS OF FEAR that we must learn to deal with. The first is real fear — the kind we experience when we're confronted with a clear and present danger. The second is anxiety — the layers of repressed fear that give birth to the anxious creations of our mind. Although these kinds of fears might appear to be real, they usually have no basis in fact.

The first kind of fear — real fear — is brilliantly symbolized in the legend of the Medusa, the snake-haired monster who roamed the hills of ancient Greece attacking villages and devouring people at will. Many brave warriors tried to kill her, but they all failed because anyone who looked upon her fearsome countenance would instantly become "petrified" (or turned to stone).

The Medusa represents real fear, the kind we experience when we're facing a clear and present danger or when life compels us to deal with some deep personal issue that we've repressed and kept hidden away in the back of our mind. These are the fears that we must confront because we can neither avoid them nor continue to postpone them by repressing them as we may have done in the past. The problem is that if we "look" at these fears in the wrong state of mind, we're liable to become petrified or "scared stiff."

Perseus, the hero who finally slew the Medusa, protected himself from her magic spell by looking at her reflection in his mirror-like shield. Over the years, I've come to call Perseus's legendary shield "the shield of detachment." Detachment is a calm, neutral state of mind that is highly prized by martial artists and spiritual seekers alike; it enables them to stay cool, calm, and collected in the face of danger. The first technique in this chapter, the Janus technique, will teach you how to use your breath like Perseus's shield to keep from becoming scared stiff when you're dealing with fear of something real.

Returning to the Land of Light

THE SECOND TYPE OF FEAR — repressed fear or anxiety — is brilliantly dramatized in the Greek legend of Orpheus. You may remember that Orpheus descended into Hades, hoping to persuade Pluto, who reigned in the underworld, to release his beloved Eurydice from the hold of death. Pluto was so impressed by the young man's courage that he gave him a chance to win her back. Eurydice would be allowed to follow Orpheus back to the land of the living, on one condition: he must never turn and look behind himself until he had reentered the land of light. If he casted even the slightest glance over his shoulder, he would lose Eurydice forever.

As Orpheus climbs the dismal stairway from hell, he is continually beset by Pluto's ferocious hounds, who snarl, and growl, and snap at his heels with every step he climbs. But Orpheus ignores their threats and never once turns around to protect himself. Just as he glimpses the light of day at the top of the stairs, he hears Eurydice cry, "Orpheus! Help!" Unable to bear the thought of losing her, Orpheus impulsively turns around to rescue her — only to find that Eurydice's cry of distress was a cruel and cynical ruse. All he can do is look on helplessly as Pluto's demons drag his beloved back to the land of the dead.

Orpheus lost Eurydice because he listened to his anxieties instead of keeping his mind focused on his primary goal: reaching the land of light. If he had treated his fear of losing Eurydice the same as he treated Pluto's hounds, he'd have brought her safely home. The second technique in this chapter, the Tippy technique, will teach you how to ignore the anxious creations of your own mind by focusing on your breathing as if it were the light at the top of the stairway from hell.

DETACHMENT TECHNIQUE #1:
JANUS

JANUS WAS A ROMAN GOD with two faces: one in the front of his head and the other in back. The Romans worshipped him as the guardian of portals and the patron of beginnings and endings. They usually placed his effigy above the gateways of temples and public buildings, where he could oversee whatever events were taking place both within and outside the walls.

I call this next practice the Janus technique because it enables us to keep our consciousness delicately poised on the dividing line between our inner and outer worlds, where we can observe the events occurring both within and outside of ourselves. This threshold between inner and outer reality is a neutral zone of consciousness that lies beyond fear and doubt (see "Witness Consciousness" in chapter 21). Warriors who enter this neutral state of consciousness become virtually untouchable during a battle because they lose all sense of concern for their personal safety.

Janus is a powerful grounding technique that steadies and strengthens the mind and breath. However, its chief virtue lies in the fact that it enables us to cultivate the same calm and detached state of mind that Perseus gained by steadily looking into his shield while fighting the Medusa. Over the centuries, the Eastern martial artists have developed many similar "gazing" techniques to cultivate the virtues of fearlessness, detachment, and one-pointedness of mind.

This is how the Janus technique is done:

1. As usual, assume a comfortable sitting position with your rubber balls held loosely in your hands, then close your eyes and begin meditating on the movements of your breath.

2. Once you've become attuned to its movements, open your eyes very gently and slowly — without losing track of your breath — and allow your gaze to rest on any spot that comfortably falls within your field of vision.

3. Your next task is to keep your attention steadily trained on that spot, without straining your eyes and without losing track of your breath. Keeping your awareness perfectly poised between your breath and the spot you're gazing at is somewhat like learning to ride a bicycle without falling to one side or the other. In this case, you're learning to keep your consciousness neutrally balanced "at center," without falling inward (toward your breath) or outward (toward your focal point).

4. As you meditate, sometimes your vision will blur and your eyes will begin to wander. When these things happen, be careful not to force your eyes to stay in focus. If you squeeze the rubber balls with one steady pressure, your eyes will regain their ability to stay in focus with no sense of effort or strain. It's also okay to blink your eyes whenever you feel the need.

5. Keeping your attention evenly suspended between your breath and the point in front of you will cause your consciousness to become delicately poised

on the dividing line between your inner and outer worlds. Within moments after starting, you'll feel a calm, steady center beginning to crystallize within you.

6. As this center of calmness becomes more firmly established, you'll begin to experience a new sense of freedom from any events taking place, both within and outside yourself. For example, you'll find that distracting influences, such as anxious thoughts, uncomfortable physical sensations, or sounds in the outside world, will have little or no effect on your feelings of calmness and stability.

7. After five to ten minutes of gazing at the external point (without losing track of your breath), you'll feel a strong urge to close your eyes and turn within. Resist this feeling for as long you can without straining. When you finally allow your eyes to close, you'll be instantly drawn into a deep state of meditation. At this point, you may continue to meditate inwardly for as long as you wish.

Janus is an excellent way to begin your daily meditations because the steadier your mind is right from the start, the deeper and more fruitful your meditations will be. Over time, the feelings of calmness and steadiness this technique produces will become part of your everyday consciousness.

DETACHMENT TECHNIQUE #2: THE TIPPY TECHNIQUE

THERE ARE SOME DAYS when we feel so beleaguered by anxious thoughts and agitated feelings that we need some sort of special help to loosen their grip on our mind. These are the best times for practicing the "Tippy technique." Believe it or not, I learned this method for bringing anxious feelings under control from my dog Tippy, an amazingly intelligent collie who lived on our family farm in Connecticut.

When Tippy and I went walking along the country roads, some of the dogs from the neighboring farms would come charging toward us, barking furiously to assert their territorial rights. Some of them acted so fierce and nasty that I'd find myself flinching or walking a bit faster to get away from them — but not Tippy. He always remained completely calm, aloof, and self-possessed because he had a foolproof system for disarming even the most hostile dog without making a single growl or menacing bark.

Tippy's method was incredibly simple: When a dog came running toward us barking, he'd completely ignore it and casually continue sniffing at trees alongside the road. This unflappable behavior would usually cause the other dog to come even closer and bark louder than ever. But no matter how close it came or how loudly it barked, Tippy would just keep on sniffing the trees and fence posts, without casting so much as a glance in the other dog's direction.

The other dog would become so nonplussed by Tippy's aloofness that he would finally stop barking and come closer to check him out. Once the dog got close enough, Tippy would suddenly turn and thrust his nose directly into its face, as if to say, "Yes? Is there something on your mind?" The dog would be so intimidated by this "Tippy treatment" that he'd immediately turn and walk meekly back home with a drooping tail.

Since then, I've used Tippy's system on any hostile dog I happen to encounter when I'm out jogging or taking a walk. If a barking dog approaches me from my right, I make it a special point to look casually off to my left. If it comes at me from behind, I never turn around to look at it, no matter how scared I might be. Above all, I never betray any feelings of fear by breaking my stride or changing my speed. This method has never once failed me. Even the most unfriendly dogs soon lose interest and wander off to look for more interesting things to do.

The old adage that says "a barking dog will never bite" is basically true — but only if we ignore the dog while it's barking. If we turn around in fear and say something like "Nice doggie!" or "Shoo! Go away!" even a dog who'd normally be too scared to attack is liable to gain the courage to bite.

The anxiety-based scenarios we create in our minds are just like those barking dogs. As long as we ignore them, they won't try to bite. Like the threats of those barking dogs, most of our fearful imaginings are simply not based in fact. However, we can turn them into reality by giving them credence, which is exactly how Orpheus lost Eurydice. Over the years, I've learned that Tippy's method for handling troublesome dogs is a great technique for dealing with the nagging thoughts and anxious feelings that shatter our peace of mind.

Tippy's techniques can be practiced in the privacy of your home, but it's better to do it outside as a walking meditation. Next time your anxious thoughts and feelings begin running out of control, just stop whatever you're doing and take your "barking dogs" out for a walk. This is how it's done:

1. As you're walking along the street, learn to ignore your worried thoughts, just as Tippy ignored those barking dogs. One of the best ways to do this is to meditate on your breathing the whole time you're walking.

2. As you're watching your breath, focus your attention on the simple, obvious things in your surroundings that you would usually take for granted. For example, you might notice the color and shape of a certain house and describe it to yourself in detail: "That's a white house with blue trim. It has a big picture window in front and two smaller windows on each side." If your anxious feelings are particularly intense or difficult to ignore, describe the things you see by speaking to yourself out loud.

3. Most important of all, never get into a dialogue with your worried thoughts. Don't try to figure them out, and don't try to push them out of your mind. These tactics will simply give them more energy and make them stronger than ever. Just keep watching your breath and ignore them like Tippy ignored those barking dogs.

4. The louder your dogs "bark" to get your attention, the more determined you must become to watch your breath and keep your mind focused on the simple things you see around yourself. Remember: Although Pluto's hounds continually growled and snapped at Orpheus's heels, they never actually bit him because, like Tippy, he ignored their threats.

5. The harder you have to work to ignore your barking dogs, the more control you're gaining over your mind. Although you may feel terribly scared and helpless, you're actually weakening your mind's crippling fascination with its own sense of fear and developing new levels of inner strength and detachment.

6. You can speed the process of quieting your mind by squeezing your rubber balls (or thumbs) with one steady pressure as you walk. The deeper and stronger your breathing becomes, the sooner your mind will quiet down.

7. No matter what steps you take to regain your composure, always remember to keep watching your breath and keep it open and flowing. This will enable you to ride the waves of anxiety until they lose some of their virulence. Once your anxiety has become a bit less intense, you can use any of the grounding, strengthening, and balancing techniques to guide your mind and body into higher states of integration than ever before.

The Lion and the Monkey

THE EASTERN WARRIORS SAY that when a lion hears a gunshot, it lifts its head and looks around to discover where the shot came from. But when a monkey hears a gunshot, it shrieks in fear and anxiously begins to check its body to see if it's been wounded. This difference in behavior illustrates the major difference between a courageous person and one who becomes the helpless victim of his own fear.

"Lion-hearted" people never let fear for their own safety interfere with their ability to cope with whatever danger might be at hand. Paradoxically, this relative lack of concern for their personal safety is the very reason why they're usually so invulnerable.

In times of crisis, our greatest protection lies in remaining calm and centered, and the only way to achieve this is to keep our breath open, flowing, and strong. Insofar as we manage to accomplish this, the powerful resources that fear can bring become just as available to us as to any great warrior. The Janus and Tippy techniques work hand in hand to help us use the energies of our fear as an ally. Janus helps us cultivate the steadiness and quiet courage of a lion, while Tippy's technique keeps us from behaving like a scared monkey and becoming a victim of our own anxious thoughts and feelings.

My students sometimes say, "These techniques work just fine when I'm meditating at home, but what should I do when I get scared out there in the 3-D world?" The first thing I advise them to do is "Keep on breathing, no matter what!" The spirit of life that dwells in your breath has incredible powers for handling pain and fear. If you remember to keep your breath open and flowing, you'll be surprised at how much more calm and solid you'll feel, even in times of crisis.

These breathing techniques really work. All you have to do is to spend some quality time making them your own. Just as an athlete learns to perform well under pressure by training regularly, your ability to keep your breathing strong, open, and flowing under fire will greatly depend on the discipline and regularity you bring to your daily practice. As a great martial artist used to say to his students:

I know not how I smite my enemies;
I simply do my practices every day.

CHAPTER TEN

LEARNING

to

TRUST YOUR BREATH

UP TO THIS POINT IN THE BOOK, you've learned so many breathing techniques that you may be wondering how you'll ever manage to practice all of them in the course of a single session. The solution to this problem is simple: Don't even bother to try! Just work with a few of the basic techniques at any given time. Any technique you practice on a regular basis will gradually change the way you breathe. As your breath learns the lessons that a technique has to offer, you can phase it out of your daily practice sessions and begin to include some of the basic techniques found in the subsequent chapters.

For example, I recommend that everyone begin by practicing the Tarzan and gentle rapid breathing techniques on a daily basis to get their breath open and flowing. As the releasing effects of these techniques begin to take root in your system, your breath will begin moving more freely of its own accord. At this point, you can gradually phase them out of your daily practice sessions and begin to include some of the grounding and strengthening techniques taught in chapter 7.

As your breathing patterns begin to change because the grounding techniques are accomplishing their work, they, too, will require less amounts of regular practice, and you can begin to include the breath-balancing techniques as part of your daily practice. Once you've become reasonably proficient with the basic techniques taught in chapters 3, 5, 7, and 8, you'll be ready to work with the more advanced techniques taught in the rest of the book.

The Wisdom of the Breath

WORKING WITH A COMPLETE and well-balanced set of breathing techniques is somewhat like playing a game of golf with a full set of clubs. When we're out on the fairway, we never use the clubs in strict numerical order because there is no way to know which club we'll need next until after we've hit the ball and seen where it lands. So once you've mastered the basic techniques, don't rigidly practice them in the same sequence you learned them. Whenever you sit to meditate, treat each session as new. Since your breathing patterns will always be evolving and changing, your breath will usually require different kinds of development each time you sit to practice.

The only technique that you *must* work with at all times is meditation on the breath. No matter which breathing techniques you decide to practice on any given day, be sure to spend plenty of time simply meditating on your breath without trying to influence its movements. This will not only give your breath a chance to practice the lessons it's learned from each of the basic techniques, it will also ensure that you continue to reap the special fruits and blessings that only meditation can bring.

As your breath regains its vigor and health, the techniques you practiced on a regular basis will spontaneously show up to support you in the course of your everyday life. For example, you might be speaking with a difficult client or having lunch with an irascible relative who grates on your nerves. Just when your patience is wearing dangerously thin, you'll suddenly hear an inner voice quietly reminding you to watch your breath, or you may find yourself secretly doing the gentle rapid breathing technique to ease your feelings of exasperation.

When you first begin working with breathing techniques, you're using your mind to guide your breath away from its old, bad habits and into healthier states of balance. Always remember, however, that the spiritual life-force that dwells in your breath is infinitely wiser than your mind will ever be. So as your breath begins to get back on track as a result of working with the basic techniques, your next challenge will lie in learning to trust your breath by allowing it to do whatever it wishes without trying to control its movements.

The farther you travel along the path of the breath, the more you'll realize that the advanced kinds of guidance you'll eventually need can come only from the natural wisdom of the breath itself. As your breathing becomes increasingly strong, healthy, and well-balanced, the spiritual life-force that dwells in your breath will not only "tell" you which techniques are best to work with at any given time, it will spontaneously modify the basic techniques you've already learned to suit the ever-evolving needs of your breath. The spirit of life that dwells in your breath is so infinitely wise, it will even create new techniques, especially for you, that you've never seen or heard of before.

PART THREE

HEALING ILLNESS

CHAPTER ELEVEN

THE INVISIBLE MAN

The real you is invisible.

— Paramahansa Yogananda

In March of 1940, the great Hindu saint Swami Paramahansa Yogananda delivered a brilliant lecture to a Western audience in which he introduced them to a vitally important but little-known part of themselves, which he called "the invisible man."

> *Within the physical body, yet invisible to the physical eyes, is an identical body of light, the astral encasement of the soul.... The astral body looks exactly like the visible one, except that its form, being made of light and energy, is*

*extremely subtle.... There is an invisible astral counterpart
for all the bodily parts. Behind your physical heart there is
an invisible heart. Without it, your visible heart would not
beat. You have invisible organs of sight and hearing, an
invisible brain, invisible bones, and nerves.... Without the
invisible self, the body would be as worthless as a corpse.*[1]

For thousands of years, saints, sages, and shamans of all cultures and traditions have taught that human beings have not one, but two different bodies. The Eastern masters called them the "physical body" and the "subtle body." In the New Testament, the early Christian fathers refer to them as the "natural body" and the "spiritual body."[2]

Our physical (or natural) body is the finite, mortal part of ourself that belongs to the earthly plane of existence. The subtle (or spiritual) body is the matrix of our soul — the celestial part of our being that belongs to the world of spirit. Most relevant to the purposes of healing, however, the subtle body is the abode of the spiritual life-force. It is also the part of our being in which we experience all of our thoughts and emotions and "trap" our feelings of fear.

Everyone knows about their physical body because it is made up of solids, liquids, and gasses. However, few people are aware that they also have a subtle (or spiritual) body. Because it is made of light and energy, the spiritual body is too subtle to be detected with our physical senses.

Although the subtle body is normally invisible to the physical eye, there have always been psychically gifted people, such as yogis, shamans, and spiritual healers, who can see its radiations with their subtle eyes. These people universally describe the subtle body as an oval halo of shimmering light that surrounds the physical body. For example, Don Juan, the famous Native American sorcerer, once told Carlos Castaneda that to the eyes of "a man of knowledge," human beings look more like "luminous eggs" than the two-legged creatures we normally see with our physical eyes.

The tradition of depicting images of saints surrounded by halos of golden-white light is not just a matter of artistic license or a figment of the artist's imagination. The subtle body of a great saint sometimes glows with such brilliance that its light can even be seen with the physical eye. In the New Testament, for example, Matthew describes how Jesus' face "... did shine like the sun, and his raiment was white as light."[3]

Over the centuries, the subtle body has been given dozens of names. Most people call it the "aura" because it appears as a colorful halo or auric glow that surrounds the physical body. It is also commonly called the "astral body" because it is made of astral matter (energy and light) and belongs to the celestial planes of existence. I call it the "human energy field" or the "field of human consciousness" because this is the dimension of our being in which we experience all forms of conscious perception — all images, thoughts, emotions, and experiences of pleasure and pain.

The Etheric Double

OVER THE CENTURIES, Hindu and Buddhist yogis developed special meditation techniques that enabled them to study the structure of the subtle body in minute detail. They learned that the subtle body consists of four concentric bands of conscious energy, which the Hindus call *koshas* (or "sheaths"), and that each sheath controls a different aspect of human consciousness (see Figure 11.1).

The first, or innermost, sheath is called the "etheric body." Some people call it the "etheric double" because it is a perfect duplicate of the physical body, except that it is made up of energy and light instead of matter. The etheric double is the "invisible man" Yogananda spoke of in his lecture. The etheric body (or double) contains the energy blueprint for the growth and development of the physical body. It also supplies the spiritual "electricities" that power all of the biological processes that take place in the physical body. Without the spiritual energies supplied by the subtle body, our physical body would be as useless as a car without a battery.

The halo immediately surrounding the etheric double is known as the "emotional body" because this is the sheath of consciousness in which we experience our emotions.

The second halo shown in the illustration represents the "mental body." As its name implies, this is the dimension of consciousness in which all forms of mental activity, such as thinking, imaging, and dreaming, take place.

The outermost sheath is called the "causal body." This is the dimension of our being in which all creative abilities and miraculous powers are found.

As you study Figure 11.1, bear in mind that the subtle body is a multidimensional energy field that is impossible to depict in a two-dimensional drawing. For example, the four sheaths are not separate units that fit inside one another like a child's nest of dolls. Although they vibrate at different frequencies, their energies continually interpenetrate and influence the rate of one another's vibrations. Together, the four sheaths comprise one whole person — a single conscious entity, complete with thoughts, emotions, and the ability to interact and create on the earthly plane by using the physical body as its host.

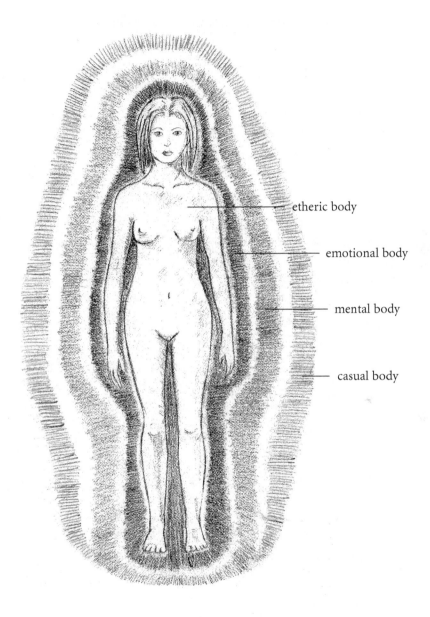

etheric body

emotional body

mental body

casual body

Figure 11.1: The Subtle Body
Note: The physical body is not shown in this drawing.

The Spiritual Electricities

THE PRANIC LIFE-FORCE ENTERS OUR BEING via a central channel in the etheric body that the Hindus call the *sushumna* (see Figure 11.2). The sushumna is the equivalent of the spinal cord in our physical body. In deep meditation, it can be seen as an exquisite column of golden-white light that extends from the base of the spine to the crown of the head. This incredibly beautiful column of light is the very core of our being, for this is where the spiritual life-force enters our body and dwells in its most pristine form for as long as we're alive and breathing.

Distributed along the length of the sushumna is a series of brilliantly colored energy centers known as *chakras* ("wheels" in Sanskrit). The chakras are equivalent to the brain and nerve plexuses found in the physical body. They serve as step-down transformers that cause the rapidly vibrating energies of prana to vibrate at the lower frequencies required by the physical body.

Radiating out from the chakras is a vast and intricate network of thread-like structures called *nadis*. The nadis are equivalent to the neural pathways of the physical body. Their function is to distribute the stepped-down energies produced by the chakras to every tissue and cell of the physical body. (For the sake of clarity and simplicity, the nadis are not illustrated in Figure 11.2.)

The physical body is like a magnificent robot that has no power supply of its own. Without the spiritual electricities supplied by the etheric body, it would become a lifeless corpse. When we die, our subtle body separates from our physical body and leaves with our very last out-breath.

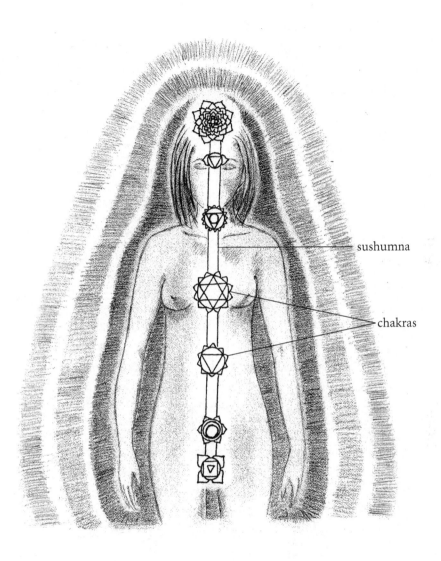

sushumna

chakras

Figure 11.2: The Sushumna and the Chakras

The organ transplants routinely performed by today's surgeons provide tangible evidence that the subtle body is the physical body's power source. The only reason that doctors can remove an organ from a dead person's body, store it in an organ bank, then revivify it in a living person's body is because the recipient still has a subtle body — and that's what brings the organ back to life.

Phantom Limbs

THERE IS A MYSTERIOUS MEDICAL PHENOMENON known as the "phantom limb effect" that doctors find difficult to explain. People who have lost a limb sometimes feel as if the amputated limb is still attached to their body. In some cases, they continue to feel pain in the phantom limb long after their wounds have healed. Some doctors theorize that these phantom impressions originate in the severed nerves of the stump. Others think that the phantom limb and sensations of pain are psychosomatic symptoms that only exist in the person's mind.

The reason the doctors are puzzled is that the sensations of pain and the impression of still having a limb have nothing to do with the physical body; both experiences originate in the person's etheric body. People who experience the presence of phantom limbs are actually sensing the presence of their etheric limbs. Although their physical limb is gone, the corresponding limb of their etheric double still exists in their energy field, giving them the impression that the missing limb is still attached to their body.

The techniques I use in my healing work clearly show that the sensations of pain in phantom limbs originate with the severely repressed feelings of pain and fear that the person experienced at the time of the injury. For example, I once worked with Dan, a stoic Iowa farmer whose leg had been amputated below the knee because of a terrible accident he'd had on his farm. Although four years had gone by since the accident, Dan lived with the constant impression that his missing leg was still attached to his body. He also experienced chronic feelings of low-grade pain, reminiscent of the pain he felt at the time of his accident.

As I worked with the vibrations in Dan's energy field, I could feel his etheric leg projecting from the stump in exactly the same place where his physical leg would have been. Several of my advanced trainees, who were observing the session, could also feel Dan's phantom leg in his energy field. After assuring Dan that his phantom sensations weren't figments of his imagination, I helped him release the feelings of chronic pain and "erased" the phantom leg from his consciousness by cleansing the fear that had stayed trapped in his energy field since the accident.

Biomagnetic Energy Fields

FOR MORE THAN A CENTURY, Western scientists have known that all living creatures are surrounded by a field of electromagnetic energy that disappears when the organism dies. Although few doctors realize that this electromagnetic field is the same as the subtle body, they've become increasingly aware of the vital role it plays in the development and healing of an organism's physical body. For example, in the early 1940s Harold Burr, a neuroanatomist at Yale University, conducted a series of experiments in which he used conventional voltmeters and electrographic images (Kirlian photographs) to study the size and shape of the energy fields that surround living plants and animals.[4]

Burr began by photographing the auras of salamanders, and discovered that the shape of their aura is approximately the same as the shape of their physical body. He then moved on to mapping the energy fields of various plants, and learned that their auras also follow the shape of the physical plant. When Burr photographed the auras of plant seedlings, however, he was surprised to find that their energy fields resemble, not the shape of the seedlings, but the shape of the adult plants they would become.

Burr received an even greater surprise when he began photographing the auras of leaves that had been cut in half. Although half the leaf was gone, his photos revealed the ghostly presence of the missing half in its energy field. This phenomenon has since become known as the "phantom leaf effect" — the plant-world analogue to the phantom limb effect that occurs in human beings. Burr's research led him to conclude that an organism's energy field contains the growth template for the development of its physical body.[5]

Some years later, Dr. Robert Becker, a New York orthopedic surgeon who was studying the regeneration of limbs in frogs and salamanders, devised an ingenious experiment that further supported Burr's conclusions. When a salamander loses an arm or leg, it grows an entirely new limb from the remaining stump. Frogs, however, don't regenerate limbs; they simply heal at the stump as humans do. Becker surgically amputated the arms of salamanders and frogs, then, as their injuries healed, studied the electromagnetic changes that took place in their energy fields. He discovered that, during the process of healing, the electromagnetic currents in a salamander's energy field undergo opposite shifts in polarity from those that occur in a frog's energy field. When he subjected the stump of a frog's arm to the reversed currents that flow through a salamander's energy field, the frog grew a new arm.[6]

Vibrational Healing

THE RESEARCH DONE BY PIONEERS like Harold Burr and Robert Becker has since given rise to the field of bioelectronics, a relatively new branch of medicine that promotes healing by influencing the electromagnetic vibrations in a person's energy field. These days, doctors routinely use various ultrasound and magnetic-field therapies to shrink tumors, heal broken bones, stimulate the growth of cartilage, and treat the symptoms of rheumatoid and degenerative arthritis. Dr. Richard Gerber describes this trend toward vibrational healing in his rich and informative book, *Vibrational Medicine:*

> *Medicine is at the threshold of discovering a hidden world of unseen energies that will help to diagnose and heal illness as well as allow researchers to gain new insights into the hidden potentials of consciousness. The etheric level of energy will be the first of these unseen worlds to be explored by enlightened scientists.*
>
> *Researchers will discover that the etheric body is an energetic growth template that guides the growth and development, as well as the dysfunction and demise, of all human beings. Based upon the evolved insights of these enlightened researchers, medicine will begin to comprehend that it is at the etheric level that many diseases have their origins.[7]*

Western scientists have only recently recognized the important role of the human energy field in healing. However, many ancient healing modalities have worked with the energies of the subtle body for thousands of years. For example, Chinese acupuncture promotes healing by correcting imbalances in the flow of chi throughout the physical body. The practitioner first reads the state of a patient's health using a sophisticated form of pulse diagnosis, then places needles at appropriate points along the acupuncture meridians to stimulate the flow of spiritual electricities from the subtle body to the physical body.

Ayurveda, the traditional healing modality of India, is also based on enhancing the flow of prana throughout the physical body. Much like Chinese acupuncturists, Ayurvedic physicians diagnose the state of a patient's health through pulse reading. They then prescribe a combination of diet, herbs, exercise, and therapeutic massage to reestablish a balanced flow of energies between the subtle and physical bodies.

For thousands of years, healers throughout the world have also used sound vibrations to change conditions within the subtle body. For example, shamanic healers and medicine men and women from all times and places have promoted healing by chanting, shaking rattles, and beating drums to influence the subtle body's vibrations. Tibetan Buddhist physicians and monks developed similar techniques over two thousand years ago, and they still use these methods for healing sick people today. Probably the most pleasant and soothing of all vibrational healing methods is practiced by East Indian musicians, who play "healing ragas" — Divinely inspired musical scales — that Hindus believe were provided by the gods to ease the pain and heal the sickness of human beings.

Mind or Matter?

IN HIS AUTOBIOGRAPHY, Bertrand Russell recalls that even as a young boy, he was irresistibly attracted to pondering metaphysical questions. When he tried to discuss such weighty matters with his parents, however, they never took him seriously. For example, when the budding genius asked the age-old question about the difference between mind and matter, they flippantly replied, "What is mind? No matter! What is matter? Never mind!"

Most Western scientists believe that the mind originates in the brain. They consider it to be some sort of "afterglow" of the bioelectrical impulses that move through a person's brain cells, but nothing could be farther from the truth. The mind and the brain are as different from each other as a computer is from the human being who operates it. The mind is an organ of cognition and perception that exists in the mental sheath of the subtle body, the dimension of consciousness in which all forms of mental activity, such as thinking, imaging, and analyzing, take place. The mental energies of the subtle body use the brain and its neural pathways to interact with the physical world.

The brain, on the other hand, is like a magnificent computer that correlates and coordinates our thoughts with our physical actions. However, it can neither interpret nor evaluate the information that passes between the mind and the physical senses because it has no intelligence of its own. Without the mental energies supplied by the subtle body, the brain would be as useless as a computer with no source of electrical power.

When a person suffers brain damage and loses some of their mental faculties, the "missing" parts of the mind haven't been destroyed along with the tissues of the brain because the mind doesn't exist in the physical body. Although the mind's ability to interact with the physical world has been impaired because the brain's circuitry has been damaged, the mind itself remains intact in the subtle body, complete with all its memories and intellectual functions.

Fear and the Subconscious Mind

THE "SUBCONSCIOUS MIND" ALSO EXISTS in the subtle body. In chapter 4, I discussed the fact that holding our breath to block feelings of fear does nothing to reduce the amount of fear in our system; it merely traps the fear in our energy field, where it turns into anxiety. In essence, what we call our subconscious mind is the accumulation of the anxious energy that's become trapped in our subtle body by suppressing our breath in fear (see chapter 14 for more on this subject).

These layers of "subconscious fear" not only complicate the healing of all injuries and illnesses, they sometimes take on a life of their own and create completely new symptoms of sickness or pain that have nothing to do with the original illness. For example, many conditions of chronic pain that are presumed to be the permanent results of an injury are actually caused by the layers of anxious energy that have been trapped in a person's energy field.

In chapter 4, I spoke about Karen, the woman who suffered from chronic pain for thirty-five years after her leg had been crushed in a childhood accident. The pain she felt all those years wasn't caused by her injury; it was caused by all the pain and fear she'd suppressed when the doctor ordered her to stop crying. As soon as I helped her release these fear-ridden impressions from her energy field, Karen's pain quickly faded, and soon it disappeared.

In the same chapter, I also told the stories of Teresa, the Brazilian woman whose bee sting was slow to heal, and Ann, whose ankle developed tuberculosis of the bone after not healing for two years. The healing these women experienced in their physical bodies actually began in their subtle bodies, where their past impressions of fear were stored. When I lifted some of the fear that was trapped in their energy fields, their pain quickly subsided and their injuries finally began to heal.

The meditation and breathing techniques described in the following chapters will teach you how to cleanse pain and fear from your energy field. These techniques will not only enable you to release the layers of subconscious fear that interfere with healing, but they'll also teach you how to direct healing prana to specific areas of your mind and body that are most in need of help. These techniques are very effective and powerful. However, your ability to promote deep self-healing will greatly depend on how well you've mastered the basic techniques taught in chapters 3, 5, 7, and 8.

As you read through the following chapters, if you come across any technique that seems too far beyond your current level of accomplishment, just read the instructions without trying to practice it, and continue reading through the rest of the book. When your mastery of the basic techniques has strengthened and matured, you can return to that technique and work with it a later time. If you end up mastering only the basic techniques, you'll still have accomplished a lot. So don't try to push the river; don't insist on working with the advanced techniques until you've become reasonably skilled in working with the basic techniques, from which they derive their powers.

CHAPTER TWELVE

THE
HEALING TRIANGLE

*If one perceives there is disharmony and discomforts in the body,
one should store the breath energy and direct it to attack where
the ailment is. The ailment will naturally be gotten rid of.*
— MASTER GREAT NOTHING OF SUNG SHAN

EVERY TECHNIQUE IN THIS BOOK PROMOTES HEALING of one
kind or another. Some techniques energize our system, others
help us to feel more calm and solid, and still others dissolve
pain, fear, and tension and heal diseased tissues by increasing
the flow of prana throughout our system. Although these healing effects can sometimes be quite powerful and dramatic,
they're merely some of the fringe benefits we get from practicing breathing techniques to restore the health of our breath. In
order to take full advantage of the breath's healing powers, we

must learn how to consciously direct healing prana to specific symptoms of illness in our mind and body. In the words of the Chinese masters:

The breath follows the will which commands the breath like magic.[1]

In this chapter, you'll learn how to work with "the healing triangle," a powerful and sophisticated meditation technique that will enable you to concentrate your breath energy and direct it to diseased parts of your body with pinpoint accuracy.

The healing triangle is based on an ancient Hindu technique called *sumyama*, which the yogis practiced to attain miraculous powers (see chapter 17). The same meditative principles can be used to cultivate extraordinary powers of self-healing. This technique is wonderfully effective for healing a wide range of physical and emotional disorders. In this chapter, you'll be learning how to use the healing triangle to work with the specific symptoms of physical illness. Later on, in chapter 15, you'll learn to use it for healing emotional problems.

THE HEALING TRIANGLE

I CALL THIS TECHNIQUE "THE HEALING TRIANGLE" because it involves three basic elements that are kept in a delicate state of balance at all times (see Figure 12.1). The first element is our consciousness (our mind in meditation); the second is the breath; and the third is the particular symptom of illness we wish to heal. Figure 12.1 depicts our consciousness as poised at the apex of a triangle, where it simultaneously watches the breath and the disturbance we're feeling in our body.

When we focus our attention on the breath and the disturbance at the same time, we're creating a three-way "electrical circuit" through which the breath's healing energies are directly transmitted to the symptom of illness. In effect, our consciousness acts like a set of jumper cables that makes a direct connection between our breath and the symptom we wish to heal.

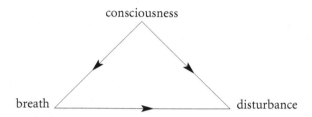

Figure 12.1: The Healing Triangle

The healing triangle is a remarkably powerful technique. However, your ability to promote deep self-healing will depend greatly on the depth of your meditation, the health of your breath, and the degree to which you've mastered the basic techniques taught in earlier chapters. The healthier and stronger your breathing is, and the greater your mastery of the basic techniques, the more effective the healing triangle will be whenever you sit to practice it. This is how it is done:

1. Sit in a comfortable posture with your rubber balls in hand, and meditate on your breath for five to ten minutes to establish a good state of meditative consciousness.

2. Next, do enough rounds of Tarzan and/or gentle rapid breathing to be sure that your breath is open and flowing.

3. Once your breath is moving more freely, keep watching your breath and use your consciousness like a radar beam. Slowly scan your body from the top of your head all the way down to your pelvis, looking for any symptoms of distress that feel as though they need some special help.

4. As you scan the inside of your body, you might come across any number of symptoms that could use some special attention. For example, there might be a burning sensation behind your eyes, a pain in your chest, tension in your stomach, and so on.

5. Work first with the symptom that is calling the loudest for your attention. For example, let's say you have a painful knot of tension in your stomach that feels more deeply disturbed than any other symptom of distress in your body.

6. Without losing track of your breath, focus your attention on the most intense part of the pain or tension, then squeeze your rubber balls firmly enough to match its intensity. This will bring your breathing tensions into synch with the tension in your stomach. On the very next inhalation, you'll find yourself breathing directly into the knot, as if your breath were selectively reaching out to touch the pain.

7. Keep the same steady pressure on the balls to keep the compression of your breath in synch with the tension you feel in your stomach, then do about five to ten seconds of gentle rapid breathing directly into the knot. This will weaken the energy blocks surrounding the knot and bring concentrated waves of healing prana directly into the tissues that feel

dis-eased. Within seconds, the knot will begin to feel a bit softer and the pain will diminish noticeably.

8. If you continue to watch your breath and keep tracking the changes taking place in your stomach, you'll notice that the pain or tension is continuing to change for the better, even though you've discontinued the gentle rapid breathing technique.

9. Still watching your breath, allow these changes to run their course for a full minute. At the end of this assimilation period, change the pressure on the balls to match the new feelings of pain or tension in your stomach. Then do another round of gentle rapid breathing to further weaken the energy blocks and bring fresh waves of prana into the tissues that need to be healed.

10. Each time you repeat this cycle, the pain and tension will grow increasingly weak, until the knot finally disappears. As the knot in your stomach begins to fade away, subtler symptoms of distress will begin to reveal their presence. These newly revealed disturbances might show up in other parts of your body, but they will usually appear somewhere in the immediate vicinity of the problem you've been working on — in this case, your stomach.

11. Whatever form these newly emerging disturbances take — feelings of irritation, pressure, burning, or anything else — treat them the same as you did the original feelings of pain in your stomach. Focus your attention on (what is now) the strongest feeling of disturbance, squeeze the balls firmly enough to match its intensity, breathe gently and rapidly into

the disturbance for five or ten seconds, then simply return to watching your breath and track the symptom's progress as it gradually melts and changes.

As this healing process unfolds, the feelings of release and relief will gradually move from one symptom to another, as if playing a slow-motion game of "healing tag." In the words of one Taoist master, "The various illnesses will retreat and disperse."[2] This gradual dispersion of symptoms will usually continue for anywhere from fifteen minutes to an hour. However, there's only so much healing your body can do in one sitting. As your body begins to reach this limit, your symptoms will gradually stop responding to the technique and the session will bring itself to a close.

What to Watch For

When you work with the healing triangle, you can expect it to bring relief and healing about 65 percent of the time. The rest of the time, it will seem to have little or no effect on your symptoms. Every so often, a symptom might even seem to get worse instead of better. If and when this happens, it usually indicates that the symptom is undergoing a "gestation period" — a stage of development in which it's not quite ready to change and be released.

Whenever your symptoms fail to respond, simply meditate on your breath as you usually do, or practice any of the basic techniques that feel right at the moment, and work with the healing triangle at a later time. Remember that the basic techniques trigger various kinds of spontaneous healing every time you work with them. When working with the basic techniques, you may not be selectively guiding the healing process; nevertheless, your body will still undergo healing of one kind or another.

Be careful not to start your practice sessions with a preconceived notion about which specific problem you intend to heal. Always begin by working with the most uncomfortable feeling revealed in your body when you scan it in meditation. When that feeling begins to heal and fade, focus your attention on the next symptom that calls loudest for attention. No matter which problem you might prefer to heal first, don't try to apply the healing triangle until and unless that problem shows up as the dominant symptom of distress in your body.

The pranic life-force is infinitely wise. As you meditate, learn to follow its movements wherever they take you. When conditions in your body are in the right state of balance, the particular symptoms you'd most like to heal will eventually show up as the dominant feelings of distress and have their turn to be bathed in the healing energies contained in your breath.

The healing triangle derives its power from your meditative consciousness, not from the gentle rapid breathing technique. During the early stages of learning to work with the healing triangle, gentle rapid breathing is used to *initiate* the healing process, which means it triggers the movement of energies between your breath and the symptom that needs to be healed. As you become more experienced, however, you'll find that your meditative consciousness can set the healing energies in motion without getting a "jump-start" from the gentle rapid breathing technique.

There are no set rules about how little or much to use the gentle rapid breathing technique during the course of any given session. Generally speaking, I might use it four or five times during the first ten minutes of my own self-healing sessions. The rest of the time, I tend to work with meditative consciousness alone, and only use gentle rapid breathing to disperse particularly stubborn energy blocks.

THE FOUNTAIN OF LOVE

In general, the more long-standing an illness is and the more severe its symptoms, the more time and skill you'll need to heal it. So if you're working with a particularly serious or protracted form of illness, it's best to look for a gradual improvement of your symptoms rather than to push for instant results. However, when an experienced meditator practices the healing triangle, it can bring remarkably immediate and dramatic results even if it's the first time the person has worked with this technique.

About fifteen years ago, I taught the healing triangle technique to Elizabeth, a fifty-five-year-old social worker who was dying of spinal cancer. Elizabeth's disease was so advanced that medications could no longer relieve the constant pain she felt in her spine. Within fifteen minutes after I began coaching her on how to work with the healing triangle, she entered an especially deep state of meditation in which she felt her pain gradually dissolve, then completely disappear. At the site where most of the pain had been, she now felt "a warm fountain of love" that gushed gently forth from her spine suffusing her mind and body with deep feelings of peace and well-being.

These glowing reports took me completely by surprise. How had Elizabeth managed to transcend her pain so quickly? She answered my unspoken question a bit later on when she told me that she'd been a nun for twenty years before leaving the cloister to become a social worker. Thanks to the spiritual disciplines she'd faithfully practiced as a nun, Elizabeth had attained unusually strong meditative powers that brought her instant mastery of the healing triangle. Although I never saw her again, I'm certain that Elizabeth's remarkable affinity for this technique helped her to die peacefully, with little or no pain.

CHAPTER THIRTEEN

HEALING RESPIRATORY PROBLEMS

Wherever there is an ailment [one may] guide the breath energy to disperse it. . . . What disease is there that cannot be removed?

— TAOIST TEXT

RESPIRATORY DISORDERS are some of the most difficult problems to work with. One reason is that the tissues of the upper respiratory system are among the most delicate and overworked tissues in the body. Another is that our sense of fear is directly linked with the health of our breath. All air-breathing animals have an instinctive fear of suffocating, but we humans tend to overreact to this fear, making our feelings of suffocation much worse than they actually are.

Whenever we feel short of breath, we tend to get scared and instinctively try to bring more air into our lungs. But the harder we try, the more we constrict the muscles and tissues of our respiratory system and the less air we actually get — which makes us feel more scared than ever. When the fear that we're going to suffocate runs out of control, it turns into feelings of panic that severely restrict our intake of air and complicate the healing of any respiratory problem, no matter what treatments we use.

So whenever you have a respiratory problem, if you begin to get scared because you feel short of breath, try to remember that the fear of suffocation usually exists more in your mind than it does in your body. Your body can function remarkably well with very little air. As long as you don't panic or exert yourself, you'll be surprised at how comfortable you can feel even when the tissues of your upper respiratory system are constricted or swollen.

Meditation and Medication

THIS CHAPTER PRESENTS a set of techniques that help reduce the symptoms of tension, inflammation, and congestion in tissues of the upper respiratory system. To tap into the benefits these techniques offer, however, it is essential that you meditate on your breathing the whole time you're practicing them. Ironically, some people who most need to access the powers of their breath are also the most afraid to pay attention to their breathing because they think it's the source of their pain and fear.

Some people with chronic breathing disorders even become angry and resentful toward their own breath because they blame it for all of their problems. This attitude of fear and resentment is their greatest obstacle to restoring the health of their breath. One of the very best ways to move beyond such negative reactions and to keep yourself from panicking is to meditate on your breathing.

The techniques taught in this chapter may be practiced by themselves, or they may be used in conjunction with conventional medications such as bronchial dilators and nasal decongestants. If you are under the care of a doctor because you have a severe or chronic breathing disorder, continue taking your prescribed medication and use these techniques to enhance their effects. As you gain skill in working with these techniques, if you are considering reducing or eliminating your need for medication, you should consult with your doctor.

RESPIRATORY TECHNIQUE #1:
THE HEALING TRIANGLE

THE HEALING TRIANGLE can also be used to reduce feelings of tension, inflammation, and congestion in tissues of the upper respiratory system. It doesn't matter whether your symptoms are due to a cold, an infection, or a chronic breathing disorder. The process of using your breath to promote healing in your sinuses, throat, or bronchial tubes is essentially the same in every case.

Before you actually begin working with this technique, you should meditate on your breath for at least five minutes to establish a good state of meditation. Whenever you work with a respiratory problem, be sure to sit up as straight as you can, without straining. This will make it much easier for your body to breathe and your symptoms to shift and change. If you feel too ill to sit up straight by yourself, try propping yourself up with pillows.

This is how to apply the healing triangle to respiratory problems:

1. Sit in a comfortable posture with your rubber balls held loosely in your hands and meditate on your breath for at least five minutes to establish your meditation.

2. Still watching your breath, scan the tissues of your upper respiratory system to discover which symptoms of distress need the most help. For example, your sinuses might feel blocked, your throat might feel sore, your bronchial tubes might feel tense or congested, and so on.

3. Let's say that the feelings of congestion in your bronchial tubes are the most uncomfortable symptom of all. Without losing track of your breath, focus your attention on those feelings. Squeeze the rubber balls firmly enough to match their intensity, then do five or ten seconds of gentle rapid breathing directly into the disturbed areas. This will help disperse the blocks in your breathing and bring concentrated waves of healing prana directly into the congested tissues.

4. When you stop, keep watching your breath and study the changes that are now taking place in your lungs. Within seconds, you'll notice that your bronchial tubes feel a bit less congested and that it is correspondingly easier for you to breathe. If you keep watching your breath and continue to track the changes taking place in your lungs, the feelings of congestion will continue to ease.

5. Keep tracking these changes for at least a full minute. Then — still watching your breath — adjust the pressure on the balls to match the newly reduced feelings of congestion and do another round of gentle rapid breathing directly into your bronchial tubes. When you stop and observe the changes this makes, you'll usually find that the feelings of congestion are gradually beginning to disappear and that it is even easier to breathe than it was before.

6. As the feelings of congestion begin to fade, other feelings of distress (such as tension or irritation) might begin to show up in your bronchial tubes. If this happens, it doesn't mean that you're trading the congestion for a different set of symptoms. The tension and irritation have always been there; they're simply being revealed as the clouds of congestion disperse.

7. Treat these newly revealed disturbances just as you did the feelings of congestion: Focus your attention on the most uncomfortable symptom. Let's say your most uncomfortable symptom is now a feeling of irritation or inflammation. Squeeze the balls firmly enough to match the intensity of this symptom, then breathe gently and rapidly into the affected tissues for about five or ten seconds. When you're through, simply meditate on your breathing and keep tracking the feelings of irritation as they gradually ease and fade.

8. As your bronchial tissues become more relaxed, other symptoms of distress may gradually reveal themselves elsewhere in the region of your sinuses, throat,

or lungs. No matter where these symptoms appear or what form they take (tension, irritation, soreness, and so on), treat them just as you did the disturbances you previously felt in your bronchial tubes.

9. Keep watching your breath and focus your attention on whatever now arises as the most prominent feeling of distress. Squeeze the balls firmly enough to match the symptom's intensity, breathe gently and rapidly into the affected tissues for five or ten seconds, then simply meditate on your breath and study the changes taking place in your upper respiratory system. As the various symptoms fade and leave, you'll find it easier and easier to breathe.

You can work with the healing triangle for as long as your symptoms continue responding to the technique. As your body approaches its limits of healing, the session will automatically wind itself down and come to a close.

Once the healing session has run its course, give your system a chance to assimilate the benefits of your work by meditating on your heartbeat and breath for at least five to ten minutes. If you wish, you can keep a steady pressure on the rubber balls to deepen your breathing and strengthen your heartbeat. By the time you return to your normal activities, you'll feel like a new person.

What to Watch For

The tissues of the upper respiratory system are some of the most delicate in your body. So whenever you apply the gentle rapid breathing technique to your sinuses, throat, or lungs, it's very important to work as gently and sensitively as you possibly can. If you breathe too forcefully, or if you become impatient and try to rush the healing process, you're liable to irritate the tissues more than ever.

As you work, if you begin to get scared because you feel short of breath, just remember that the feeling of suffocation is more often an emotional fear than a physical fact. If you pay attention to the needs of your body and ignore the feelings of anxiety in your mind, the panicky feeling of suffocation will soon fade away.

Should you begin to get impatient or angry because you find it hard to breathe, don't treat your breath as an enemy. Always remember that your breath is the best friend you have in the world; it works every second of every day to sustain your life and heal your body, and it will continue to take care of you until the very last breath of your life.

Working with Sinus Congestion

THE MUCOUS MEMBRANES that line our sinus cavities are some of the most overworked tissues in our body, largely because they serve as our first line of defense against harmful airborne substances. Just as canaries were once used to detect poisonous gases in coal mines, the delicate tissues in our sinuses serve as an early warning system against airborne pollutants. Another of their tasks is to act as filters that intercept harmful particles and keep them from reaching our lungs.

The habit of suppressing our breath in fear creates tension and stress in the upper respiratory tract, which cause the sinus tissues to become overly sensitive to substances that wouldn't bother us when present in normal concentrations. These chronic conditions of tension and stress not only make it difficult for our sinuses to do their work in some people, they can eventually lead to allergies.

Considering their delicate nature and their difficult task of protecting our lungs, it's amazing that the sinus membranes manage to stay healthy and functional for as long as they do. But as strong and resilient as they are, they do have their limits. When these delicate membranes finally become inflamed or swollen, they need all the gentleness and meditative sensitivity we can muster as we work to relax and heal them.

These next two techniques — "the solidifying technique" and "relaxing the throat" — will help you create more breathing space in your sinuses when they feel pressured, constricted, or swollen. As you practice these techniques, remember to work as gently as you can. The more gentle and sensitive your work is, the more immediate and powerful the healing effects will be.

RESPIRATORY TECHNIQUE #2:
THE SOLIDIFYING TECHNIQUE

IN CHAPTER 7, you learned to use the solidifying technique to deepen and strengthen your breathing. This remarkably versatile technique can also be used to increase the volume of air that enters your lungs when your sinuses feel blocked or swollen. This is how it's done:

1. Sit in a comfortable upright position with your rubber balls held loosely in your hands and begin meditating on your breath.

2. As you breathe in and out, get a sense of how relatively open or blocked your nasal passages are by

noticing the amount of air that moves through your sinuses without forcing your body to breathe.

3. Next, squeeze the rubber balls with one steady pressure, then study the effects this has on your sinuses. As soon as you squeeze the balls, your breathing will deepen and the amount of air moving through your nasal passages will noticeably increase. If you check out your sinuses, you'll find that they feel a bit more open and relaxed than they did before.

4. The next step is to give your sinus tissues a chance to assimilate these changes. To do this, keep meditating on your breath and continue squeezing the balls for two or three minutes with the same steady pressure. As you meditate (still squeezing the balls), you can increase these new feelings of openness by imagining that the air is entering your body as if from between your legs.

5. At the end of the assimilation period, keep meditating on your breath and release the pressure on the balls very gradually and carefully, so as not to disrupt the new balance of tensions in your sinuses. If you do this correctly, your sinuses will continue to feel as open and free as they did while you were squeezing the balls.

You can repeat steps one through five for as long as the technique continues to bear fruit. However, there is a limit to how much you can practice any breathing technique before it begins to lose its effectiveness. If you go too far, it might even create some sort of backlash. So as you work, be on the lookout for any signs of diminishing returns. When the technique seems to be losing its effectiveness, you can either switch to a different technique or stop working on your sinuses altogether and resume this kind of work at a later time.

Respiratory Technique #3: Relaxing the Throat

MANY FACTORS CAN CAUSE our sinuses to become constricted or swollen, such as allergies, infections, and airborne pollutants. No matter what the original cause, however, all sinus problems are greatly exacerbated by the chronic tensions almost everyone holds in their pharynx and throat. Most people are unaware these tensions even exist because they are part of the habitual blocks in their breathing. If we know how to access these normally hidden tensions and help them relax, our sinuses will instantly open, too.

This is how "relaxing the throat" is done:

1. Sit in a comfortable upright position and begin to meditate on the movements of your breath. As you breathe in and out, tune in to your sinuses and get a sense of how relatively open or blocked they feel. To do this, simply notice the amount of air that easily moves through your sinuses, without forcing your body to breathe.

2. Still watching your breath, focus your attention on the back of your throat, then swallow as gently and sensitively as you possibly can. The instant you swallow, your sinus blocks will suddenly ease. The next time you inhale, you'll notice a definite increase in the amount of air that can easily move through your sinuses.

3. Next, give your throat and sinuses a chance to re-adjust their tensions by allowing your breath to

move in and out of your body for several cycles of breathing — then repeat the technique of swallowing gently to relax your throat. Each time you repeat this technique, your throat and sinuses will feel a bit more relaxed and your breathing will be somewhat freer.

When the technique of relaxing your throat begins to lose its effectiveness — usually within five to eight trials — you can consolidate the gains you've made and help your sinuses open up a bit more by picking up your rubber balls and working with the solidifying technique for an additional three or four minutes. This is how it's done:

1. Once you're through working with relaxing the throat, squeeze your rubber balls with one steady pressure and hold the pressure constant for three or four minutes. As soon as you squeeze the balls, your breathing will become a bit deeper and your sinuses will open a tiny bit more. You can increase these new feelings of openness even more by imagining that the air is entering your body as if from between your legs.

2. The next step is to give your sinus tissues a chance to assimilate these changes. To do this, keep watching your breath and continue squeezing the balls with the same steady pressure for two or three minutes more.

3. When you're ready to release the pressure on the balls, be sure to do so very carefully and gradually. If you do this correctly, your sinuses will continue to feel as open, free, and well supported as they did while you were squeezing the balls.

What to Watch For

At times, the signs of opening in your sinuses might seem to be relatively small and insignificant, but don't be discouraged or fooled. Even the slightest improvement in the condition of your sinuses will greatly speed their healing.

As you work, if you begin to get scared because you're having difficulty breathing, be careful not to force or strain to take in more air. Remember that the harder you try to breathe, the more you'll constrict the tissues of your sinuses and the less air you'll actually take in. Just accept whatever air your sinuses can supply without forcing them, and learn to ignore the fear that you are liable to suffocate. As long as you don't panic or tense up in fear, you'll be surprised at how comfortable you can feel, no matter how constricted or congested your sinuses are.

The Invisible Demon

THERE IS AN ANCIENT SUFI PARABLE about a traveler who is out walking alone in the desert. He happens to glance back over his shoulder and notices a set of footprints following close behind him in the sand. Not realizing that these are his own footprints, the man thinks that an invisible demon is silently stalking him from behind. Seized with fright, he begins to walk a bit faster. When he looks over his shoulder to see if he is outdistancing his pursuer, he's dismayed to find that the footprints are just as close as ever! And the faster he walks to get away, the faster the demon walks, too.

With mounting fear, the man breaks into a run, hoping to leave the demon behind. But each time he glances back over his shoulder, the demon's footprints are right there behind him. By this time, the man has become so terror-stricken that he begins racing across the sand dunes, using every last ounce of his strength. Eventually he falls unconscious to the desert floor, where he dies of exhaustion — running from nothing but his own fear.

Like the tragic story of Orpheus, this Sufi parable illustrates the harm we can do to ourselves by believing in the anxiety-ridden creations of our own minds. This story also contains a perfect description of why some people with particularly severe asthma sometimes die of suffocation. It is commonly believed that asthma is caused by external factors, such as allergenic substances and environmental pollutants. Although these can certainly play a major role in the development of asthma, I've found that they're usually not its primary cause. The breathing techniques I've developed over the past thirty years have shown me that asthma isn't a true disease; it's a bad habit of suppressing one's breath in fear.

Whenever we hold our breath in fear, we create stressful tensions in the tissues of the upper respiratory system. These fear-ridden tensions in our pharynx, throat, and chest are the very embodiments of our breathing blocks. When asthmatics clutch on the in-breath to block their feelings of fear, they create more tension in their bronchial tubes than in any other tissues of their respiratory system. The more they clutch on the in-breath, the more they constrict their bronchial tubes and the harder it becomes for them to breathe. The less air they get, the more scared they get — and the more they clutch on the in-breath.

On rare occasions, this vicious cycle can spiral so far out of control that some people literally suffocate themselves to death. No amount of oxygen or medication can counteract the strangling effects of their own feelings of fear. The good news, however, is that the cycles of fear and tension that underlie all asthma attacks can be gently interrupted and gradually brought under control.

Controlling the Symptoms
of Asthma

IF YOU HAVE ASTHMA ATTACKS, you can use any of the following techniques to interrupt the cycles of tension and fear that cause your bronchial tubes to constrict. These techniques may be practiced with or without the aid of medication, so it's perfectly fine to use bronchial dilators or nasal decongestants whenever you think you need them. As you become increasingly skilled at using your breath to control your asthmatic reactions, you can gradually reduce, or even eliminate, your need for medication — but always consult with your doctor.

THE SOLIDIFYING TECHNIQUE

If you're having an asthma attack, one way to increase your intake of air is to use the solidifying technique. Sit in a comfortable upright position and meditate on your breathing. Once you're attuned to its movements, squeeze your rubber balls with one steady pressure. The moment you squeeze the rubber balls, your breathing will immediately deepen, the amount of air that enters your lungs will increase, and your feelings of anxiety will become a bit weaker.

Still watching your breath, continue to squeeze the balls with the same steady pressure for two or three minutes more. When you're ready to release the pressure, do so very gradually and slowly. If you release the pressure gradually enough, your breathing will feel nearly as open and free as it did while you were squeezing the balls. The more open and free your breathing becomes, the weaker your feelings of anxiety will become.

BREATHING-RELEASE TECHNIQUES

Another way to bring in more air is to work with the Tarzan technique. This will help disperse the breathing blocks that keep your bronchial tubes locked up in fear. As you're watching your breath, make an outgoing sound of "aahhh" and tap on your chest for five or ten seconds, just forcefully enough to make your voice crack. Then give your bronchial tubes a chance to readjust their tensions.

If the asthma attack is particularly severe, work very gently at first. Make a gentle sound of "aahhh" and tap on your chest gently (but firmly enough to make your voice crack) for no more than five seconds at a time. As your bronchial tubes begin to relax, you can make the sound stronger and tap your chest more vigorously for longer periods of time. As your breath begins moving more freely, your feelings of anxiety will gradually fade and disappear.

You can also relax the tensions you hold in your bronchial tubes by working with the gentle rapid breathing technique. As you're watching your breath, breathe rapidly and gently (for five or ten seconds) into any feelings of constriction or tension that exist in the region of your lungs. When you stop, keep watching your breath and give your bronchial tubes a chance to assimilate the relaxing effects of this technique. As your bronchial tubes begin to relax and your breath begins moving more freely, your anxious feelings will become correspondingly weaker.

Whenever you practice these techniques, be sure to work as sensitively and gently as if you were working with the tissues of a newborn baby. This will ensure that you don't create additional irritation for your respiratory tissues rather than helping them to relax.

RELAXING THE THROAT

The technique of swallowing gently to relax your throat can also be used to relax the tensions you hold in your bronchial tubes. The instant you swallow, the tensions in your sinuses and bronchial tubes will soften and ease. On the next inhalation, you'll notice a definite increase in the amount of air that is entering your body.

GENTLING THE IN-BREATH

Another way to relax your breathing and increase your intake of air is to work with gentling the in-breath (the balancing technique taught in chapter 8). One of the main reasons that asthmatics have difficulty breathing is that their habit of clutching on the in-breath is so strong that, as they inhale, their bronchial tubes become constricted and rigidly locked up in fear. Gentling the in-breath (breathing in as if from between your legs) weakens this clutching reaction making it easier to breathe. Gentling the in-breath can also be especially helpful for reducing the symptoms of wheezing.

STRENGTHENING THE OUT-BREATH

You can also help your bronchial tubes relax by working with strengthening the out-breath to weaken the habit of clutching as you breathe in (see chapter 8). To refresh your memory: At the end of the out-breath, thrust the air from your body with a short, sudden stroke by contracting your diaphragm with a moderate degree of force. As soon as you thrust from your diaphragm, the air will immediately reenter your body with new feelings of ease and strength.

Once you are breathing more easily, you can help your

bronchial tubes stay relaxed and control your symptoms of wheezing by continuing to gentle your in-breaths. Whenever you inhale, remember to bring the air into your body as if breathing in from between your legs.

THE HEALING TRIANGLE

Once your breath is moving more freely from working with these techniques, you can further reduce any feelings of irritation and constriction in your bronchial tubes by working with the healing triangle, as described earlier in this chapter.

What to Watch For

You may repeat any of these techniques as many times as you wish. Remember, however, that there is a limit to how long you can work with any technique before it begins to lose its effectiveness. When it comes to working with respiratory problems, short regular practice sessions are much more effective than working too long at one sitting.

To avoid creating a backlash, be on the lookout for any signs of diminishing returns as you work. When a technique seems to be losing its effectiveness, either switch to a different technique or simply stop practicing and give the tissues of your respiratory system a chance to assimilate the work you've already done.

As you work with these techniques, it is vitally important to keep your mind quiet by watching your breath. If you begin to get scared because you feel short of breath, don't force to bring more air into your body. Remember that the harder you try to breathe, the more you'll constrict your bronchial tubes and the less air you'll actually get.

No matter how obstructed your breathing may feel, learn to

accept whatever amount of air your body can comfortably provide, without forcing it to breathe. Remember that your body can do remarkably well with very little air. If you keep watching your breath and learn to ignore any fear that might enter your mind, your feelings of suffocation will soon fade away.

Should your fear be so great that it's difficult to keep watching your breath, try working with the Tippy technique (described in chapter 9): Open your eyes and focus your attention on the simple objects you see around you, without losing track of your breath. If you keep watching your breath and ignore your anxious feelings (as Tippy ignored those barking dogs), the fear will gradually leave. Once your anxiety begins to subside, you can close your eyes again and continue dissolving the blocks and relaxing the tensions that keep you from breathing easily.

Over the years, my clients and students have had varying degrees of success in using these techniques to control their asthma symptoms. Some whose symptoms were relatively mild to begin with have managed to become completely free by spotting the early signs of an impending attack and nipping it in the bud. People with particularly severe and longstanding asthmatic reactions usually find it more difficult to become free of their symptoms. No matter how deep-rooted anyone's symptoms of asthma may be, however, at the very least they can learn to use these techniques to lessen their symptoms and bring their attacks under better control.

CHAPTER FOURTEEN

FEAR
and
EMOTIONAL ILLNESS

*An agitated mind produces suffering even in the midst of
affluence; it doesn't seem to know how to become quiet or still.*
— SWAMI MUKTANANDA

WHAT ARE EMOTIONS? Where do they exist — in our mind or
in our body? Just what is the subconscious mind, and how does
it relate to emotional illness?

Our emotions originate in our judgments — our evalua-
tions of the events that touch our lives. Imagine three people
entering a newly painted room. The first person exclaims, "How
lovely! I'd like to paint my own bedroom that color." The
second person thinks, "Ugh! This reminds me of my dentist's
office." The third person scarcely notices the color and doesn't

respond at all. The first person feels delight, the second feels anxiety, and the third feels indifference — yet all three are responding to the same event. This principle is the basis of our emotional reactions to all situations, great or small. A tragic news story that evokes compassion in one person might evoke rage in another, helplessness in a third, and evil delight in a fourth. Over a lifetime of making such personal assessments about events in our lives, we develop emotional habit patterns that gradually take on a life of their own.

Although our judgments initially shape our emotions, the judgments we make with our minds should no more be confused with the emotions themselves than a potter should be confused with the clay he shapes. Emotions are a form of energy that exists in the subtle body, and their function is to link our thoughts with our actions.

Just as our eyes need light in order to see an object, our mind needs a connecting medium to link up with events in its field of awareness. The emotional energies serve as this connecting medium. And just as our eyes organize random rays of light to bring a specific object into focus, our mind organizes the emotional energies to bring a selected experience into focus and establish its relationship with that event. This is why the ancient Hindu yogis referred to emotions as the *dikhari* (or "relational") energies.

Emotions and Body Chemistry

MANY PEOPLE THINK THAT OUR EMOTIONS originate in the biochemical reactions that take place in the physical body. It's true that our emotions and body chemistry are so closely linked that any change in one produces corresponding changes in the other. However, to conclude that our biochemistry is the cause of our emotions is like thinking that sunlight is the cause of the sun. In fact, it's just the opposite: Our emotions cause the biochemical reactions.

The energies that constitute our emotions exist in the subtle body, not the physical body. For example, when we feel scared, the sensations we feel in our physical body (such as an accelerated heart-beat or tension in the chest) are not the emotion of fear itself. They are the physical counterparts of the vibrations of fear that we feel in our subtle body.

Psychiatrists routinely prescribe drugs to treat emotional problems such as chronic anxiety, depression, and psychosis. Unfortunately, medications can neither eliminate the cause of neurosis nor cure mental illness because they can't remove anxiety from the subtle body — only the breath can accomplish this task. At best, mood-altering drugs can temporarily shunt the anxiety aside by forcing changes in the body's chemistry that can't be naturally maintained. This is why patients who take these medications on a long-term basis must continually have their prescriptions readjusted. It is also why these medications often cause undesirable side effects or lead to permanent dependency.

Although doctors are fully aware of these drawbacks, they continue to prescribe mood-altering drugs because they know of no other way to effectively control these problems. However, I've worked with dozens of people who, with the help of their doctors, have been able to greatly reduce or eliminate their need for medication by using their breath to reduce the level of anxious energy stored in their subtle body.

The approach I take is very simple. I give my clients a head start on their problems by using my breath to reduce the amount of anxious energy trapped in their subtle body. I also teach them meditation and breathing techniques that enable them to control their anxiety on a day-to-day basis.

One of the most striking examples of how effective this approach can be happened with Carol, a forty-year-old woman who suffered from chronic pain and weakness in her legs because of congenital deformities in her feet. Carol came to me because she'd always wanted to play tennis, but the problems in her legs and feet had kept her from doing so. Her legs improved so much in a single session that she signed up for tennis lessons the next day. About a month later, Carol sent me the following note:

The healing session was like a miracle. My fears subsided and I'm free of antidepressants for the first time in fifteen years.

These words came as a complete surprise to me. Carol had never mentioned that she also suffered from depression. What happened? Through further conversation with Carol, the picture became clear: Over the years, the feelings of pain and fear in her feet and legs had given rise to discouraged and anxious feelings, which gradually caused her to become depressed. When we helped her feet by reducing the levels of anxiety stored in her subtle body, her depression spontaneously lifted and disappeared.

The Subconscious Mind

THIRTY YEARS OF WORKING WITH EMOTIONAL PROBLEMS have convinced me that the dark and mysterious entity Freud called the "subconscious mind" is little more than the accumulation of anxious energy that we've trapped in our subtle body by suppressing our breath in fear. How does the anxiety get stuck there? It's a two-step process. First, we hold our breath to block our fearful impressions, then we hold our breath again to block the anxiety we've created by holding our breath to suppress our fear.

Ironically, holding our breath does nothing to reduce the amount of fear in our system; it only reduces our awareness of how scared we actually feel. The fear isn't gone; it's only been pushed deeper inside and is now unable to shift and change as emotions should naturally do.

Our subconscious mind isn't made up of all the specific thoughts or traumatic memories that we've repressed in fear. It consists of all the anxiety we've created by holding our breath to block our feelings of fear. In truth, there is no such thing as the Freudian subconscious mind. There is only the accumulation of anxious energy that we've left trapped in our subtle body to avoid feeling scared and weak.

The resulting split in awareness leads us to think that we have two different minds, which we call our "conscious" and "subconscious." We like to believe that our conscious mind is our "right" mind, and our subconscious mind is "not who we really are." The truth is, however, that both minds are one and the same. The problem is that the part we call our "rational" mind is too scared to either feel or admit to its own troubled feelings.

As a teenager during World War II, I remember seeing newsreels of great battleships that were so constructed as to be virtually unsinkable. When these ships were hit by a torpedo, the sailors would seal off the flooded compartments to keep the ship from sinking. This tactic usually kept the ship afloat, but its fighting capabilities were so badly impaired it was forced to head back to port for repairs, limping all the way home.

Our mind is just like one of those crippled battleships. The part we call our conscious mind is like the upper decks that are still accessible to us. Our subconscious mind is like the flooded compartments we've sealed off in fear. The fear that stays trapped in the lower decks is the very substance of our subconscious mind — not the particular memories associated with that fear.

Fear and Emotional Issues

STRANGE AS IT MAY SEEM, fear is the only emotion we ever block. For example, we don't really block feelings of our anger; we only block our *fear* of feeling angry, or of showing our anger to other people. After all is said and done, it doesn't matter which emotion we *think* we're blocking — anger, sadness, or even love — what we're really trying to block are the feelings of fear associated with those emotions.

Suppressing our fearful emotions can bring temporary feelings of strength and control, however, it does nothing to actually make us stronger. All it does is postpone the fear and create new waves of anxious energy that add to the levels of subconscious fear already stored in our subtle body.

This reservoir of repressed fear gives rise to a chronic sense of anxious "holding on" that permeates our mind and body, and secretly influences every aspect of our life. By day, it distorts our perceptions, weakens our sense of confidence, and undermines the effectiveness of every action we take. At night, it spoils our sleep and fills our dreams with fear.

All of the anxiety-ridden emotions and thoughts that we

call our "fears" and "issues" are like the different kinds of balloons we see being sold at a circus. No matter how different they may be in size, shape, or color, all the balloons are filled with helium that comes from the same tank. Moreover, each balloon is only as big as the amount of helium it contains. Once it loses its helium, it also loses its size, its shape, and its usefulness as a balloon.

Our various fears and issues are just like those balloons, except that they're filled with anxiety instead of helium. As with a balloon, every issue becomes just as big as the amount of fear we pump into it. If we can remove that fear, the issue loses its power over our mind and ceases to be an issue. This is true whether our emotional issues stem from a traumatic memory, a mental illness, or a worrisome injury that threatens our health. No matter how different they appear to be on the surface, every one of our issues is filled with the same anxious energy that comes from the reservoir of fear that we've trapped in our subtle body.

Negativity, Neurosis, and Evil

BASICALLY SPEAKING, there are two kinds of emotion. I call them our *primary* and *secondary* emotions. The primary group includes emotions such as joy, sadness, love, and fear, which arise naturally in all human beings. The secondary group includes the neurotic or distorted emotions, such as anxiety, frustration, and resentment, which we create by blocking our primary emotions in fear.

Over time, the emotions we block become so distorted and unreliable that we begin to mistrust our feelings. This sense of mistrust and doubt toward our own feelings lies at the root of all neurotic behavior. If our habits of blocking become especially severe, our (already) neurotic emotions can become so terribly bent and twisted that they develop into every dark, negative, and evil emotion that afflicts the human race.

Anger provides one of the best examples of how this dynamic works. Basically speaking, there are two kinds of anger: healthy anger and unhealthy (or distorted) anger. Like fear, anger is actually a positive form of emotional energy that enables us to protect ourselves against unscrupulous, hostile, or evil people who are trying to do us harm.

If we repeatedly suppress our anger because we're too scared to speak up for ourselves, the anger that remains stuck inside us eventually breeds feelings of frustration and resentment. If we suppress these frustrated, resentful feelings (because we're afraid to express them, too), they gradually become dark, brooding emotions, such as paranoia and hostility. As these darker emotions take root in our mind, they gradually evolve into evil feelings of hatred and cruelty toward others.

Without a doubt, repressed anger is the most dangerous and destructive of all human emotions. In my opinion, repressed anger was the real cause of World War II. Both the war and the evil deeds committed by Hitler and his henchmen were the results of their deeply repressed feelings of anger and their collective feelings of paranoia. The economic depression of the thirties and the crushing debt that the League of Nations imposed on the German people were some of the pretexts the Nazis used to gain power and wage a war in which they could project their fear and inflict their hatred onto non-Aryan people.

The tragic events of World War II represent just one of the many kinds of harm we create by repressing our anger in fear.

For example, when we turn our repressed anger in toward ourselves — instead of inflicting it on others as the Nazis did — it
gives rise to destructive feelings of angry self-criticism. However, the harm we do to our emotional health doesn't end there.
The habit of harshly criticizing ourselves spawns yet another
family of neurotic and self-destructive emotions, such as feelings of inadequacy, worthlessness, and guilt.

When people get caught in this downward emotional spiral,
they try to escape the lash of their own anger by indulging in
maudlin feelings of self-pity. All they succeed in doing, however, is reinforcing their helpless, hopeless feelings and making
them worse than ever. This tendency to swing uncontrollably
between angry self-criticism and maudlin self-pity is, I believe,
the main reason why people become alcoholics.

Anger and Psychosis

I HAVE OBSERVED MANY CASES where repressed anger also lies at
the root of severe mental disorders, such as psychotic breaks,
schizophrenia, and obsessive-compulsive behavior. Of these three,
psychotic breaks provide the simplest and clearest example of
how people can become mentally deranged by repressing their
angry feelings. Anger is one of the most intense and explosive of
all emotions. When people habitually repress their anger in fear,
the charge of anxious energy that builds gradually in their
system can one day explode into seemingly uncontrollable and
inexplicable feelings of rage.

Over the years, I've worked with at least twenty people who
had been medically diagnosed as schizophrenic, all of whom
exhibited various degrees of abnormally aggressive or violent
behavior. In most cases, I was able to help them significantly by

using my breath to reduce the levels of anxiety stored in their subtle body, and by teaching them how to use their own breath to continue the process at home.

One especially gratifying case was that of Delores, a woman in her late thirties who had spent seventeen years in and out of mental hospitals. Delores had been diagnosed as "schizo-phrenic, with obsessive-compulsive behavior." She was also prone to having severe psychotic breaks. After seventeen years of taking antipsychotic medications, Delores had become so estranged from her own emotions that her psychotherapist warned me, "Here at the clinic, people call her 'Stone Face' because she never smiles."

In my first session with Delores, as I worked to reduce the layers of fear trapped in her subtle body, I'd sometimes tell her a joke to see how she'd respond — but all she'd do was stare at me blankly. When I tried the same tactic during our second ses-sion, Delores smiled for the first time in years. During our third session, she actually laughed out loud at one of my jokes. After our fourth session, she went home and tried to tell one of my jokes to her husband — but she couldn't remember the punch line. When she came for her fifth session, she told me a joke she'd heard from her husband — and even remembered the punch line.

In all, Delores and I worked together about fourteen times over a period of seven months. By the time we completed our work, her anxiety and compulsive behavior had become dra-matically weaker. Most important of all, instead of continually repressing her angry feelings as she'd always done in the past, Delores learned to accept them well enough in her daily life to eliminate all signs of her psychotic breaks. Her emotional state was so greatly improved that she returned to college to complete her education, which had been interrupted by her illness nearly eighteen years before.

As we were saying good-bye at the end of our last session, Delores gave me a grateful hug and said, "Thanks for helping me make friends with my demons." As she spoke these words, her face lit up with one of the warmest smiles I've ever seen. When we spoke on the phone a year later, Delores told me that she was still pursuing her college studies. She was also teaching meditation and yoga to patients at the mental hospital where she'd once been a patient herself.

CHAPTER FIFTEEN

FEAR
and
EMOTIONAL HEALING

A disturbed breath leads to a disturbed mind. A steady breath leads to a steady mind. The two go together. Hence cultivate a steady and quiet breath. Thereby the mind is controlled.

— The Hatha Yoga Pradipika

AS OUR BREATH GOES, SO GO OUR EMOTIONS. For example, the way we breathe when we're angry is completely different than the way we breathe when we feel joyful or sad. Our breath and our emotions are so closely linked that we can actually change the way we feel by changing the way we breathe. In chapter 8, for example, I described how all feelings of anxiety are created by clutching on the in-breath; feelings of discouragement are created by collapsing on the out-breath; and all feelings of apathy, lethargy, and depression are created by lingering in the pause at the end of the out-breath. Thus, whenever we practice breath-balancing techniques, we're not only restoring the health of our breathing, we're also bringing our mood swings under control by changing the way we're breathing.

Every technique in this book helps to balance and heal our emotions in one way or another. Some help us feel calm and solid, others increase our feelings of strength and confidence; still others lift our spirits and literally make us feel strong of heart. The healthier our breathing patterns become from practicing the basic techniques, the healthier our emotions also become.

In this chapter, you'll learn to carry the process of healing your emotions to even higher levels of conscious control. Instead of depending on the relatively random kinds of healing produced by the techniques we've covered so far, you'll be learning how to use your breath for healing specific emotional problems.

Who Shot the Arrow?

IN THE EAST, THE BUDDHA IS REVERED as a great and compassionate healer of minds who did most of his teaching in silence. One famous story tells about an overly intellectual monk who was extremely "stuck in his head." He continually asked the Buddha trivial questions that he thought were relevant to becoming enlightened: "Please tell me, Master, does *The Diamond Sutra* have a secret meaning that you should reveal to me?" But whenever he asked such irrelevant questions, the Buddha would simply ignore him.

After several months of receiving this silent treatment, the frustrated monk brashly confronted the master and said, "What kind of teacher are you? Whenever I ask you a question, you never give me the answers I need to become enlightened! If you are as great and wise as people say, why are you so stingy about sharing your knowledge?" The Buddha looked quietly up at the monk, then finally answered by telling him this story:

> There was once a poor man who went into the forest to gather food for his family. While he was picking berries in a thick clump of bushes, someone shot him with a poisoned arrow. The man stumbled home to his wife and family, who immediately sent for the doctor. When the doctor came to remove the arrow, the man said, "Wait just a minute, doctor! Before you take the arrow out, you must answer three questions for me: Who shot me? Why did he shoot me? And what kind of poison did he put on the arrow?"

The Buddha ended his story by saying, "Oh, monk, you are acting just like that man."

Raking Over the Coals of the Past

MANY PEOPLE BELIEVE THAT, in order to heal our emotional wounds, we must first recall the past events that originally caused our feelings of conflict. The theory is that once we've brought certain memories back to the light of consciousness and analyzed them with our rational mind, we will then become free of our fear.

Some people carry this idea one step farther by suggesting that, in one way or another, we must reenact or relive the experiences that originally created the fear that keeps us stuck in our problems. Although both of these approaches have a certain degree of merit, in and of themselves neither one can set us free.

Unless we actually experience the subconscious charge of anxious energy that is keeping us stuck and release it from our system, little healing can possibly take place.

At best, recalling or reenacting the details of our past traumas can help us reconnect with the anxiety we felt at the time, but this is only the first stage of healing. Once we're in touch with that anxiety, we must then attend to the most important task of all: releasing it from our system.

When it comes to healing our emotional disturbances, it doesn't matter how, why, or when we originally got scared. Just as the doctor in Buddha's story could have removed the arrow without knowing the name of the man who shot it, we can cleanse the subconscious layers of anxiety from our system without knowing a single fact about what originally scared us — and we can accomplish this with our breath.

If you examine your thoughts at any given moment, you'll find that they perfectly reflect the state of your emotions. No matter how you're feeling — happy, sad, optimistic, discouraged, or anything else — every thought you create in your mind will be colored by that emotion. When you're feeling happy, your thoughts will be naturally buoyant and bright; when you're feeling sad, all of your thoughts will be tinged with the color of sadness.

When we feel scared or insecure, our mind has a terrible habit of trying to avoid feeling its fear by escaping into the world of its thoughts. We like to believe that if we can just "figure things out," everything will be okay. Most of the time, however, this is just an excuse our mind makes to avoid feeling the fear itself. And the more we try to escape by indulging in our thoughts and fantasies, the more firmly entrenched the fear becomes in the deeper layers of our mind.

Meditative consciousness enables us to look past our

thoughts and mental images and perceive the underground streams of anxiety that are really causing our problems. Once we're in touch with these subconscious streams of anxious energy, we can gradually dry them up with our breath. As the anxiety begins to lift from our system, our various emotional disturbances (conflicting emotions, feelings of insecurity, recurring traumatic memories, and so on) will become correspondingly weaker and gradually fade from our life.

EMOTIONAL HEALING TECHNIQUE #1:
CALMING A TROUBLED MIND

AN ANCIENT HINDU TEXT known as *The Yoga Vashishtha* says:

A disturbed breath leads to a disturbed mind. A steady breath leads to a steady mind. Hence cultivate a steady breath and quiet breath. Thereby the mind is controlled.[1]

This next technique, "calming a troubled mind," will teach you how to quiet your mind by stabalizing the movements of your breath. As long as you manage to keep your breathing steady (without forcing), your mind will be steady, too. You'll find this technique especially helpful when your worried thoughts and anxious feelings are beginning to run out of control. Once your mind becomes quiet and stops trying to figure things out, it's amazing how the answers you need usually show up all by themselves.

This is how the technique is done:

1. Sit in a comfortable meditation posture, with your rubber balls held loosely in your hands, then close your eyes and begin to meditate on your breath.

2. Once your mind is attuned to your breathing, get in touch with your troubled thoughts. Don't try to argue or reason with them, and don't try to shut them out of your mind. This will only give them more energy and make them stronger than ever.

3. If you keep watching your breath and look "behind" your troubled thoughts, you'll discover that there are subtle undercurrents of anxious energy flowing through your mind and body. These normally hidden streams of anxiety are the true source of your worried thoughts and stressful feelings in your body.

4. Once you're in touch with these underground streams of anxiety, you can use the solidifying technique to slow them down and bring them under control. To do this, keep watching your breath, then squeeze the rubber balls with one steady pressure to deepen and strengthen your breathing. As soon as your breathing becomes deeper and stronger, your anxious feelings will become less intense and your thoughts won't be quite so frantic.

5. Once your mind has become a bit quieter, the next step is to use the healing triangle technique to clear some of the anxiety from your system. To do this, keep watching your breath; tune into the feelings of anxiety as clearly as you can; squeeze the rubber balls firmly enough to match their intensity; then do about ten seconds of gentle rapid breathing directly into the anxious feelings to help them shift and change.

6. When you are done, keep watching your breath, release your hold on the balls very gradually and

gently, then study the changes that are taking place in your mind and body.

7. The first thing you'll notice is that your breathing has become much more stable and is now stronger than before. Along with these changes in breathing, you'll also notice that your anxiety now feels less intense, and your mind has become correspondingly quieter.

8. You may repeat this technique as many times as you wish. Once your thoughts begin to quiet down and the charge of anxious energy has become less intense, you can then work with any of the balancing, grounding, and strengthening techniques to deepen and strengthen your breathing. The more balanced and stable your breathing becomes, the quieter and stronger your mind will be.

Making Friends with Your Troubled Feelings

WE ALL HAVE OUR PERSONAL DEMONS of fear that secretly lurk at the back of our mind and trouble our thoughts and emotions. Scary as they can sometimes be, these demons aren't malicious enemies who are out to do us harm; they're simply the scared and conflicted parts of ourselves that we've abandoned in fear. If we think of them as dangerous foes whom we must confront and do battle with — or avoid at all costs — we'll never get free of our problems. Remember that everything we call an "issue" is an issue only because it's filled with fear. In order to heal our emotional wounds or resolve our feelings of conflict, we must become a quiet and supportive friend to the fear-ridden thoughts and insecure feelings that we normally try to hide away in the dim recesses of our mind.

All "issues" or symptoms of emotional distress can be greatly helped — if not completely healed — by reducing their underlying charge of anxiety. This is true whether we're suffering from a diagnosed mental illness, post-traumatic stress disorder, or a neurotic fear, such as "No one will ever love me." If we're willing to experience the charge of anxious energy that creates and sustains our problems, we can use our breath to clear it from our system. As the clouds of anxiety begin to disperse, our conflicted feelings and emotional traumas will gradually weaken and fade away to exactly the same degree.

Sadness and grief provide excellent examples of how this process works. Sadness is the emotion we feel when we've lost someone or something we dearly love. It is one of the finest and healthiest emotions we can possibly feel, because it is filled with so much love. If we focus our mind on the feelings of love, instead of our feelings of loss, the sadness becomes a gift from God. For example, whenever we think of a close friend who has died, we'll experience feelings of love that are sweeter and stronger than those we felt while our friend was still alive.

Grief, on the other hand, is a distorted form of sadness. It results from trying to hold on to the person we love despite the fact that they're gone. If we focus on our feelings of loss — instead of our feelings of love — our sadness instantly turns into grief. In order to heal our painful feelings, we must be willing to experience the hidden layers of anxiety that power our grief and cleanse them from our system. As the clouds of anxiety begin to disperse, our grief-stricken feelings will gradually weaken and fade away. The feelings of sadness that remain will not only be free of anxiety and distress, they'll also become like faithful lifelong companions who always bring sweet memories and feelings of love that will stay with us the rest of our life.

EMOTIONAL HEALING TECHNIQUE #2: HEALING DISTURBED EMOTIONS

THE HEALING TRIANGLE IS A GREAT TECHNIQUE for healing most kinds of emotional problems, no matter what their original cause. Whenever you're feeling emotionally distressed, you can use this technique to quiet your mind and disperse the waves of anxious energy that are causing your troubled feelings. When you practice this technique properly, you can actually feel the anxiety leaving your system as slowly and gently as a meadow mist in the morning sun. As the charge of anxious energy weakens, your distressed feelings will begin to fade away of their own accord.

The following instructions will teach you how to work with the emotions of sadness and grief. You'll find, however, that you can apply these instructions to heal most feelings of distress or conflict, no matter which emotions are involved.

This is how it's done:

1. Sit in a comfortable meditation posture (rubber balls held loosely in your hands), then close your eyes and begin meditating on your breath. Once your mind is attuned to your breathing, begin to study the symptoms of emotional distress or conflict as they appear in your mind or body.

2. Let's say, for example, that your mind is filled with grief-stricken thoughts because a close friend has recently died. The first step in healing your grief is to

steady your mind to keep your worried thoughts and anxious feelings from running out of control.

3. To do this, use the technique for calming a troubled mind (described earlier in this chapter): Keep watching your breath, and squeeze the balls with one steady pressure. As soon as your breathing becomes deeper and stronger, your anxiety will become a bit less intense and you'll find it much easier to keep your mind from getting trapped in its own scared thoughts and helpless feelings.

4. If you keep watching your breath and look "beneath" the worried thoughts, you'll discover a subtle vibration of anxiety that is secretly present in a deeper part of your mind. Keep ignoring the thoughts and allow yourself to feel this anxious vibration as clearly as you can. Then — without losing track of your breath — change the pressure on the balls to match its intensity. Do about five or ten seconds of gentle rapid breathing directly into the anxious feelings, then keep watching your breath and notice how the technique has changed your emotional state.

5. One thing you'll notice is that your feelings of grief and insecurity have become a bit less intense. If you take the time to study your grief a bit more closely (without losing track of your breath), you'll see that it is being caused by a deep inner feeling of "holding on" to resist your sense of loss. This feeling of anxious holding is the real source of your grief — not the loss of your friend.

6. To weaken your grief even further, continue ignoring any thoughts that enter your mind and keep your attention focused on whatever anxious feelings may still remain. Squeeze the rubber balls firmly enough to match their intensity, then do about five or ten seconds of gentle rapid breathing to help them leave your system. As the clouds of anxiety begin to disperse, so too will your sense of grief.

7. If you keep watching your breath and track the waves of anxious energy, they'll continue to shift and change all by themselves, just as the physical feelings of pain and tension change when you work with the healing triangle technique. Eventually, you'll be left with only your feelings of sadness, free of your fear and your sense of loss.

8. Then, when you think of your friend who has died, you'll experience poignant feelings of love and gratitude rather than anxiety, grief, and helplessness. The sweet memories and feelings of love that sadness naturally brings to mind will be like precious heirlooms that will always be part of your life.

Anxiety and Excitement

ONE OF THE MOST IMPORTANT SECRETS to healing emotional problems is to realize that anxiety and excitement have exactly the same vibration. These two emotions feel so much alike that people often get them confused. For example, we often hear people say that they are "anxious" to do something, when they really mean they're eager or excited about doing it. If you look back over the events of your life, you'll find that some of the most exciting times were also some of the scariest.

Anxiety and excitement are so much alike that one can easily become the other in the blink of an eye. When we accept these emotions just as they are, and permit their rapidly vibrating energies to move freely through our system, they'll fill us with feelings of enthusiasm and boost our sense of power. On the other hand, if we resist their vibrations by closing our breath down in fear, we'll instantly begin to feel nervous and scared.

Great athletes are continually faced with the problem of taking in the energies of an excited crowd without turning them into anxiety. The bigger and more excited the crowd is, the more self-possessed the athlete must be to keep from getting nervous. If an athlete knows how to keep a steady mind and ride the waves of excitement like surfing waves at the beach, the energy from the fans will act as a mood-lifter and a strength-booster. This is what the great hockey player Bobby Orr meant when he said, "What I love most about playing hockey is playing the puck off the roar of the crowd."

We can use this same approach to heal our fear-ridden emotions and reclaim the feelings of enthusiasm and buoyancy we once had as a child. If we learn how to keep our mind steady and ride the waves of anxious energy as they go coursing through our system, the anxiety itself will lift us out of our emotional ruts and restore our spirited feelings.

Riding the waves of anxiety is something like riding a frisky horse that has a mind of its own. If we can manage to stay on the horse's back for even a little while, it will eventually quiet down and become compliant enough for us to lead it wherever we will.

EMOTIONAL HEALING TECHNIQUE #3:
BREAKING FREE OF UNRULY THOUGHTS

IN PREVIOUS CHAPTERS, we've spoken in terms of healing the mind and body by cleansing the layers of anxious energy from our system. There are times, however, when we feel so beleaguered by unruly thoughts and emotions that we need some special help to loosen their grip on our mind. These are the times when waves of anxious energy come rushing up to the surface of our own consciousness with so much intensity that we may not be strong enough to control them by stabilizing our breath. When this happens, all we can do is ride the waves of anxiety until they lose some of their strength. As soon as they've become a bit less intense, we can use our breath to calm our agitated feelings and lead them to quieter pastures.

You'll find this next technique — "breaking free of unruly thoughts" — extremely helpful for working with particularly intense and turbulent emotions, such as anger and frustration. The first step in bringing them under control is to free our mind from the grip of its own negative, scared, and unruly thoughts. If we learn to look past the confused ideas and turbulent thoughts that are entering our mind, we can then work with the underlying charge of anxious energy that is actually causing our mind to run out of control. As soon as this anxious charge begins to weaken, we can use our breath to rein in our anxious feelings.

"Breaking free of unruly thoughts" can also be used to regain control of intense and dogged emotions, such as jealousy, paranoia, and obsessive-compulsive feelings. The key to healing such intensely distorted emotions is to avoid getting caught in their mental traps and to work directly with the subconscious charge of anxiety that powers them. The more we ignore the neurotic thoughts that such emotions create in our mind, and learn to ride their underlying waves of anxious energy, the sooner those feelings will lose their strength and begin to fade from our life.

This is how the technique is done:

1. Sit in a comfortable meditation posture, with your rubber balls held loosely in your hands, then close your eyes and begin to meditate on your breath. Once you're in touch with your breathing, tune in to the angry or frustrated thoughts that are buzzing around in your mind.

2. Don't let your mind get caught in these thoughts. Accept the fact that they exist, but don't react to them. Don't talk back to them, and don't try to force them out of your mind. Remember, the more attention you give them, the stronger they'll get. The best way to break their hold on your mind is to keep watching your breath and learn to ignore them, just as Tippy ignored those barking dogs (see chapter 9).

3. Another way to loosen the grip of these thoughts on your mind is to use the solidifying technique to deepen and strengthen your breathing. Begin by watching your breath, then squeeze your rubber balls with one steady pressure. As soon as your breathing becomes deeper, your mind will become a bit quieter and your angry thoughts will immediately begin to weaken.

4. If your angry feelings and runaway thoughts are abnormally intense, try meditating with your eyes open, as you learned to do with the Tippy technique. If you keep watching your breath and focusing your attention on the objects in your surroundings, you will find it much easier to ignore the angry or frustrated thoughts that are trying to control your mind. If your thoughts and feelings are still too strong to ignore, just keep watching your breath — get to your feet — and take your "barking dogs" out for a walk.

5. Another way to break free of your unwanted thoughts is to work with the Janus technique (described in chapter 9). The detached state of mind that Janus fosters will not only take the angry edge off of your thoughts, it can also help you completely suspend your thinking.

6. Once your mind has become a bit quieter, you can then work with any of the grounding, strengthening, and balancing techniques to harmonize your system. The more balanced and stable your breathing becomes, the more quiet and stable your mind will become and so to will your emotions.

What to Watch For

The techniques described in this chapter can be used to heal almost any kind of emotional problem, whether old or new. The secret to using these techniques most effectively is to keep your mind steady and strong by keeping it anchored in your breathing. If you keep watching your breath and stay in meditation the whole time you're working, you'll find it surprisingly easy to cope with the waves of anxious energy that create and sustain your problems. As the charge of anxiety grows weaker, the problems will either disappear or become so feeble they can no longer control your life.

There may be times when your feelings of anger and frustration are so intense that all you can do is to burn off some of their energy by engaging in some sort of vigorous physical activity, such as jogging, swimming, or chopping wood. At other times, you might have to vent these feelings in reasonably safe and harmless ways, such as screaming out the window of your car as loudly as you can while speeding along the highway.

One of my own favorite ways to blow off steam is to go for a swim in a nearby lake, where I can thrash about and scream as loud as I wish while swimming underwater (that way, it's only the fish who get bothered). No matter what kind of venting techniques you might prefer, however, always remember to keep your mind stable by ignoring the unruly thoughts that enter your mind and by watching your breath to keep it open, flowing, and steady.

When it comes to healing any emotional issue or conflict, there are two basic facts you should always keep in mind:

1. Most emotional problems result from the habit of rejecting our feelings in fear. These include even the symptoms of post-traumatic stress disorder, the aftermath of particularly intense and traumatic experiences. So it's extremely important that you learn to be kind, accepting, and patient with yourself, especially when you're feeling scared and helpless.

2. The more intense and long-standing a problem is, the more time it will take to heal, so don't expect any deep-rooted problem to disappear overnight. As Mark Twain so aptly put it:

   Habit is habit, and not to be flung out of the window by any man, but coaxed downstairs a step at a time.[2]

CHAPTER SIXTEEN

PRANIC ENERGY HEALING

When a person can use the breath energy in his body to produce breath energy for other people's five viscera, he has achieved a wonderful success.

— TAOIST TEXT

ONCE WE LEARN HOW TO USE OUR BREATH for healing ourselves, we can then learn to use it for healing others. The Chinese masters considered this to be one of the highest of all breathwork attainments. I call this skill "pranic energy healing" because it's based on the healer's ability to consciously transmit healing prana (or chi) into another person's system. This transfer of healing prana from one person to another is possible because the pranic life-force is the same in all living creatures. The secret to this transfer is a meditative state of consciousness known as "entrainment." In the state of entrainment, the breath energies of two individuals come into mutual resonance within their subtle bodies.

The word *conspirator* perfectly describes the state of communion that exists between people whose breath energies have become entrained. *Conspirator* is derived from the Latin word *conspirare,* which means "to breathe together," "to unite," and "to agree." Thus, the word *conspiracy* refers, not to a band of sinister people who are secretly plotting to do evil, but to any group of people who are so like-minded that they're literally "breathing as one." Pranic energy healers are able to induce this state of shared breath energies at will.

Entrainment is not an altered state of consciousness that only a yogi or healer can enter. On the contrary, we often experience this communion of breath energies in our daily life without realizing it. For example, a newborn baby lives in a constant state of entrainment with its mother and, thus, shares most of her feelings. Mothers also become entrained with their babies, but to a much lesser degree.

We often commune with lovers, spouses, and intimate friends through the medium of shared breath energies. This is especially evident in those intimate moments when we instinctively know exactly what our partner is feeling or thinking without saying a word to each other. The breaths of a husband and wife can spontaneously become entrained while they're sleeping together. This is the basis of the mysterious phenomenon of shared dreams. Our breath can even become entrained with that of a beloved pet. Like newborns, however, pets are entrained to a much greater degree with their masters' breath (and, therefore, with their masters' feelings) than the other way around.

In the East, the state of entrainment has been consciously cultivated for both healing and spiritual purposes. For example,

Tibetan Buddhist physicians have learned to enhance their diagnostic abilities by bringing the movements of their own breath into synch with those of their patients. Tibetan Buddhist monks use similar techniques for entraining their breathing with that of dying people in order to help them make a peaceful transition from this world to the next.

Pranic energy healing is an inborn talent in everyone. Since accomplished teachers of this art have always been extremely rare, however, most people who've learned to heal with their breath have intuitively developed this gift on their own. Pranic energy healers have never been easy to find, but they do pop up here and there, especially in traditional societies. Some of the *curanderos* (folk healers) of Brazil are known to use their breath in this way. The same is true of certain folk healers in India and China. Individuals the world over have been born with some form of this natural healing ability. For example, I once heard of an old woman in a small coal-mining town in Ohio who could use her breath to "blow the fire out of burns." As long as the injured person was immediately brought to her for treatment, the burns would heal rapidly without pain or blistering. She was even able to pass this ability on to her granddaughter.

Working with Chronic Pain

THE STATE OF SHARED BREATH ENERGIES enables a pranic energy healer to lift pain, fear, and tension directly from another person's system. This is an incredibly powerful tool for alleviating even the most stubborn conditions of chronic pain. For example, I once treated a woman for a chronic headache she'd had for twenty-three years. By the end of a single session, her headache was gone; to the best of my knowledge, it never returned.

In chapter 4, I described an even more dramatic example of

the breath's power to control pain: At one of my seminars on pranic energy healing, I worked with a woman named Karen, who had been in constant pain for thirty-five years after her leg had been crushed in a childhood accident. As soon as I began to work with her leg, the pain began to subside, and within twenty minutes it was gone.

The techniques of pranic energy healing are so sensitive that they enable the healer to detect symptoms of pain that are too subtle to either detect or relieve with conventional methods of treatment. Over the years, I've helped dozens of people who suffered from various kinds of aches and pains for which their doctors could find no apparent physical cause.

Around the time when I first discovered that I could use my breath to heal others, one of my guitar students called to ask me to help his brother Damon. Damon had slipped on a concrete floor and gotten a nasty blow to the head that knocked him unconscious for twenty-four hours. While he was out, his doctors had performed a spinal tap to diagnose his condition. When Damon regained consciousness, he complained of a splitting headache and a nagging pain in his back where the spinal tap had been done. His doctors had unsuccessfully tried to relieve his pain with various medications, but eventually had to discharge him from the hospital, saying there was nothing more they could do to help him.

At that point in my career, I had no idea whether I'd be able to help Damon; I'd only been using my breathwork to help my students overcome the anxious feelings and muscular tensions that interfered with their playing guitar. To my great surprise, however, Damon's headache and the pain in his spine cleared up within ten minutes after we began our work.

Pranic energy healing is able to produce such immediate

and powerful results because of its unique ability to cleanse pain and fear from a person's system. Over the years, I've found that remarkable numbers of physical problems — from migraine headaches and slow-healing fractures to chronic infections and gastrointestinal problems — respond readily to this method of healing. As I work with my clients, they can actually feel their pain, tensions, and anxious feelings gradually leaving their mind and body.

In order for this kind of healing to occur, however, one condition must always be met: People who want to be healed must be willing to meditate on their breath and make friends with their pain and fear. Self-acceptance is the guiding force that connects our breath with the symptoms that need to be healed. Unfortunately, when some people get sick they resent their body and treat it as their enemy. People who are too angry or impatient with their own body to watch their breath and acknowledge their body's complaints will get little or no permanent help from this kind of work.

As I mentioned in chapter 13, some people with chronic breathing disorders are afraid to meditate on their breath and pay attention to its movements because they think it's the source of their pain and fear. Some even become angry and resentful toward their breath and blame it for all their problems. This attitude of fear, resentment, and self-rejection is their greatest obstacle to healing.

Neuromuscular Problems

THERE ARE CERTAIN NEUROMUSCULAR DISORDERS for which doctors can find no physical cause. My own experience has been that many of these "mysterious" diseases are psychosomatic illnesses that are caused by blocking one's feelings of anger and fear. For example, several years ago I worked with a thirty-five-year-old man named Michael who suffered from uncontrollable facial twitches, an impaired sense of balance, and recurring episodes of faintness and dizziness. The doctors had diagnosed his condition as "benign paroxysmal positional vertigo," but they could neither determine its cause nor help bring his symptoms under control.

During our first session, I discovered that Michael's symptoms were being caused by his deeply repressed feelings of anger. When I inquired into his personal life, he told me that he was often plagued with angry feelings and paranoid thoughts. He easily lost his temper, and he often picked fights with other men for little or no reason. In an effort to curb his aggressive behavior, Michael had learned to repress his angry thoughts and hostile feelings before they could create trouble with other people. Since he neither expressed nor resolved (but only repressed) his conflicted feelings, they took the form of nervous tensions that disrupted his sense of balance and made his face twitch.

By the end of our first session, Michael's symptoms had greatly improved. Not only was he more calm and relaxed, but he also felt more present in his body than he'd ever felt in the past. By the end of our second session, his symptoms were almost gone. The greatest benefit to Michael, however, was that our work put him in touch with long-repressed feelings of anger he'd been harboring since childhood. In the following months, Michael became totally free of his symptoms by learning to modulate his feelings of anger and paranoid thoughts, using the techniques described in chapter 15.

Over the years, I've worked with at least six people who had

Bell's palsy and trigeminal neuralgia, which produce painful spasms or loss of facial-muscle control. As with Michael, each person's symptoms were rooted in their deeply repressed feelings of anger. I was especially struck by the fact that all of these people turned most of their anger inward on themselves instead of outward at other people. Although we spent relatively brief amounts of time working together, I was able to help these people reduce the intensity of their symptoms enough to make an appreciable difference.

Betty's story provides an example of how repressed fear can create neuromuscular problems that have no apparent physical cause. Betty was a sixty-five-year-old woman who had to wear special shoe supports to keep from losing her balance and falling onto her face whenever she tried to walk. Within minutes after we started working, I discovered that Betty was harboring deep-rooted feelings of fear and weakness in her legs and feet. As the session progressed, she remembered that the first signs of her problem showed up at the age of ten, when she was sent to live in an orphanage because her mother abandoned her.

The sudden loss of her mother's support had left Betty feeling so scared and weak that her legs constantly trembled. In an effort to strengthen her legs, she had developed an unconscious habit of continually tensing her muscles to control her shaky feelings. These fear-ridden tensions in her legs and feet were disrupting her equilibrium by sending misleading information to the areas of her brain that controlled her sense of balance.

By the time Betty's session with me was over, we had cleared so much tension and fear from her legs that she was able to walk normally, without shoe supports, for the first time in fifty years.

A few weeks after our session, Betty called to give me some exciting news: "Guess what, Andy! I've just fulfilled one of my heart's desires. Today I went out and bought my first pair of Reeboks!"

An Eye for an Eye

IN CHAPTER 14, I mentioned that I've worked with at least twenty people who were diagnosed as schizophrenic, all of whom exhibited various kinds of aggressive or violent behavior. One thing I noticed is that they all shared an unusual pattern of tension in their neck and shoulders and in the erector muscles along their spines. I've also noticed that this characteristic pattern of muscular rigidity perfectly matched their compulsive behavior and their rigid ways of thinking. Whenever I helped them reduce the tension they held in these particular muscle groups, the rigidities in their thinking eased up to the same degree.

One of the most striking examples of this happened with Fred, a thirty-two-year-old man who had been diagnosed as having an "extremely hostile, paranoid, schizophrenic personality." Fred was a remarkably intelligent, congenial, and likeable person who loved to read poetry and study books on philosophy. But he could suddenly become extremely hostile and violent the instant he thought he'd been wronged.

During our second session, Fred told me about an event that had taken place a few years earlier. He had been living in a stormy relationship with a woman and her baby (who was not his child). One day while Fred was out of the house, the woman spitefully burned his beloved books in the fireplace. When Fred came home and saw what she'd done, he became so furious that he threatened to kill her baby. (Fortunately, he never followed through with this threat.)

I said, "Fred! How could you even *think* of killing her baby just because she burned your books?"

"Like it says in the Bible, 'an eye for an eye and a tooth for a tooth.' Those books were the most valuable thing in the world to me, and I figure that her baby was the most valuable thing in the world to her."

"You can't possibly equate a stack of books with a baby's life. Can't you see how wrong that is?"

"Yeah? Well, that's what all my other therapists told me, too. But I don't see anything wrong with it. 'An eye for an eye' is nothing but fair."

Realizing that it was impossible to reason with him, I had Fred meditate on his breath while I worked to reduce the tension in his neck, shoulders, and back. As the tone of his muscles softened, tears began to run down Fred's cheeks and I heard him quietly say, "Oh, yes, it would have been wrong."

Surprised by his words, I said, "What are you talking about, Fred?"

"I can see now why it would have been wrong to kill that baby."

The Asthmatic Chihuahua

A NUMBER OF DOCTORS AND PSYCHIATRISTS who've watched me work have attributed the success of my treatments to the ill-defined force called "the power of suggestion." My answers to this charge are quite simple. For one thing, the healing powers of the breath can be demonstrated and validated in clinical settings and under controlled laboratory conditions. For another, pranic energy healing works just as well with animals as it does with human beings, and animals are not as subject to suggestions or placebos as humans are.

Over the years, I've worked with dozens of animals, ranging from household pets and farm animals to zebras, seagulls, and goldfish. This has always been one of the most rewarding aspects of my healing work, because even wild animals become remarkably cooperative and grateful once they realize you're trying to help them. One of my most memorable experiences involved a Chihuahua named Pepe who belonged to one of my clients. Pepe's owner, Jane, was a woman in her early fifties. Jane suffered from an unusually severe case of asthma. When her attacks were particularly strong she'd come to me for help.

One day, Jane called me on the phone — but this time it wasn't for herself. Close to tears, she said, "Andy, my dog Pepe is terribly sick. The vet says he's dying and there's nothing more he can do. Would you come to my house as soon as you can and see if you can help him?" When I arrived at Jane's house, she led me into the living room, where Pepe was lying in a well-padded basket that served as his bed. He was extremely feeble, and obviously close to death.

As I worked with Pepe, Jane watched the proceedings with tears in her eyes. Every so often, she'd anxiously plead, "Oh, Pepe! Please don't die! I can't bear to lose you." Pepe was so entrained with his owner's feelings that, at that moment, he began to have a full-blown asthma attack — a response he'd picked up from his years of living with Jane. Before I could provide Pepe with any more help, I had to banish Jane from the living room and make her wait in the adjoining kitchen. After helping Pepe as much as I could, I went into the kitchen to sit with Jane and tell her what I'd learned:

"Listen, Jane. Pepe is old, he's sick, and he's ready to die. I don't think you realize what a great strain you're putting him under by begging him to stay. He loves you so much that he's trying to stay on just to please you. But he can't keep it up any longer. You've got to let him go."

"Please, Andy, can't you help him to stay alive for just a few more weeks?"

"I don't think so, Jane. I've managed to make him a lot more comfortable, but he's very feeble and tired inside; it's his time to go."

As I was speaking, Jane suddenly exclaimed, "Andy! Look at Pepe!"

When I looked into the living room, I could scarcely believe my eyes. Pepe was sitting up in his bed and wagging his tail! When I went over to check out his energy, I was completely mystified by this sudden, almost miraculous, change in his health.

"I don't understand how this happened, Jane. Pepe's life-force is still pretty feeble, but he's definitely stronger than he was. It looks as though Pepe will last a bit longer after all!"

"If I could only have him for two more weeks!"

"You might just get that. But for Pepe's sake, I want you to promise that next time he's ready to go, you won't try to hold him back."

"I promise, Andy. I'll let him go."

A few weeks later, I received a beautiful card from Jane. On the cover was a life-like drawing of a Chihuahua that looked just like Pepe. The message inside said:

Dear Andy,
Pepe lived exactly two more weeks. When he died, I was
finally able to let him go. Thank you so much for helping.
It was a beautiful gift to both of us.

Beneath her signature, Jane had also inscribed these words
of Jesus:

As ye have done unto the least of my brethren, so ye have
done unto me.[1]

PART FOUR

EXPERIENCING
the
DIVINE

CHAPTER SEVENTEEN

THE BREATH
of
CREATION

Tao is the breath that never dies.
It is a mother to all creation.

— LAO TZU

WHERE DOES THE BREATH GET ITS CREATIVE POWERS? How are these powers related to God? In order to answer these questions, it is important to know a few basic facts about the origin of the universe and the divine forces that created it.

There are two dimensions, or poles, of reality. The first is *Godhead,* the formless dimension of reality that gives birth to the physical world. The second is *Creation,* the physical universe of space, time, and material things. Everyone is familiar with the created world because we can perceive its elements with our physical senses. Relatively few people are aware of the Godhead, however, because its spiritual energies are beyond the reach of our physical faculties of perception.

Over the centuries, Godhead has been given many names. The Hindus call it *Brahman,* the Chinese call it *Tao,* and Christians call it *Godhead,* while Buddhists call it *Sunyata,* which means "the great emptiness." The term that sages and mystics of all traditions most commonly use is "the void," because Godhead is completely *devoid* of created things. This is why the great Christian mystic Meister Eckhart once described Godhead as "a place in which nothing is."

When our sages and mystics say there is "nothing" in Godhead, what they actually mean is that there are no *things* in Godhead, because this formless dimension of reality exists just prior to the creation of the physical world. Paradoxically, there is something in Godhead; however, it is unlike anything we know in the created world. That "something" is pure Divine Consciousness, the irreducible "substance" from which everything in the universe is made.

Godhead is not a place where Divine Consciousness "dwells"; it is a term that denotes Divine Consciousness in its formless aspect. The Eastern masters sometimes refer to this nonmoving dimension of reality as "Divine Consciousness reposing in its eternal stillness." In contrast, the physical world we know so well is the manifestation of Divine Consciousness in its moving or creative phase. Accordingly, I sometimes refer to Godhead and Creation as "the stillness" and "the movement."

As Divine Consciousness emerges from the stillness of Godhead, it begins vibrating at different frequencies to create the infinite numbers of separate things that comprise the physical world. Everything in this universe — from the subtlest thought wave to the hardest diamond — is simply a form of Divine Consciousness in its creative (or moving) phase. In air-breathing creatures like us, Divine Consciousness takes the form of Prana, the spiritual life-force that causes our breath to move.

Both dimensions of reality — the stillness and the movement — are perfectly reflected in the movements of our breath. Every inhalation and exhalation is an expression of Divine Consciousness in its moving aspect, while the pauses that briefly occur at each end of the breath provide fleeting glimpses of the stillness of Godhead. Since our breath is a direct extension of the pranic life-force, every cycle of breathing duplicates the movement of cosmic energies between Godhead and Creation. Thus, as we breathe in and out, we are literally creating our own personal version of the universe.

According to the Eastern sages, by mastering the creative forces that dwell in our breath, we can not only become enlightened, we can also gain various kinds of miraculous powers. For example, according to *The Shiva Sutras*, one of India's most ancient and sacred spiritual texts, a person can acquire supernormal powers over the elements through the practice of meditation, austerities, and breath control.

Miraculous Powers

BUDDHA IS THE MOST FAMOUS HINDU YOGI who attained enlightenment by mastering the forces that dwell in the breath. Along with the gift of enlightenment, his mastery of the pranic life-force also brought him the full range of miraculous powers that all great spiritual masters are said to possess. The Buddhist writings contain numerous stories about his abilities to float in the sky, heal with his touch, and calm the raging waters of a river in flood. According to one story, Buddha once demonstrated his mastery over the elements of nature by causing a great column of fire to issue forth from one side of his body while an equally spectacular column of water gushed up toward the heavens from his other side.

About five hundred years after Buddha died, an Indian master named Bodhidharma brought the teachings of Zen Buddhism to China, where the Buddhist teachings and breathing practices merged with those of the Taoist masters. One remarkable offspring of this cultural cross-pollination was the Tibetan Buddhist science of breath known as *Dumo*, the "mystic heat yoga." Dumo embodies a rigorous set of breathing techniques that are practiced in combination with various mantras (sacred sounds) and visualization techniques. This combination of disciplines enables the practitioner to accomplish some extraordinary yogic feats.

For example, monks who are adept in the practice of Dumo can sit naked in the snow on a freezing night and generate enough body heat to dry wet sheets placed on their backs. This feat is usually accomplished, not once, but as many as fifteen times during the course of the night. However, this ability to generate great quantities of heat within one's body seems relatively insignificant compared to some of the other feats that are said to be possible for a Dumo adept. According to an ancient Tibetan Buddhist text known as *The Six Yogas of Naropa*:

> He who can fully master the Five Pranas (five stages of Prana), or hold them in their respective Centers, will gain the following merits:

- *[he can] radiate beams of light from his body*
- *make his body vanish*
- *work various kinds of miracles*
- *transform stones into gold*
- *walk on water without sinking*
- *enter fire without being burned*
- *melt a snow mountain with his Dumo heat*
- *travel to a distant cosmos in a few seconds*
- *fly in the sky and walk through rocks and mountains*[1]

The ancient yogic texts of India describe many of these same powers. For example, in his famous *Yoga Sutras* the great Hindu sage Patanjali not only describes some of the altered states of consciousness in which miracles can be performed, he also provides detailed instructions on how to cultivate specific powers, such as the ability to levitate or to make oneself invisible. Patanjali's teachings are so basic and timeless that they are currently being studied by more people in our time than ever before in history. During the late 1970s, for example, a number of major television documentaries and magazine articles featured Maharishi Mahesh Yogi, the famous master of meditation who was teaching his followers how to levitate on the basis of Patanjali's instructions.

Patanjali's *Yoga Sutras* also describe an ancient technique called *sumyama* (pronounced "soomi-yahma"), which brings various kinds of extraordinary powers. (To refresh your memory, sumyama is the basis of the healing triangle technique described in chapter 12.) It should be noted, however, that Patanjali's instructions contain no magic words that make it possible to instantly walk on water or float in the sky. The success of his techniques greatly depends on the depth of one's meditative consciousness and the degree of yogic control a person has gained over his or her mind and body.

In countries such as Tibet and India, there are numerous swamis and mendicant monks who earn their living by displaying various kinds of miraculous powers. Some of them can levitate; others materialize objects from thin air or read a person's mind; still others can suddenly appear within (or vanish from) the midst of a crowd of people. In *Autobiography of a Yogi*, Swami Yogananda recounts some wonderfully instructive and amusing stories about a number of mendicant monks he'd personally met who used their magical powers to attract followers. One of the most colorful was a swami named Ghanda Baba, who was also known as "the perfume saint." Ghanda Baba was a Tibetan yogi who could materialize a person's favorite foods from thin air on demand, or imbue an object with the scent of any flower a person might request — hence the name "perfume saint."

Spiritual Practices and Miraculous Powers

SOME PEOPLE INADVERTENTLY ACQUIRE supernatural powers through the regular practice of spiritual disciplines. For example, Saint Teresa of Avila practiced her religious austerities with such fervor and devotion that she often slipped into intense states of rapture that caused her to float uncontrollably up toward the ceiling:

> ...*great powers raised me up from the very soles of my feet.... I don't know what to compare these powers to;*

they were much greater than in the other spiritual experiences.[2]

Teresa was especially troubled by the fact that her levitations sometimes occurred in public:

Once, when there were some ladies of nobility present in order to hear a sermon . . . I began to see the Lord was going to raise me up. . . . I stretched on the floor and the nuns came and held me down; nonetheless, this was seen.[3]

Most Catholic theologians, and even the saints themselves, are at a loss to explain just how or why some people gain various miraculous powers and charisms during the course of their spiritual evolution. For the most part, they simply accept such powers as part of the mysterious ways in which God works through a few chosen people. Saint Augustine was one of the few Catholic authorities to realize that miracles are based in natural laws that are poorly understood.

Powers of Healing

THE WRITINGS OF THE TAOIST MASTERS say relatively little about using one's breath to cultivate miraculous powers. One Taoist treatise titled *The Utmost Secrets of Methods of Breathing* mentions a few of the extraordinary powers that the mastery of breath can bring:

If one learns the wonder of using the breath energy, the spirits will make the body walk and move on air.[4]

The same treatise also speaks most respectfully about a mysterious eighth-century magician named T'ung Hsuen:

*As T'ung Hsuen came unexpectedly, no one knew whose son he was. From his great ease in magical transformations, he might be some great immortal from ancient times...his breathing secret is the secret treasure of Taoists.*5

For the most part, however, the ancient Taoist masters showed much more interest in using the breath to cultivate powers of healing than for gaining magical powers. The Taoist, Hindu, and Buddhist writings universally affirm the healing powers contained in the breath; however, they give little practical information on how to actually develop these skills. This is partly because healing with the breath has traditionally been considered esoteric knowledge to be withheld from the uninitiated, and partly because some of this knowledge is impossible to convey in words. It can only be passed directly on from master to disciple. In the words of one Taoist master:

*[The Original Breath] has many secrets that are only orally taught...it is not possible to record them with a brush on paper.*6

In my own case, whatever powers of healing I possess spontaneously appeared as the natural result of regularly practicing spiritual disciplines. During a particularly intense and concentrated phase of my spiritual development, besides working with my daily routine of breathing practices, I also devoted at least two hours a day to chanting various sacred texts and mantric sounds. To increase the power of my chanting, I'd bring the rhythms of my breath and heartbeat into synch (as described in chapter 7), then I'd sing in perfect time with my heartbeat for the entire duration of the chant.

After two or three months of chanting in this multidisciplined way, I noticed that I was inadvertently picking up on my guitar students' thoughts and emotions. At other times, I could discern feelings of tension and stress in various parts of their bodies, which they weren't aware of themselves. As these psychic abilities grew stronger with time, I also discovered that I could use my breath to vacuum pain, fear, and tension from another person's system. Eventually, I also learned that I could use my breath to awaken the same powers of healing in other people.

In all the years I've worked as a teacher and healer, I've never deliberately tried to cultivate any of the psychic abilities or healing powers I use in my work. Whatever powers I happen to possess have always appeared of their own accord as the natural results of faithfully practicing spiritual disciplines — especially those involving meditation on the breath. To this very day, whenever I focus my mind on my heartbeat, I hear the mantric sounds that I practiced so many years ago spontaneously repeating themselves in perfect time with the beat of my heart and the flow of my breath.

CHAPTER EIGHTEEN

SAMADHI:
The
BREATHLESS STATE

When there is effortless suspension of breathing, it is the supreme state of... pure infinite consciousness. Who reaches this state does not grieve.

— *THE YOGA VASHISHTHA*

THERE ARE MANY LEVELS OR DEGREES of meditative consciousness. The deepest and most powerful of all is a state of profound meditative absorption that the Hindus call "samadhi." Samadhi is the highest goal of all spiritual practices because it is from within this state that our most profound experiences of Divine communion and spiritual liberation take place. The Hindus also call it "the breathless state" because, at the deepest levels of samadhi consciousness, one's breath completely stops moving for minutes — or even hours — at a time, without harm to the body. As we enter the state of samadhi, our breathing becomes so slow and refined that its movements are nearly imperceptible. At deeper levels of samadhi consciousness, our breath completely stops moving, our mind becomes profoundly peaceful, time stands still, and we feel that we are standing in the presence of Eternity itself.

This experience of deep stillness and peace is our first direct experience of God's formless aspect. The saints and mystics of all traditions call it "the peace of god." Saint Paul called it "the peace that passeth all understanding." The peace of God and the stillness of Godhead are one and the same phenomenon. Each is simply a different way of experiencing Divine Consciousness reposing in its own stillness. During a weekend workshop, one of my students who entered this state of deep stillness and peace heard an inner voice say, "I am the Eternal One."

Divine Communion

WHEN WE ENTER THE STATE OF SAMADHI, our experiences of Divine communion can take countless forms, including visitations from celestial beings, visions of one's chosen deity, or revelations of future events. In general, the content of religious and mystical experiences will reflect the religious and cultural background of the person to whom they are happening. For example, a Hindu will tend to see visions of Krishna or Rama, while Christians will tend to see visions of Mary or Christ. By the same token, when Native Americans go out on a vision quest, they tend to see visions of indigenous animals, such as sacred crows or buffaloes. Eskimo shamans, on the other hand, tend to see visions of arctic animals, such as seals and whales, but — understandably enough — they never see crows or buffaloes.

However, God is neither a person, a place, nor a creaturely thing. The entity we call God is Divine Consciousness — the pure disembodied Spirit that exists beyond all names and forms. If we want to see God as God really is, our mind must be perfectly still and totally free of all preconceptions. In the words of Meister Eckhart:

Nothing in all creation is so like God as stillness... who is to hear the Word of God (where all is quiet), must be quiet himself and void of ideas and forms.[1]

The Hindu sage Patanjali expressed these same ideas in a slightly different way:

Union with God comes about through stilling the thought waves of the mind.[2]

The Bible expresses these same truths in the briefest way of all — it simply says:

Be still and know that I am God.[3]

The peace of God is one of the purest experiences of Divine communion we can possibly have, because it is totally free of all subjective content, such as visual images or preconceptions about the nature of God that stem from our religious or cultural background. Zen Buddhists consider this experience of stillness and peace to be one of the highest prizes we can attain as we travel the path to enlightenment. You might also be interested in knowing that samadhi is the level of meditative consciousness in which Zen Buddhist monks can "hear" the "sound of one hand clapping" — the soundless sound of Unity relating only to itself.

Unfortunately, many people who attain these feelings of stillness and peace from practicing spiritual disciplines fail to recognize their true significance because their experience of Divine communion didn't take the form of a mystical vision of heaven or a visit from an angelic being. Most of my students enter the state of samadhi at least three or four times during the course of a weekend workshop. When I invite them to share their experiences with the rest of the group, some people typically say, "Well, my mind became very peaceful. But aside from that, nothing significant happened."

The Bliss of Samadhi

ALONG WITH THESE FEELINGS OF STILLNESS and peace, we also experience subtle feelings of joy and well-being that arise from a source deep inside. As our state continues to deepen, these quiet feelings of inner joy gradually turn into the ecstatic, blissful feelings that the Hindus call "the bliss of samadhi." The sages and saints of Islam call it "god-intoxication." To the mystics and saints of the Western world, this experience of heavenly joy is known as *ecstasis* (or ecstasy).

Teresa of Avila was a Christian saint who never heard of samadhi, yet she clearly describes how her breathing would "gradually subside" whenever she entered the blissful states in which she experienced union with God:

The soul feels such a sweet and wonderful delight that almost everything falls away — it falls into a kind of swoon. The breathing and all bodily functions gradually

*subside.... All exterior strength is lost, and the soul's
strength increases so that it can more thoroughly enjoy the
bliss.... [U]nion and rapture or elevation, or what they
call flight of the spirit or transport... these are all different
names for the same thing which is also called ecstasy.*[4]

When we enter the state of samadhi and our breath stops
moving, it's a sign that we've made a transition from "outer"
breathing to "inner" breathing, as the Taoist masters would say.
The reason we no longer need to breathe air through our lungs
is that our consciousness has completely merged with prana in
the form of the "breath of God" that dwells in our subtle body
(see chapter 11).

The Hindus call this transition from outer to inner breathing "sushumnal breathing" because it takes place within the
sushumna, the central channel of golden light that exists in
the subtle body. To refresh your memory, the sushumna is the
very core of our being; this is where the life-force initially enters
our system and dwells as the breath of God that causes our
breath to move. When our physical breath stops moving, it indicates that our consciousness has entered the central column of
golden light and we're breathing directly with God's own breath.

The Four Stages of Samadhi

THERE ARE FOUR STAGES OR LEVELS of samadhi consciousness. The first is called *nimilena samadhi*, or "introvertive
samadhi." The Hindus call it introvertive samadhi because
when we enter this level of meditative consciousness, we lose all
track of time; we become oblivious to our physical surroundings and even lose consciousness of our body. Our mind

becomes so deeply immersed in the peace of God that it tends to blank out as it does in deep sleep. We don't realize that we've been in samadhi until our mind "wakes up" again and returns to the world of movement.

The second level is called *nirvikalpa samadhi,* or "thought-free samadhi." Here, too, we lose all track of time; we lose consciousness of our body and become oblivious to events taking place in our physical surroundings. This time, however, when our mind becomes filled with the peace of God, it doesn't blank out. This level is called thought-free samadhi because our mind becomes perfectly still. It stops creating its usual stream of random thoughts and becomes a silent witness to events taking place in the inner dimensions of consciousness. This is also the level of samadhi in which most mystical visions and experiences of Divine communion take place.

The third level is called *nirvythana samadi,* or "extrovertive samadhi." At this level of samadhi consciousness, our mind becomes perfectly still and free of all thoughts as it does with introvertive samadhi. This time, however, we're not only aware of events taking place in the inner dimensions of consciousness, we remain fully aware of our body and of events taking place in our physical surroundings.

When we open our eyes and return to the outside world, it appears surprisingly different. Although our breath has begun to move again, our mind stays immersed in the stillness of Godhead. Although we've returned to the world of movement, we're *still* in deep meditation. Instead of meditating on events taking place in the inner dimensions of consciousness, however, we're now meditating on events taking place in the outside world.

While we're in this state, our mind is so peaceful and quiet, it alters the way we experience time and changes our perception of reality. For example, the physical world takes on a somewhat transient and illusory quality. It doesn't appear quite so solid and real as it does in our everyday state of mind. Although we're clearly aware of the passage of time, time (itself) seems somewhat unreal. Life feels more like one long and continuous moment, rather than a series of separate events succeeding each other in space and time. There is never a sense of dwelling on the past, nor of projecting our thoughts into the future. There is only the present moment.

The fourth and deepest level of samadhi consciousness is called *sahaja samadhi,* which means "the great samadhi" in Sanskrit. At this level, we not only experience the same qualities of peace and detachment that we do in extrovertive samadhi, we also experience the state known as "unity consciousness." Our consciousness becomes so completely merged with God's that we lose all sense of our limited self. All boundaries between inner and outer reality seem to disappear, and we have the experience of being at one with God and all created things.

The following quotes from Swami Yogananda's book *Man's Eternal Quest* provide an excellent description of the changes that take place in our mind and body as we enter the state of sahaja samadhi:

> *When the profound ecstasy of God falls over you, the body becomes absolutely still, the breath ceases to flow, and the thoughts are quiet — banished, every one, by the magic command of the soul. Then you drink of God's bliss and experience an intoxication of joy that not a thousand draughts of wine could give you.... When you can feel your presence in all creation, and also know the Joy that is beyond creation, then you are a God-like being.... You are*

in every blade of grass and on the mountaintop; and you
can feel every cell of your body and every atom of space.[5]

Healing and Transformation

SAMADHI IS THE MOST TRANSFORMATIVE STATE of consciousness
our mind can possibly enter. It is also the most challenging to
master. It's extremely difficult to enter this state without blanking out because the peace and bliss of God are like powerful
intoxicants that cause an untrained mind to become drowsy
and fall into a sleep-like state. Even when our mind blanks out,
however, we still derive great benefits from having been in this
state. Whenever we enter the state of samadhi, our mind and
body undergo tremendous amounts of spontaneous healing.

The healing and restorative powers of samadhi are many
times greater than those of deep sleep, because when we "fall
asleep" in samadhi, we're literally resting in the arms of God. By
the time we "wake up" and return to the outside world, we're
never quite the same. Each experience of being in samadhi not
only brings healing and restoration to our mind and body, it
also leaves our everyday mind a bit freer of fear and more
deeply tinged with the peace of God.

The only people who can enter the depths of samadhi without losing consciousness are highly disciplined yogis or fully
enlightened and God-realized beings. In fact, fully enlightened
and God-realized beings live in a permanent state of sahaja
samadhi, because samadhi consciousness is the very essence of
enlightened and God-realized states.

People who regularly practice spiritual disciplines are likely
to enter the state of samadhi at one time or another. It can also
happen to exceptionally creative and gifted people, such as

scientists, athletes, and artists who've become totally absorbed in a task that requires periods of intense and prolonged concentration (see chapter 20).

Some people inadvertently enter this state after being subjected to extreme and prolonged conditions of mental and physical duress: for example, prisoners in the Nazi concentration camps or soldiers who've been caught in extremely harrowing battle conditions for an extended period of time. Still others have entered this state as the result of ingesting psychedelic substances, such as LSD, peyote, or psilocybin (sacred mushrooms). However, all such experiences of samadhi consciousness soon fade away. In most cases, the person to whom it happens can neither maintain the experience nor repeat it later at will.

It takes tremendous amounts of self-discipline to enter the state of sahaja samadhi and never leave it again. Fully enlightened and God-realized beings are the only people who've mastered this task, which is precisely why we call them "perfected masters." Until we become fully enlightened, every samadhi experience we have will be relatively short-lived.

No matter how brief it might be, however, every experience of samadhi permanently affects our everyday mind. When our mind returns to the outside world, the feelings of stillness and peace might seem to vanish, but once we've experienced these God-given feelings, they always stay with us in one form or another and become part of our everyday consciousness.

MEDITATION ON THE SPACE OF GOD

IN CHAPTER 17, I described how the two dimensions of reality — the stillness and the movement — are perfectly reflected in the movements of our breath. Every inhalation and exhalation is a manifestation of Divine Consciousness in its moving aspect, while the pauses that briefly occur at each end of the breath provide fleeting glimpses of the stillness of Godhead.

The Hindus call these pauses the *kumbhak,* which means "pot" or "vessel" in Sanskrit. They consider each pause to be a sacred vessel or chalice that holds the nectar of pure Divine Consciousness. I call them "the space of God" because they can be used as "gateways" into the stillness of Godhead.

This next technique — "meditation on the space of God" — will teach you how to use the pause at each end of the breath to enter the stillness of Godhead and partake of the peace of God. Before you try to work this technique in earnest, you should be reasonably skilled with the balancing techniques taught in chapter 8. If you haven't been working to improve the balance of tensions between your in- and out-breaths, you won't have enough control of your breath to effectively use this technique.

One of the best times to practice this technique is immediately after working with your daily breathing practices, or after practicing spiritual disciplines such as meditation, chanting, or prayer. Another excellent time is immediately after working with meditational movement disciplines, such as hatha yoga, Tai Chi, or Chi Kung. When they are correctly practiced, all of these time-honored spiritual disciplines will help to deepen and balance your breathing. The deeper and slower your breathing becomes and the more evenly balanced your in- and out-breaths are, the longer the pauses will last.

This is how meditation on the space of God is done:

1. Sit in a comfortable posture, then close your eyes and meditate on the rhythm of your breath as the air swings in and out of your body. This time, instead of

watching its movements (as you usually do), focus your attention on the pause that briefly appears at the turnaround points in your breathing.

2. If you stay alert and study these pauses, you'll see that they are more than just empty spaces. Within each pause, there are palpable feelings of stillness and peace. Study those feelings of peace and allow them to fill your mind. That peace you feel is the peace of God — the energy of Divine Consciousness reposing in its own stillness.

3. When your breath begins to move again, keep remembering the feelings of peace in your mind until you experience them again in the pause that occurs at the other end of your breath.

4. Each time you enter the space of God, the feelings of peace will become deeper and stronger. As your mind becomes filled with these feelings of peace, they'll begin to overflow into your body like tea that spills from a brimming cup and overflows into the saucer.

5. The more peaceful and quiet your mind becomes, the more slowly your breath will move and the longer each pause will last. As you enter the early stages of samadhi, your breathing will become so slow and refined that its movements will be nearly imperceptible.

6. At the deeper levels of samadhi consciousness, your breath will completely stop moving and only the pause will remain. When your breath becomes still, your mind will become still and completely immersed in the peace of God.

7. Along with these feelings of stillness and peace,
    subtle feelings of joy and well-being will begin to
    arise from a source deep inside. As your state of
    samadhi deepens, these subtle feelings of inner joy
    will gradually turn into the ecstatic feelings known
    as the bliss of samadhi.

In the words of Swami Yogananda:

*When the divine joy comes, immediately, I am lifted into
the Spirit. I feel the bliss of a thousand sleeps rolled
into one, and yet I don't lose my ordinary consciousness.*[6]

What to Watch For

If you find it difficult to focus your mind on the pauses, it's a
sign that your in- and out-breaths aren't well balanced enough
to work with this technique. When this happens, you can finish
the session by meditating on your heartbeat instead.

If your mind blanks out at any time while practicing this
technique, it doesn't mean that you've done something wrong.
Remember that it is extremely difficult to enter the state of
samadhi without losing consciousness, because the untrained
mind isn't strong enough to fully contain the peace of God.
With enough time and disciplined practice, however, you can
learn how to enter the deeper levels of samadhi consciousness
— and stay for a while without blanking out.

The length of time you spend in samadhi will depend on the
depth of your meditation and the state of balance that exists
between the tensions of your in- and out-breaths. The state of
suspended breathing can last anywhere from several minutes to
several hours. Most experienced meditators manage to stay in

samadhi for an hour at most, before their mind and breath become active again and their consciousness returns to the outside world.

The suspension of breath that takes place in samadhi can't be induced by holding our breath and forcing it to stay still. Our breath must stop moving of its own accord, with no sense of strain or feelings of suffocation. All of the time-tested spiritual disciplines, such as meditation, prayer, chanting, yoga, and the repetition of sacred names, can bring us into samadhi because they were specifically developed to quiet the mind so that it can receive the peace of God. When these practices bear their highest fruit, our breath stops moving, our mind becomes still, and we're drawn into the depths of samadhi when we least expect it.

Each time we practice our disciplines, we're building a charge of meditative energy that accumulates from one session to another. When this charge reaches a critical mass, our breath will stop moving — all by itself — and we'll enter the depths of samadhi with no conscious effort of our own.

CHAPTER NINETEEN

BREATH-RETENTION TECHNIQUES

If one meditates on the pause that occurs between one's inhalations and exhalations, one will experience the state of pure Divine Consciousness.

— *THE VIJNANA BHAIRAVA*

OVER THE CENTURIES, the Hindu and Taoist masters developed special techniques called *bhandas,* or "locks," to keep their breath from moving for extended periods of time. The main purpose of these breath-retention techniques is to duplicate the suspension of breath that takes place in the state of samadhi. In and of themselves, retention techniques are incapable of bringing anyone directly into samadhi. When correctly practiced, however, these techniques can prepare the breath for entering into the breathless state and even bring brief experiences of the peace and bliss that are part of samadhi consciousness.

Unfortunately, most of the ancient retention techniques are so forceful and demanding that relatively few people can practice them without running the risk of incurring negative side-effects, such as panic attacks, arrhythmia, or shortness of breath. In response to this problem, I've developed a number of less rigorous, but equally effective, retention techniques that are much easier and safer to work with.

The techniques described in this chapter — "balancing the stick," "solidifying the breath," and "prolonging the space of God" — are considerably gentler and easier to work with than most of those passed down by the ancient masters. These techniques will not only prepare your breath for entering into the breathless state, they'll also prepare your mind to enter the depths of samadhi and stay for a while without blanking out.

Once again, I'd like to remind you that you should be reasonably skilled with the balancing techniques taught in chapter 8 before trying to work with these techniques in earnest. If you haven't worked on balancing the tensions of your in- and out-breaths, the techniques taught in this chapter will be relatively less effective and more difficult to do.

RETENTION TECHNIQUE #1:
BALANCING THE STICK

I CALL THIS TECHNIQUE "BALANCING THE STICK" because it reminds me of a game we played as children. The object of the game was to balance a stick on the tip of our finger and keep it standing up straight as long as we could without moving our hand. When the stick began to tip over, we'd move our hand adroitly from side to side to keep the stick from falling down. As soon as we got the stick standing up straight again, we'd keep our hand as still as we could — until the stick began to tip over again.

This technique works in much the same way. The object is to bring your breath to stillness, then keep it from moving for as long as you can without forcing it to stay still. When your breath tries to move (either in or out), gently resist its movement and coax it to stay still for as long as you can without creating undue feelings of stress or strain. When your breath reaches the point at which it *must* move again, allow it to move as it pleases — but only for as long as it takes to bring it back to stillness.

This is how "balancing the stick" is done:

1. Sit in a comfortable upright posture and meditate on your breath. Once you're attuned to its movement, do a few rounds of the gentle rapid breathing technique to enliven your breath and ensure that it's reasonably open and flowing.

2. Once your breath is moving more freely, spend a few minutes balancing the tensions of your in- and out-breaths by working with any of the balancing techniques (see chapter 8) that feel appropriate. As soon as your in- and out-breaths feel more evenly matched, you're ready to work with "balancing the stick."

3. Once again, do a few rounds of gentle rapid breathing to enliven your breath. When your breath has readjusted its movements, gently suspend your breathing. Keep your breath from moving for as long as you can without forcing to make it stay still.

4. You may keep your breath suspended at any point between breathing in or breathing out. What matters

most is that you keep it from moving without forcing. When your breath tries to move either in or out,
coax it to stay still for as long as you can without
causing feelings of suffocation or strain.

5. No matter how long you manage to keep your
breath still, it will eventually insist on moving again.
Once your breath has reached its limits, allow it to
move in any direction (and with any rhythm) it
chooses.

6. As soon as your breath has reestablished a steady
flow, repeat the process of balancing the stick. Hold
your breath gently and keep it from moving for as
long as you can. When your breath tries to move
either in or out, coax it to stay still a bit longer.

7. When your breath finally *insists* on moving again,
allow it to do whatever it pleases to regain a steady
and comfortable flow. As soon as it's moving freely
again, bring your breath to stillness as soon as you
can without causing undue feelings of stress or
strain.

8. After you've done three or four rounds of balancing
the stick, give your breath a full minute to assimilate the changes this technique produces. By the
time your breath has readjusted its tensions, you'll
find that your breathing has become a bit deeper,
stronger, and more evenly balanced.

9. Along with these increased feelings of balance and
strength, your breath will be moving a bit more
slowly. You'll be feeling much more peaceful and
quiet in both your mind and your body.

What to Watch For

You may work with this technique for as long as you wish. When it begins to produce diminishing returns, it's time to move on to a different set of practices or bring the session to a close.

Should you begin to feel anxious or find yourself gasping for air, it means that you're either working too hard to keep your breath still, or you're keeping it still beyond the point at which it should begin moving again. If you work gently with your breath and remain sensitive to the feelings in your body, these kinds of problems won't occur.

RETENTION TECHNIQUE #2:
SOLIDIFYING THE BREATH

EASTERN YOGIS AND MARTIAL ARTISTS traditionally use retention techniques for building great reserves of spiritual strength and power. The process of restraining one's breath to accumulate inner reserves of spiritual energy is something like storing water behind a dam or creating tension in a bowstring before letting the arrow fly. The Chinese masters refer to the process of restraining the breath as one of "accumulating great breath energy." In the words of one Taoist master:

> *Having breath energy in the body is like having water in a river.... When there are deep waters, unusually large ships can be carried. When tremendous breath energy is accumulated, unusual life can be maintained.*[1]

This next technique — solidifying the breath — is a combination of balancing the stick and the solidifying technique (taught in chapter 7). It will not only prepare your breath to enter the breathless state by teaching it how to slow down, but it will also help you build the inner reserves of meditative energy that will draw you effortlessly into samadhi. This technique begins in the same way as balancing the stick. This time, however, you'll be holding the rubber balls in your hands the whole time you are practicing.

This is how it's done:

1. Sit in a comfortable posture with your rubber balls held loosely in your hands and begin to meditate on your breath. Once you're attuned to its movement, do a few rounds of gentle rapid breathing to enliven your breath, then spend a few minutes on balancing your in- and out-breaths. When your in- and out-breaths feel more evenly matched, you're ready to include the solidifying technique as part of your retention practices.

2. Do a few more rounds of gentle rapid breathing to enliven your breath. As soon as your breath has readjusted its movements, begin to balance the stick, which means keep your breath from moving for as long as you can without forcing it to stay still.

3. When your breath insists on moving again, squeeze the balls with one steady pressure and your breath will instantly lose its urge to move for at least ten or fifteen more seconds. When your breath tries to move again, just squeeze the balls a bit harder and you'll find it surprisingly easy to keep your breath still for another ten or fifteen seconds.

4. You can squeeze the balls harder as many as three or four times in succession to keep your breath from moving. No matter how much longer you manage to keep your breathing suspended, however, there is always a point at which it will have to move again.

5. When your breath has reached this limit, keep the same steady pressure on the rubber balls and allow your breath to move as it pleases. By the time your breath has readjusted its tensions, your breathing will be noticeably steadier and stronger. It will also be moving a bit more slowly and will feel more evenly balanced.

6. If you study the effects in your mind and body, you'll find that your mind has become more peaceful and your body feels much more solid and grounded.

7. Once your breath has readjusted its movements, release the pressure on the rubber balls very gradually and slowly. If you do this correctly, your breath, your mind, and your body will feel nearly as steady, calm, and solid as they did while you were squeezing the balls.

What to Watch For

You may repeat steps two through seven as many times as you wish. When the technique begins to lose its effectiveness, it's time to practice other techniques or bring the session to a close.

If you begin to feel anxious or short of breath during any phase of this practice, you're either forcing to keep your breath from moving, or it's not the right time to work with retention techniques.

Balancing the stick and solidifying the breath are an extremely versatile combination of breathing techniques. In this chapter, you're using them as retention techniques to prepare your mind and breath for entering the state of samadhi. However, these techniques can also be used to steady your mind when you're filled with doubt and confusion, or for grounding yourself in your body whenever you're beginning to feel scattered or out of control.

RETENTION TECHNIQUE #3: PROLONGING THE SPACE OF GOD

PROLONGING THE SPACE OF GOD is the same technique as meditation on the space of God, which you learned in chapter 18. The only difference between them is that, in this case, you'll be using balancing the stick and the solidifying technique to prolong the pauses and deepen the feelings of stillness and peace that exist in the space of God.

Some of the best times to work with this technique are immediately after practicing breathing techniques or other kinds of spiritual disciplines, such as meditation, chanting, yoga, or prayer. These are the times when the movements of your breath will usually be fairly deep, well balanced, and healthily slowed down.

This is how prolonging the space of God is done:

1. Sit in a comfortable posture with your rubber balls held loosely in your hands, and begin to meditate on your breath. This time, however, instead of watching the movements of your breath as you usually do, focus your attention on the pause that appears at the end of the breath.

2. If you stay alert and study these pauses, you'll see that they're more than just empty spaces. Within each pause, there are palpable feelings of stillness and peace. Focus your attention on those feelings of peace and allow them to fill your mind.

3. When your breath tries to move again, you can prolong the pause by balancing the stick — which means, hold your breath gently to keep it from moving. The longer you keep your breath still by balancing the stick, the stronger the feelings of peace will become.

4. When you've reached the point at which you can no longer keep your breath from moving by balancing the stick, it's time to squeeze on the rubber balls. As soon as you squeeze the balls, your breath will instantly lose its urge to move and the pause will last even longer.

5. Whenever your breath tries to move, just squeeze the balls a bit harder. As soon as you squeeze on the rubber balls, your breath will lose its urge to move and the pause will last longer. The longer you make the pause last, the deeper the feelings of stillness and peace will become throughout your mind and body.

6. You might be able to increase the length of the pause by squeezing the balls harder three or four times in succession. No matter how hard or how often you squeeze the balls, however, there is always a point at which your breath will have to move to freshen the air in your body.

7. When it's time to let your breath move again, keep your mind focused on your breathing, then release

the pressure on the rubber balls and allow your breath to do whatever it needs to regain its freedom of movement. As your breath readjusts its movement, keep remembering the feelings of peace in your mind until the next time you bring your breath to stillness and reenter the space of God.

8. As soon as your breath regains its feelings of comfort, you can repeat the process of prolonging the pause at each end of the breath by balancing the stick and squeezing the balls.

Each time you prolong the pause and enter the space of God, the feelings of stillness and peace will become deeper, stronger, and more firmly established throughout your mind and body. The more peaceful and quiet your mind becomes, the more slowly your breath will move and the longer the pauses will last.

As you enter the early stages of samadhi, your breathing will become so slow and refined that its movement will be nearly imperceptible. At the deeper levels of samadhi consciousness, your breath will stop moving completely. When your breath becomes still, your mind will become equally still and fully immersed in the peace of God.

What to Watch For

When you enter the state of samadhi and your mind becomes filled with the peace of God, this is the point at which you'll tend to blank out because God's peace and bliss are Divine intoxicants that only a highly disciplined mind can imbibe without losing consciousness.

I once read that Josef Stalin respected Winston Churchill more than any other man he knew — not so much because Churchill was an astute politician and a courageous warrior, but mostly because the crusty old British bulldog was the only man who could drink as much vodka as Stalin and still keep his wits about him.

If we want to reap the finest fruits that samadhi can bring, we must follow Churchill's example. This doesn't mean that we should be able to drink as much vodka as he could without passing out; it means that we must learn how to keep our mind sober and clear no matter how much of God's peace we imbibe.

The feelings of peace and bliss that arise in samadhi are two of the greatest rewards to be gained from practicing spiritual disciplines. In fact, some highly accomplished yogis practice retention techniques primarily for the sake of inducing these euphoric feelings. Whenever we enter the state of samadhi, it's perfectly fine to enjoy these God-given feelings. But if we make the mistake of indulging in them, our mind will soon drowse off and go under.

In chapter 18, I pointed out that we can't enter the state of samadhi by forcing our breath to stay still. Samadhi is a gift from God — a state of grace we attract to ourselves by faithfully doing our practices. So as you travel the spiritual path, always remember that self-effort and grace are inseparably linked. The more committed you are to experiencing God, the more of God's grace you'll attract. This is the meaning of the old adage "God helps those who help themselves."

CHAPTER TWENTY

THE GATEWAY
to
CREATION

Within humanity lies the key to the door of creation.

— LAO TZU

CONTEMPORARY PHYSICISTS have fairly well proven that the universe was created by a massive explosion — a cosmic "big bang" — that occurred many billions of years ago. As the energies released by this explosion spread out into space, they began to vibrate at increasingly slower frequencies and eventually "condensed" to become all the forms of matter that exist in the physical world. Since matter consists of condensed vibrations, some physicists describe our universe as being made of "frozen sound."

Thousands of years ago, the Eastern masters came to some remarkably similar conclusions. Like the scientists, they also say that it was created by a cosmic explosion, and that all forms of matter are made of "condensed" or "frozen" sound. There are, however, some extremely important differences in how the spiritual masters and scientists gained their knowledge. The scientists arrived at their conclusions by studying the physical world with the aid of sophisticated laboratory instruments and systems of mathematics. The Eastern masters arrived at essentially the same conclusions by using spiritual practices to study the innermost workings of Godhead.

Within the depths of samadhi, the sages heard hundreds of thousands of mantric sounds emanating from Godhead. They realized that these sounds were the vibrational frequencies of the cosmic energies that create the universe. When they traced these vibrations back to their source, they discovered that all of the different mantric sounds originated in one supreme mantra that had the sound of *Om*.

According to the Eastern masters, Om is the source of all forms of matter and energy that exist in the physical world. When viewed from the perspective of Godhead, Om is the sound Divine Consciousness makes when it begins "moving" to create the universe. When viewed from the perspective of the physical world, Om is the sound of the big bang itself.

As Divine Consciousness emerges from the stillness of Godhead, it begins to vibrate at various frequencies to create everything that exists in the universe, from all the "solid" stuff we can perceive with our physical senses to the subtlest of nuclear energies. Thus, from the point of view of the Eastern masters, Divine Consciousness is both the Creator of the universe and the basic "substance" from which all things are made.

The Opening of the Eye of God

OVER THE CENTURIES, saints and mystics have given Godhead many different poetic names such as "the kingdom of the Heavenly Father" or "the abode of God." But these terms shouldn't be taken too literally, because there is no "father" or "God" in Godhead. Godhead is not a "place" where "the Creator" dwells; it is an infinite field of conscious energy — the energy of pure Divine Consciousness reposing in its own stillness.

God (the Creator) comes into being when Divine Consciousness emerges from the stillness of Godhead and begins to create the universe. The Hindus refer this initial moment of Creation as "the opening of the eye of God," as if God had been asleep within Godhead and were just waking up to create the physical world of time, space, and infinite numbers of separate things.

The Judeo-Christian Bible uses a remarkably similar metaphor to describe the moment in which the universe first came into being. According to Genesis 1:3 (AV), the creation of the universe began at the instant in which God said, "Let there be light." This "light" that God commanded not only refers to the dawn of the first day; it also refers to the dawning of the light of Consciousness. Thus, the Hindu expression "the opening of the eye of God" and the biblical phrase "Let there be light" are remarkably similar metaphors for the instant in which Divine Consciousness "awakens" from its slumber in Godhead and begins to create the universe.

The Gateway to Creation

As DIVINE CONSCIOUSNESS EMERGES from the stillness of Godhead, it crosses a threshold in consciousness that I call "the gateway to Creation." This "gateway" is a neutral zone of consciousness in which the elements of the physical world have not yet taken form. In the *Tao Te Ching*, Lao Tzu calls this neutral zone of consciousness "the door to creation."[1] In another verse of the *Tao Te Ching*, he describes this neutral zone of consciousness as "a preface to nature and a prelude to God"[2] because this is the dimension of consciousness in which God (the Creator) and the physical world are just about to be born.

During the course of their spiritual development, some people have experienced this gateway and watched their universe come into being. Meister Eckhart was referring to this very experience when he said:

> *Prior to creatures, in the eternal now, I have played before the Father in His Eternal stillness.*[3]

Most people who are fortunate enough to have watched their universe being born have found it an ecstatic and awesome experience. For some, however, it can be extremely confusing and frightening because they think they're losing their minds. Some years ago, I happened to meet one such person while returning from a month-long spiritual retreat at an ashram in Ganeshpuri, India.

While sitting in a coffee shop in London's Heathrow airport, I found my attention drawn to a woman (about thirty-eight years old) who was sitting a few tables away from mine. To my surprise, I heard an inner voice say, "Go sit with that woman. She needs your help." My first response was to ignore the voice because I preferred to be by myself. But the voice insisted: "Go sit with that woman!" So with no further resistance, I walked over to her table and introduced myself.

The woman told me that her name was Lindsay. She was an artist who lived in California. As she spoke, I recognized her as one of the people who had also attended the month-long retreat. When I mentioned that she looked a bit troubled, Lindsay replied, "You're right. I'm afraid I'm losing my grip on reality. Whenever I wake up, the world is gone and takes a while to appear. In the meantime, I feel as though I'm living in some sort of vacuum and I keep hearing the sound of 'Ommm.' It's scary to have the world disappear like that. I'm afraid something's going wrong with my mind. Ever since it all began, I've also been getting terrible headaches."

Lindsay was suffering from a headache at that very moment and she gratefully accepted my offer of help to ease her pain. As I expected, her headache disappeared as soon as she let go of some of her fear and allowed herself to relax. I said, "You don't have anything to worry about, Lindsay. You're not getting sick. In fact, you're undergoing a rare and wonderful transition in consciousness because your spiritual practices are beginning to bear some wonderful fruits."

After telling Lindsay a few basic facts about the gateway to Creation, I said, "You're actually having one of the greatest creative experiences an artist can possibly have. The reason you're getting those headaches is that when you get scared of the changes taking place in your consciousness, you create tension and stress throughout your mind and body. As soon as you learn to relax and just flow with these experiences, your headaches will disappear."

On the airplane, I met up with Lindsay again. It turned out that she had been sitting directly in front of me ever since we'd first boarded the plane in Bombay. On the flight back to New York, Lindsay fell asleep for an hour or so. When I noticed that she was beginning to wake up, I tapped her gently on the shoulder.

"How is your headache?" I whispered.

"Fine; it's all gone."

"Has the world come back into focus?"

Her eyes still closed, Lindsay smiled gently and said, "No, not yet. But the engines are making the most glorious sound of 'Oooommm.'"

"Well, I'm jealous. Let me know when the world reappears, will you?"

Judging from the blissful smile on her face, however, Lindsay was obviously enjoying the inner show so much that she was in no hurry to see the world reappear in its usual form.

The Twilight Zone of Consciousness

Everyone is familiar with that brief period when we're neither asleep nor awake, but somewhere in between. For a few confusing moments, we don't know *who* or *where* we are because our mind is in a state of limbo. It is no coincidence that Lindsay watched her world being born during the initial stages of waking up, because "the twilight zone" between waking and sleeping is the same dimension of consciousness as the gateway to Creation. Just as Divine Consciousness moves through a neutral zone of consciousness when it first "wakes up" and begins to create the universe, our mind similarly moves through the twilight zone when it's just waking up to (re)create our personal version of the world.

All creative abilities and miraculous powers originate within this neutral dimension of consciousness where thoughts, images, and physical forms have not yet taken shape in our mind. *The*

Spanda Karikas, one of India's most ancient and sacred texts, speaks of the powers of creation that exist in this twilight zone of consciousness:

> *When sleep has not yet fully appeared and all objects of experience have faded out of sight, the state of the supreme Goddess of Creation will reveal herself.*[4]

The Hindus call this twilight zone the "transcendental state of consciousness" because it transcends — or lies beyond — the ordinary states of waking and sleeping consciousness. In his book *Man's Eternal Quest,* Swami Yogananda refers to the transcendental state as "superconsciousness." He also describes some of the extraordinary powers that exist in this neutral zone between waking up and falling asleep:

> *In the superconscious state, you can see that your body and mind are sleeping and yet have total consciousness of all happenings. I can go into the depths of sleep and enjoy the sleep state and at the same time be with the world. Sometimes I sleep just as the ordinary person does, and again, I can sleep and consciously watch myself sleeping or I can sleep and dream and at the same time also hear everything that is going on around me.... Those who go deep into superconsciousness develop unusual spiritual powers and control over natural forces.... In superconsciousness you can see or know anything you wish to — not by imagination, but in reality. I can sit in this chair and transfer my mind to India and see exactly what is going on in my old home.*[5]

Samadhi, Breath, and Creation

THE GATEWAY TO CREATION has been mentioned by the great masters of all spiritual traditions, although each describes it uniquely. For example, Saint Augustine once spoke of "a heavenly door for the soul into the Divine nature where somethings are reduced to nothing."[6] In the *Tao Te Ching*, Lao Tzu called this heavenly door "the door of creation." The ancient Chinese master of breath even provides us with this cryptic clue as to where the key to this "door" can be found:

> *Can you control your breathing so that it is as soft and gentle as a newborn babe's?*[7]

People who haven't studied the science of breath would never guess that Lao Tzu's door of creation is the breathless state of samadhi. Nor would they guess that the breath holds the key to opening that door.

Whenever we make a transition from being awake to falling asleep (or the other way around), our mind passes through the twilight zone and we have a fleeting experience of samadhi consciousness. Samadhi and the twilight zone are one and the same state of consciousness. The only difference between them lies in their duration. Most of the time, our experience of being in this neutral zone of consciousness is so short-lived that we're not even aware it has happened.

Samadhi, on the other hand, is a much longer-lasting experience that we can learn to cultivate and even control by practicing spiritual disciplines. Anyone who learns how to enter this neutral dimension of consciousness — and stay for a while without blanking out — can study the secrets of Creation and learn to control the shape of events taking place in the physical world.

EMANUEL SWEDENBORG:
SCIENTIST, MYSTIC, AND MASTER OF BREATH

Alfred North Whitehead, the distinguished British mathematician and philosopher, once wrote:

> [God's] creation is a continuous process. . . . Insofar as man partakes of this creative process does he partake of the divine.[8]

Nowhere can this fact be more clearly seen than in the life of Emanuel Swedenborg (1688–1774), an incredibly gifted genius whose accomplishments as a scientist and inventor rival those of da Vinci, Galileo, and Newton. During the last twenty-seven years of his life, Swedenborg became equally renowned as a great mystic and lover of God whose spiritual attainments easily compare with those of Meister Eckhart and Teresa of Avila. What few people seem to realize, however, is that this incredibly gifted genius was the first known master of breath in the history of Western civilization.

The list of Swedenborg's scientific and spiritual accomplishments is much too long to enumerate here. However, the following thumbnail sketch will give you a sense of the incredible scope of his talents and highlight some of the most important milestones in his remarkably long, rich, and often controversial career.

Swedenborg was a distinguished member of the Swedish Parliament who also worked in the Royal Department of Mines as special advisor to the King. However, his expertise extended far beyond the realms of mineralogy and mining engineering. Not only was he well versed in every existing branch of science (from anatomy and paleontology to physics and mathematics), he also made original contributions to knowledge in every one of these fields. Like da Vinci and Galileo, Swedenborg was also an inventor who designed a submarine, a flying machine, a compressed-air machine gun, and many other mechanical devices that he anticipated hundreds of years before their time.

At the age of fifty-five, Swedenborg was stricken with a mysterious illness that plunged him into a state of profound spiritual crisis and forced him to retire from public service for two years. During this time, he had two experiences of communion with Jesus. He also gained the ability to visit other planes of existence to converse with celestial beings, and he acquired a number of psychic powers, such as the gifts of prophecy and clairvoyance.

By the time his "illness" lifted, Emanuel Swedenborg had been miraculously transformed from one of Europe's most distinguished scientists, engineers, and inventors into one of the greatest sages, seers, and mystics the West has ever known.

According to Swedenborg, his spiritual experiences and creative powers originated within a trance-like state of consciousness that he called the "hypnagogic state," which he clearly identified as the twilight zone between waking and sleeping consciousness. Since early childhood, Swedenborg had observed that whenever he entered the hypnagogic state, his breath would stop moving as he made the shift from "external" to "internal" breathing:

> My respiration was so formed by the Lord that I could respire inwardly for a considerable time without the aid of external air... in order that I may be with the spirits and speak with them... I sometimes scarcely breathed by inspiration at all for the space of a short hour.... I was first accustomed thus to respire since early childhood when

saying my morning prayers and occasionally afterwards when exploring the harmonies of the heart and lungs and especially when deeply engaged in writing.[9]

Perhaps the greatest — but least recognized — of all of Swedenborg's accomplishments was his discovery and mastery of some of the deepest secrets of breath control, completely on his own. Even more remarkable is the fact that he did this nearly one hundred years before any Westerner had even heard of the Eastern methods of breath control.

It is highly unlikely that Swedenborg had ever heard of samadhi or the transcendental state of consciousness. Nevertheless, he not only learned that this twilight zone was the source of both his creative powers and spiritual experiences, over the years he even developed his own special set of breathing techniques for bringing his breath to stillness to enter this state at will. By the age of fifty-seven, his mastery of breath was so highly evolved that he lived in a permanent state of sahaja samadhi — the fourth and deepest level of samadhi consciousness.

CHAPTER TWENTY-ONE

THE SACREDNESS
of the
BREATH

Prayer is nothing but inhaling and exhaling the One Breath or Spirit of the universe.

— HILDEGARDE VON BINGEN

THE CONCEPT OF GOD USING HIS BREATH to create the universe can be found in the scriptures and oral teachings of many religious traditions. Another belief that many religions commonly share is that after using his breath to create the physical world, God favored human beings above all other creatures by sharing his breath with them. For example, in Genesis 2:7 (AV), the Bible says that, after fashioning human bodies from the dust of the earth, God used breath to create human souls and bring their bodies to life:

God breathed the breath of life into man's nostrils, and man became a living soul.

Although the connection between our breath and the spiritual life-force is frequently mentioned throughout the Bible, very few Jews or Christians have realized that the breath can be used as a way to enter into communion with God. Over the centuries, a relative handful of Christian monks developed techniques for including the breath as part of their spiritual practices, because they intuitively recognized its direct connection with God.

For example, a fifth-century order of Christian monks known as the Hesychasm used to repeat their prayers in perfect time with the rhythm of their breath. A thirteenth-century monk named Nikophoros the Solitary developed a special meditation technique for guiding his inhalations directly into his heart as a way to experience the bliss of God.

The saints and sages of all religions have regarded the breath as sacred because it is the only thing in the physical world that is directly connected with God. For example, Hildegarde Von Bingen, the great Christian mystic, said:

Prayer is nothing but inhaling and exhaling the One Breath, or Spirit of the universe.[1]

In the *Tao Te Ching*, Lao Tzu makes an extremely similar statement about the breath's connection with Tao:

Tao gives all things life.... Every creature honors Tao [through] its own living and breathing.[2]

So whenever you sit to meditate, set a few minutes aside to honor the sacred bond that exists between your soul, your breath, and God.

Contemplations on the Sacredness of the Breath

EACH OF THE FOLLOWING CONTEMPLATIONS is a form of prayer that will help you cultivate a greater awareness of the presence of God within your breath. After reading the following guiding thoughts, sit in a comfortable posture, get in touch with the flow of your breath, then contemplate the thoughts of your choice and follow them wherever they go. No matter where your thoughts may take you, always remember to keep watching your breath.

CONTEMPLATION #1

The biblical passage that says, "The breath of the Almighty hath given me life" is not just a poetic metaphor; it is a physical matter of fact. So whenever you meditate on your breathing, meditate with the awareness that you're entering into communion with God as the spiritual life-force that dwells in your breath.

CONTEMPLATION #2

The life-force does more than give you the gift of life and heal your mind and body. It is a ray of pure Divine Consciousness that keeps your earthbound soul in constant touch with God. So whenever you practice your breathing techniques (for any reason at all), meditate with the awareness that you are strengthening the sacred bond that exists between your breath, your soul, and God.

CONTEMPLATION #3

Your breath is the best friend you have in the world. No matter how sick or tired you may feel, the spiritual life-force works every second of every day to replenish and heal you in body, mind, and spirit, and it will never stop taking care of you until you take your very last breath. So whenever you're feeling tired, alone, or discouraged, remember the ancient Hindu saying: "God is as close as your very own breath," for God is always with you as the spiritual life-force that dwells in your breath.

Witness Consciousness

"WITNESS CONSCIOUSNESS" is one of the greatest rewards we can gain from practicing spiritual disciplines. It transforms a worried, scattered mind into a calm and powerful ally. It also bestows spiritual powers and perceptive abilities that are beyond the reach of our everyday mind. Just who is the "witness"? The witness is our inner self. It is God in the form of pure disembodied consciousness. Just as Divine Prana is "the Breath of our breath," the witness is "the Mind of our mind" and "the Consciousness of our consciousness."

For example, the witness is the source of the healing powers that dwell in our breath. Whenever we work with the healing triangle technique (chapter 12), the witness is the one who perceives the symptoms of illness and the underground streams of anxiety that are veiled from our everyday mind. The witness is also the Divine part of us that can send concentrated waves of healing Prana to the specific areas of our mind and body that need to be healed.

Witness consciousness occurs naturally as we meditate. As soon as we begin watching our breath, our mind begins to slow down, our body begins to relax, and all sense of effort starts melting away. As our mind becomes increasingly peaceful, it begins to shift into "neutral." Instead of analyzing its experiences, as it usually does in its everyday state, it observes the events in its field of awareness without judgment or expectations.

Nothing in the physical world can touch or affect the witness because it exists in a neutral dimension of consciousness that lies beyond fear, pain, and desire. Great saints and realized beings live in the witness state twenty-four hours a day. Their consciousness is so completely merged with God's that no amount of pleasure or pain can entice them, or force them, to abandon their state.

Great martial artists and warriors have learned how to enter the witness state when their life is in danger or when they're faced with a painful death at the hands of their enemies. The deeper and stronger their state is, the more peaceful, detached, and alert they become. As long as they stay in the witness state, they have no fear, nor do they "mind" feelings of pain as they would in their everyday state of consciousness.

Entering into the witness state is fairly easy to do. Once we're in it, however, it's not so easy to stay there — especially when we're subject to intense feelings of pain, fear, or desire. The story of Samson and Delilah provides a classic example of how desire can cause even the greatest warriors to lose control by abandoning their witness state. Samson was invincible in the midst of a battle, but he lost his state of witness detachment — and thereby lost his strength — by succumbing to the charms of the beautiful Delilah.

WHERE IS THE WITNESS?

EDGAR ALLEN POE ONCE WROTE a story about a politically incriminating letter that was stolen from its owner, then hidden in such an obvious place that no one was able find it. That's just what the witness is like. Whenever we sit to meditate, our mind automatically enters the witness state. Like the purloined letter in Poe's story, the witness exists in such an obvious place that it's extremely easy to overlook it. Where does the witness lie hidden? The witness belongs to the inner dimension of stillness. It exists at the "other" end of your breath.

This next technique — witness consciousness — will help you enter the witness state and study its characteristics. Once you're in witness consciousness, this technique will also teach you how to recognize just "who" and "where" the witness is.

This is how it's done:

1. Sit in a comfortable upright posture and begin to meditate on your breath. Once you're attuned to its movements, do a few rounds of gentle rapid breathing to enliven your breath and make it reasonably open and flowing.

2. As soon as you're breathing more freely, keep watching your breath and become aware of any sounds in your surroundings. For example, you might hear the sound of a passing car, the hum of a fan in your room, or a bird chirping outside your window.

3. Don't "reach out" with your consciousness to gather these sounds to yourself; just keep watching your breath and let the sounds come to you. No matter what these sounds are like — loud, soft, pleasant, or harsh — allow them to reach your consciousness without analyzing, judging, or reacting to them in any way at all.

4. If you keep your attention neutrally poised between watching your breath and listening to the sounds, a peaceful center of consciousness will gradually begin to crystallize within you and you'll feel as if

your consciousness is becoming the very center of the universe.

5. As this center becomes more firmly established, you'll discover that you can be aware of many different sounds at the very same time without shifting your attention from one sound to another — and without losing track of your breath.

6. As your witness state grows deeper, you'll begin to experience a new sense of freedom from any sounds or impressions that enter your field of awareness. For example, you'll find that distracting influences (such as loud noises or uncomfortable feelings in your body) don't bother you nearly as much as they normally would. The deeper and stronger your state is, the more peaceful and detached you'll become.

7. This peaceful, detached state of mind is known as witness consciousness. But just who and where is the witness? The witness is the part of you that is watching your breath and observing the sounds. If you'd like to "see" the witness apart from the events it is observing, this is how you can do it:

8. Once it's easy to notice sounds in the outside world — without losing track of your breath — carefully shift your attention to the part of you that is hearing the sounds and watching your breath. In other words, instead of focusing your attention on the sounds that are entering your field of awareness, become aware of the awareness itself.

9. The part of you that is hearing the sounds and watching your breath is not your everyday mind —

it is the witness. It is God in the "form" of pure dis-embodied consciousness.

What to Watch For

At times, you might become so absorbed in listening to the sounds that you forget about watching your breath. Whenever this happens, just bring your attention back to your breath, then return to the process of allowing the sounds to become part of your meditation.

As you enter the witness state, your breathing will become much more gentle and quiet. When your state becomes deep enough, your breath will slow way down — or completely stop — as it does in the state of samadhi. In fact, witness consciousness and samadhi consciousness are essentially one and the same. The witness is the part of you that stays conscious even after you've entered the depths of samadhi and your breath has completely stopped moving.

Whenever you practice the witness technique, you're not only entering into communion with God in the form of pure consciousness, you're also cultivating the same fearless and detached state of mind that Perseus did by looking into his mirror-like shield while battling with the Medusa. In fact, the Janus technique (described in chapter 9) is another way to cultivate the witness state. The more you practice the witness and Janus techniques, the easier it will be for you to enter the deeper levels of samadhi without having your mind blank out.

If you don't experience the witness as the consciousness that is distinct from the events it is observing, there's no need to worry. As long as your attention is neutrally poised between watching your breath and listening to sounds in the outside world, your consciousness is in the right place.

Witness consciousness is a peaceful, detached, thought-free state in which your everyday mind goes into neutral. So once your mind begins to think again — to analyze, judge, and react — it's a sign that you've lost your neutrality and slipped out of the witness state. Nevertheless, with time and disciplined practice, the feelings of calmness and detachment that you gain from working with this technique will gradually become part of your everyday consciousness.

"I Am" Consciousness

THOUSANDS OF YEARS AGO, the Hindu sages discovered a powerful mantra that lies hidden within the breath. That mantra is *Ham Sah,* which means "I am That" in Sanskrit. Ham Sah (pronounced "hum saah") is the vibration of Prana — the spiritual life-force that dwells in our breath. As we breathe in and out, the Pranic life-force is continually repeating "I am That" with every cycle of breathing.

Meditation on the sound of Ham Sah brings a special experience of union with God that is known as "I am" consciousness. The experience of "I am" is mentioned in the scriptures of most great religions. For example, when Moses stood before the burning bush and asked for God's name, God replied, "Tell your people I am that I am."[3] In effect, God was saying to Moses, "I have no name, I have no form. There is nothing in the world to compare me with. I am simply That which I am."

Another reference to "I am" consciousness can be found in the New Testament, in the passage where Jesus says, "Before Abraham was, I Am."[4] These words may sound puzzling to most people's ears, but Jesus wasn't speaking in riddles; he was simply describing his permanent state of oneness with God.

The message he was trying to convey to his listeners was "I am That which existed even before Abraham was born."

MEDITATION ON THE HAM SAH MANTRA

IN THE HINDU TRADITION, meditation on the Ham Sah mantra is considered to be a complete and self-contained path for attaining the state of union with God. In fact, the repetition of "I am That" as a path to God is an important practice of other great Eastern religions. For example, members of the Sufi tradition repeat the mantra *Anal-Haqq,* which means "I am That" in Arabic. Japanese Buddhists repeat the phrase *Kono Mama* — the Japanese equivalent of Ham Sah and Anal-Haqq.

The Hindu masters call Ham Sah "the techniqueless technique" because it is not a mantra we repeat in our mind or speak with our tongue. It is a sacred sound that we listen for within the movements of our breath. As we breathe in and out, the Pranic life-force spontaneously repeats the syllables "Ham" and "Sah" as a constant reminder that God is closer to us than our very own breath. When working with the Ham Sah mantra, all you have to do is meditate on your breathing and listen for the subtle sounds of Ham and Sah that are implicit in the movements of your breath.

Listening to the sounds of Ham and Sah is a very ancient and powerful meditation technique. The more evenly balanced the breath becomes from working with the basic techniques, the more effective your practice of the Ham Sah mantra will be. At the very least it can quiet our mind and body and fill us with the peace of God. When this practice bears its highest fruits, it can carry us into samadhi and bring the experience of "I am That" — the experience of oneness with God.

This is how meditation on the Ham Sah mantra is done:

1. Sit in a comfortable posture, then close your eyes and begin to meditate on your breath. Once you're attuned to its movements, do a few rounds of gentle rapid breathing to enliven your breath and make it reasonably open and flowing. As soon as your breath is moving more freely, become aware of the sound of your breath as the air enters and leaves your body.

2. If you listen carefully to your inhalations, you'll notice that the inrushing air makes a subtle whispering sound of "huuumm." As you exhale, your breath makes a gentle sighing sound of "saaahh."

3. There is no need to mentally repeat the syllables "Ham" and "Sah" or try to synchronize these sounds with your breathing. The spirit of life that makes your breath move is already "speaking" these sounds with every in- and out-breath. All you have to do is meditate on your breathing and let the mantra repeat itself.

4. As you breathe in, listen for the whispery sound of "huuumm" as the air comes into your body. As you breathe out, listen for the sighing sound of "saaahh" as the air is leaving your body.

5. As you listen to the sounds of "Ham" and "Sah," your mind will gradually begin to quiet down and enter the witness state. As your meditation grows deeper, your breathing will become increasingly gentler, slower, and more peaceful.

6. Along with these changes in breathing, the mantric syllables "huuumm" and "saaahh" will gradually move past the level of physical sound and will begin to feel like a subtle vibration or a mild tingling sensation that lies at the core of your breathing. That

tingling sensation is the vibration of Prana — the breath of God that gives you life and causes your breath to move.

7. When your meditation becomes deep enough, you'll enter the breathless state of samadhi and the physical sounds of "huuumm" and "saaahh" will fade from your consciousness. Instead of appearing as a subtle vibration within your breath, the mantra will assume the form of an even subtler vibration that arises from the innermost core of your being.

8. When your physical breath stops moving, it signifies that you've made a transition from outer to inner breathing. This means that you are now breathing directly with God's own breath because your consciousness has merged with the spirit of life that dwells within the sushumna — the central column of golden light that is the core of your subtle body.

9. When your consciousness merges with God's own breath, your sense of being a finite creature will disappear. In its place will be the experience of "I am That" — the experience of oneness with God.

CHAPTER TWENTY-TWO

THE PATH
of the
BREATH

HUMAN BEINGS CREATE RELIGIONS because their souls have a deep yearning to become reunited with God. This desire to become reunited with the Creator is woven into the very fabric of human language. For example, the word *religion* comes from the Latin *religare*, which means "to tie together again." The Sanskrit word *yoga* means "to yoke together." Thus, the words *religion* and *yoga* have the very same meaning. Both refer to the process of reuniting our souls with the Divine force that created us.

The word *yoga* is often translated as "path" or "way" because all religions are like pathways that lead to the house of God. Of the countless ways human beings have created for reaching God's house, the path of the breath is one of the simplest, most ancient, and most powerful of all. According to the Eastern sages, who masters the forces that dwell in their breath can even become immortal. To quote the Taoist masters:

> *If one knows a method to nourish the breath he is able to become immortal.*[1]

> *By carefully and constantly controlling the breath, one will naturally become divine.*[2]

The breathing techniques taught in this book comprise just such a method for "nourishing" your breath and learning to control its movements. As they strengthen and balance your breathing, they're also preparing your mind and body to experience the Divine within. As your in- and out-breaths become more evenly matched, the pause that occurs at each end of the breath will begin to shrink and become more like a pivot point. Instead of pausing briefly at the turnaround points, your breath will pivot in such a way that it enters and leaves your body with little or no break in its flow. As the turnaround points become more evenly matched, it will become increasingly easy to gently suspend your breathing and enter the space of God at will.

Every technique in this book is a way of entering into communion with God. For example, whenever you meditate on your breathing, you're entering into communion with God as the spiritual life-force that dwells in your breath. When you use your breath for healing your mind and body, your connection with the spirit of life becomes even deeper and stronger. When your mastery of breath becomes great enough, you'll enter the state of samadhi and have the experience of oneness with God.

Breathing with God's Own Breath

WHEN YOU ENTER THE STATE OF SAMADHI and your physical breath stops moving, it signifies that your consciousness has merged with God's and you're breathing directly with God's own breath. This experience brings the realization that there is no difference between you and God because you are made of the same primordial "substance" as the Divine force that created you. When your meditations become deep enough, you'll enter the state of sahaja samadhi. Sahaja samadhi is the highest goal of all spiritual endeavors because it brings the experience of unity consciousness — the experience of being as one with God and all created things.

Whenever we enter the breathless state, God, our soul, and the life-force are in such a perfect state of attunement that all three become as one. This state of triadic union between God, our soul, and the life-force is the basis of immortality. However, the occasional experiences of union with God that we get from practicing spiritual disciplines do not guarantee that we will someday become immortal. Immortality is a prize that is granted only to those highly gifted and extremely persistent people who have learned to keep their consciousness in an unbroken state of union with God's twenty-four hours a day.

Those who have mastered this state can keep their consciousness perfectly poised on the "dividing line" between Godhead and Creation. This state of conscious equipoise between inner and outer reality enables them to live in both dimensions at once. They can enter the depths of samadhi without losing track of the physical world, or return to work in the outside world and still be in samadhi consciousness. It takes tremendous amounts of discipline to enter the state of sahaja samadhi and never leave it again. Fully enlightened and God-realized beings are the only people who have mastered this task.

Enlightenment and God-Realization

ENLIGHTENMENT AND GOD-REALIZATION are essentially one and the same state of consciousness. The main difference between them is that those who have become God-realized tend to focus their attention on God "the Creator" — or Divine Consciousness in its moving aspect. Enlightened beings, on the other hand, tend to focus their attention on the stillness of Godhead, or Divine Consciousness in its resting phase.

Thus, when Jesus preached to the multitudes, he urged his followers to be as perfect as the "Father" who lives in heaven. In marked contrast, Buddha preferred to teach in silence. On those rare occasions when he spoke to his monks, he urged them to attain *nirvana* — the state in which one's mind becomes perfectly still and one's consciousness merges with the "great emptiness" of Godhead. Despite their different predilections, however, Jesus and Buddha shared the same profoundly peaceful and compassionate state of consciousness that is characteristic of all perfected beings.

Becoming fully enlightened is something like trying to climb Mount Everest. It's such a difficult and demanding task that very few people who try it make it all the way to the top. In order to become fully enlightened, we must completely transcend our sense of fear. This means that we must cleanse our system of every last ounce of fear that's been trapped in our subtle body and become so free of our fear-based view of reality that we never create fear in our mind again. This is by no means an easy task for anyone to accomplish.

The good news, however, is that we needn't be fully enlightened to enter into communion with God or live a life that is filled with genuine peace and contentment. There are many degrees of enlightened consciousness. The better we handle our sense of fear, the more peaceful and quiet our mind will become, and the more we'll experience the presence of God in all our daily activities.

The Path of the Breath

THE SAGES AND SAINTS OF ALL RELIGIONS AGREE that there is but one Divine force that creates the universe. Most of them call this force God. No matter what name they give it — Yahweh, Allah, Brahman, Tao — they also agree that the Divine force that gives us life is manifest in our breath. Regardless of how different the various religions appear to be, every religion begins and ends on the path of the breath because the breath is the only thing in the physical world that is directly connected with God. If it weren't for the spirit of life that causes our breath to move, there would be neither souls nor religions nor the precious gifts of life and consciousness with which to worship God.

The path of the breath is one of the simplest, fastest, and most powerful ways for attaining the state of enlightenment or uniting our soul with God because all experiences of pain and fear are directly controlled by the breath. The more we use the breath to quiet our mind or cleanse the layers of fear we've trapped in our subtle body, we "enlighten" our consciousness and the closer we grow to God.

The freer we become of our sense of fear, the more we begin to realize that despite their overt differences, the people of all races, nations, and religious traditions belong to the same human family. In truth, we are closer than biological brothers and sisters because at the very core of our being all of us share the same breath of Divinity. In light of this understanding, I'd like to end by invoking the prayers and blessings with which this book began:

May the knowledge of breath contained in this book
bring greater health and inner peace
to everyone who reads it.

May the spiritual knowledge this book offers bring greater
respect and understanding among the people
of all nations and all religious traditions.

NOTES

Note for biblical citations: Only two versions of the Bible have been cited in this book. In the text and in the notes, when the Authorized (King James) Version is cited, it is abbreviated AV, and when the New American Bible is cited, it is abbreviated NAB.

Chapter One

1   Robert Bly, *The Kabir Book* (Boston: Beacon Press, 1977), 33.

2   Jane Huang and Michael Wurmbrand, *The Primordial Breath: An Ancient Chinese Way of Prolonging Life through Breath Control* (Torrance, Calif.: Original Books, 1987), vol. 2:211.

3   Ibid., vol. 1:17.

4   Jay Ramsay, *The Illustrated Tao Te Ching* (London: Element, 1993), 37.

5   Genesis 1:2 (AV).

6   Exodus 14:21 (NAB).

7   Exodus 15:8–10 (NAB).

8   Job 33:4 (AV).

9   Luke 24:46 (AV).

10   John 20:22 (NAB).

Chapter Two

1   Jane Huang and Michael Wurmbrand, *The Primordial Breath: An Ancient Chinese Way of Prolonging Life through Breath Control,* (Torrance, Calif.: Original Books, 1987), vol. 1:106–7.

2   Ibid., vol. 1:75.

3   Ibid., vol. 2:26.

4   Ibid., vol. 2:43.

5   Ibid., vol. 2:55.

6   Ibid., vol. 1:75.

7   Ibid., vol. 1:18.

Chapter Three

Epigraph: As a follower of Swami Muktananda, I heard him say this many times in lectures.

Chapter Four

Epigraph: Jane Huang and Michael Wurmbrand, *The Primordial Breath: An Ancient Chinese Way of Prolonging Life through Breath Control* (Torrance, Calif.: Original Books, 1987), vol. 1:106–7.

1   Ibid., vol. 2:79.

2   Ibid., vol. 1:107.

3   Paramahansa Yogananda, *Man's Eternal Quest* (Los Angeles: Self-Realization Fellowship, 1982), 82.

4   George Bennett, ed., *The Heart of Healing: A Handbook of Healing* (Evesham, U.K.: Arthur James Ltd., 1971), 57–60.

Chapter Five

Epigraph: Jane Huang and Michael Wurmbrand, *The Primordial Breath: An Ancient Chinese Way of Prolonging Life through Breath Control* (Torrance, Calif.: Original Books, 1987), vol. 2:79.

1   Ibid., vol. 2:87.

Chapter Six

Epigraph: Frank J. MacHovek, *The Book of Tao* (White Plains, N.Y.: Peter Pauper Press, 1962), 5.

1   Ibid., 7.
2   Psalms 23:4 (AV).

Chapter Seven

1   Jane Huang and Michael Wurmbrand, *The Primordial Breath: An Ancient Chinese Way of Prolonging Life through Breath Control* (Torrance, Calif.: Original Books, 1987), vol. 2:249.

Chapter Eight

Epigraph: Jane Huang and Michael Wurmbrand, *The Primordial Breath: An Ancient Chinese Way of Prolonging Life through Breath Control* (Torrance, Calif.: Original Books, 1987), vol. 2:109.

1   Ibid., vol. 1:39.

Chapter Eleven

Epigraph: Paramahansa Yogananda, *Man's Eternal Quest* (Los Angeles: Self-Realization Fellowship, 1982), 263.

1   Ibid., 261–62.
2   1 Corinthians 15:44 (NAB).
3   Matthew 17:2 (AV).
4   Richard Gerber, *Vibrational Medicine: New Choices for Healing Ourselves* (Santa Fe: Bear & Company, 1988), 65.
5   Ibid.
6   Ibid., 95.
7   Ibid., 65.

Chapter Twelve

Epigraph: Jane Huang and Michael Wurmbrand, *The Primordial Breath: An Ancient Chinese Way of Prolonging Life through Breath Control* (Torrance, Calif.: Original Books, 1987), vol. 2:38.

1   Ibid., vol. 1:96.
2   Ibid., vol. 2:45.

Chapter Thirteen

Epigraph: Jane Huang and Michael Wurmbrand, *The Primordial Breath: An Ancient Chinese Way of Prolonging Life through Breath Control* (Torrance, Calif.: Original Books, 1987), vol. 2:151.

Chapter Fourteen

Epigraph: Swami Muktananda, *In the Company of a Siddha* (South Fallsburg, N.Y.: The SYDA Foundation, 1985), 64.

Chapter Fifteen

Epigraph: Irene Ringawa, "It's All in the Breath," *Darshan Magazine* 72 (1993): 6.
1   Ibid., 6.
2   Mark Twain, *The Tragedy of Pudd'nhead Wilson* (New York: Penguin Putnam, 1994).

Chapter Sixteen

Epigraph: Jane Huang and Michael Wurmbrand, *The Primordial Breath: An Ancient Chinese Way of Prolonging Life through Breath Control* (Torrance, Calif.: Original Books, 1987), vol. 2:213.
1   Matthew 25:40 (AV).

Chapter Seventeen

Epigraph: Jay Ramsay, *The Illustrated Tao Te Ching* (London: Element, 1993), 37.

1   Garma C. Chang, trans., *The Six Yogas of Naropa: Teachings on Mahamudra* (Ithaca, N.Y.: Snow Lion Publications, 1963), 78–79.

2   Kieran Kavanaugh, *The Collected Works of St. Teresa of Avila* (Washington, D.C.: ICS Publications, 1987), 174.

3   Ibid.

4   Jane Huang and Michael Wurmbrand, *The Primordial Breath: An Ancient Chinese Way of Prolonging Life through Breath Control* (Torrance, Calif.: Original Books, 1987), vol. 2:214.

5   Ibid., vol. 2:212.

6   Ibid., vol. 1:55.

Chapter Eighteen

Epigraph: Swami Venkatesananda, *The Concise Yoga Vashishtha* (Albany, N.Y.: State University of New York Press, 1984), 285.

1   Raymond B. Blakney, trans., *Meister Eckhart: A Modern Translation* (New York: Harper & Row, 1941), 134, 243.

2   Swami Anantananda, "Unexpected Joy," *Darshan Magazine,* 36, (1990), 11.

3   Psalms 46:10 (AV).

4   Cathleen Medwick, *Teresa of Avila: The Progress of a Soul* (New York: Knopf, 1999), 107–8.

5   Paramahansa Yogananda, *Man's Eternal Quest* (Los Angeles: Self-Realization Fellowship, 1982), 107–8.

6   Ibid., 161.

Chapter Nineteen

Epigraph: Jaideva Singh, trans., *Vijnana Bhairava: Divine Consciousness: A Treasury of 112 Types of Yoga* (Delhi: Motilal Benarsidass Publishers, 1979), 22.

1   Jane Huang and Michael Wurmbrand, *The Primordial Breath: An Ancient Chinese Way of Prolonging Life through Breath Control* (Torrance, Calif.: Original Books, 1987), vol. 2:19–20.

Chapter Twenty

Epigraph: Frank J. MacHovek, trans., *The Book of Tao* (White Plains, N.Y.: Peter Pauper Press, 1962), 5.

1   Ibid.

2   Ibid., 7.

3   Daisetz Teitaro Suzuki, *Mysticism, Christian and Buddhist* (London: Ruskin House, George Allen and Unwin, Ltd., 1979), 12.

4   Jaideva Singh, trans., *Spanda Karikas: The Divine Creative Pulsation* (Delhi: Motilal Benarsidass Publishers, 1980), 131.

5   Paramahansa Yogananda, *Man's Eternal Quest* (Los Angeles: Self-Realization Fellowship, 1982), 162–63.

6   Suzuki, 11.

7   MacHovek, 28.

8   Lucien Price, *The Dialogues of Alfred North Whitehead as Recorded by Lucien Price* (Boston: Little, Brown & Co., 1954), 366.

9   Signe Toksvig, *Emanuel Swedenborg: Scientist and Mystic* (New York: The Swedenborg Foundation, 1983), 218.

Chapter Twenty-One

Epigraph: Michael Slater, "Three Extraordinary Lives," *Darshan Magazine* 89 (1994): 20.

1   Ibid.

2   Jonathan Star, trans., *Tao Te Ching: The Definitive Edition* (New York: Penguin Putnam, 2001), 64.

3   Exodus 3:14 (AV).

4   John 8:58 (AV).

Chapter Twenty-Two

1   Jane Huang and Michael Wurmbrand, *The Primordial Breath: An Ancient Chinese Way of Prolonging Life through Breath Control* (Torrance, Calif.: Original Books, Inc., 1987) vol. 1:101.

2   Ibid., vol. 2:222.

BIBLIOGRAPHY

Avalon, Arthur. *The Serpent Power: The Secrets of Tantric and Shakti Yoga.* New York: Dover Publications, 1974.

Bennett, Bija. *Breathing into Life: Recovering Wholeness through Body, Mind & Breath.* New York: HarperCollins, 1993.

Bennett, George, ed. *The Heart of Healing: A Handbook of Healing.* Evesham, U.K.: Arthur James Ltd., 1971.

Besant, Annie. *Man and His Bodies.* London: Theosophical Publishing House, 1975.

Blakney, Raymond B. *Meister Eckhart: A Modern Translation.* New York: Harper & Row, 1941.

Bly, Robert. *The Kabir Book.* Boston: Beacon Press, 1977.

Borysenko, Joan. *Seven Paths to God: The Ways of a Mystic.* Carlsbad, Calif.: Hay House, 1997.

Capra, Fritjof. *The Tao of Physics.* New York: Bantam Books, 1977.

Captchuk, Ted, and Michael Croucher. *The Healing Arts: Exploring the Medical Ways of the World.* New York: Summit Books, 1987.

Chang, Garma C., trans. *The Six Yogas of Naropa: Teachings on Mahamudra.* Ithaca, N.Y.: Snow Lion Publications, 1963.

Chopra, Deepak. *How to Know God: The Soul's Journey into the Mystery of Mysteries.* New York: Harmony Books, 2000.

————. *Perfect Health: The Complete Mind/Body Guide.* New York: Bantam Books, 1991.

————. *Quantum Healing: Exploring the Frontiers of Mind/Body Medicine.* New York: Bantam Books, 1989.

————. *Return of the Rishi: A Doctor's Search for the Ultimate Healer.* Boston: Houghton Mifflin, 1988.

Dossey, Larry, M.D. *Healing Words: The Power of Prayer and the Practice of Medicine.* New York: HarperCollins, 1993.

————. *Reinventing Medicine: Beyond Mind-Body Healing to a New Era of Healing.* San Francisco: HarperSanFrancisco, 1999.

Dyer, Wayne. *Wisdom of the Ages: Sixty Days to Enlightenment.* New York: HarperCollins, 1998.

Einstein, Albert. *Ideas and Opinions.* New York: Crown Publishers, 1954.

Emerson, Ralph Waldo. *The Essential Writings of Ralph Waldo Emerson.* New York: Random House, 2000.

Gerber, Richard. *Vibrational Medicine: New Choices for Healing Ourselves.* Santa Fe: Bear & Company, 1988.

Hamilton, Edith. *Mythology: Timeless Tales of Gods and Heroes.* New York: Meridian Books, 1969.

Huang, Jane, and Michael Wurmbrand. *The Primordial Breath: An Ancient Chinese Way of Prolonging Life through Breath Control,* vols. 1 and 2. Torrance, Calif.: Original Books, 1987.

Iyengar, B. K. S. *Light on Pranayama: The Yogic Art of Breathing.* New York: Crossroad Publishing Company, 1992.

Kavanaugh, Kieran, and Rodriguez Otilio. *The Collected Works of Saint Teresa of Avila,* vol. 1. Washington, D.C.: ICS Publications, 1987.

Kohn, Sherab Chodzin. *The Awakened One: A Life of Buddha.* Boston: Shambhala Books, 1994.

MacHovek, Frank J. *The Book of Tao.* White Plains, N.Y.: Peter Pauper Press, 1962.

Marshall, George N. *Buddha: His Quest for Serenity.* Rochester, Vt.: Schenkman Books, 1978.

Medwick, Cathleen. *Teresa of Avila: The Progress of a Soul.* New York: Knopf, 1999.

Merton, Thomas. *The Way of Chung Tzu.* Boston: Shambhala Books, 1965.

Moyers, Bill. *Healing and the Mind.* New York: Doubleday Books, 1995.

Muktananda, Swami. *In the Company of a Siddha*. South Fallsburg, N.Y.: The SYDA Foundation, 1985.

Neihardt, John G., and Black Elk. *Black Elk Speaks: Being the Life Story of a Holy Man of the Oglala Sioux*. Lincoln, Neb.: University of Nebraska Press, 1992.

Powell, A. E. *The Astral Body*. Wheaton, Ill.: The Theosophical Publishing House, 1972.

———. *The Etheric Double: The Health Aura of Man*. London: The Theosophical Publishing House, 1969.

Price, Lucien. *The Dialogues of Alfred North Whitehead as Recorded by Lucien Price*. Boston: Little, Brown & Co., 1954.

Ramsay, Jay. *The Illustrated Tao Te Ching*. London: Element, 1993.

Schweitzer, Albert. *Out of My Life and Thought: An Autobiography*. New York: Holt, Rinehart & Winston, 1933.

Siegel, Bernie S. *Love, Medicine and Miracles*. New York: Harper & Row, 1988.

Singh, Jaideva, trans. *Spanda Karikas: The Divine Creative Pulsation*. Delhi: Motilal Benarsidass Publishers, 1980.

———. *Vijnana Bhairava: Divine Consciousness: A Treasury of 112 Types of Yoga*. Delhi: Motilal Benarsidass Publishers, 1979.

Smith, Huston. *The Religions of Man*. New York: Harper & Row, 1958.

Star, Jonathan, trans. *Tao Te Ching: The Definitive Edition*. New York: Penguin Putnam, 2001.

Steward-Wallace, John, and Swami Ghanananda. *Women Saints of East and West*. Hollywood, Calif.: Vedanta Press, 1979.

Suzuki, Daisetzu T. *Mysticism, Christian and Buddhist*. London: Ruskin House, George Allen and Unwin, Ltd., 1979.

Toksvig, Signe. *Emanuel Swedenborg: Scientist and Mystic*. New York: The Swedenborg Foundation, 1983.

Twain, Mark. *The Tragedy of Pudd'nhead Wilson*. New York: Penguin Putnam, 1994.

Venkatesananda, Swami. *The Concise Yoga Vashishtha*. Albany, N.Y.: State University of New York Press, 1984.

Yogananda, Paramahansa. *Man's Eternal Quest*. Los Angeles: Self-Realization Fellowship, 1982.

RECOMMENDED READING

Books on Spirituality and Religion
by Contemporary Masters

Chidvilasananda, Swami. *Inner Treasures*. South Fallsburg, N.Y.: SYDA Foundation, 1995.

———. *My Lord Loves a Pure Heart: The Yoga of Divine Virtues*. South Fallsburg, N.Y.: SYDA Foundation, 1994.

———. *The Union of Bliss and Emptiness*. Ithaca, N.Y.: Snow Lion Publications, 1988.

———. *The Yoga of Discipline*. South Fallsburg, N.Y.: SYDA Foundation, 1995.

Dalai Lama. *Ethics for the New Millennium*. New York: Riverhead Books, 1999.

Hanh, Thich Nhat. *Breathe! You Are Alive*. Berkeley: Parallax Press, 1988.

———. *Going Home: Jesus and Buddha as Brothers*. New York: Riverhead Books, 1999.

———. *The Miracle of Mindfulness: A Manual on Meditation*. Boston: Beacon Press, 1976.

Kapleau, Philip. *The Three Pillars of Zen*. New York: Anchor Books, 1980.

Muktananda, Swami. *I Have Become Alive: Secrets of the Inner Journey*. South Fallsburg, N.Y.: SYDA Foundation, 1994.

———. *Meditate*. Albany, N.Y.: State University of New York Press, 1980.

———. *The Play of Consciousness: A Spiritual Autobiography.* South Fallsburg, N.Y.: SYDA Foundation, 1985.

———. *Sadgurunath Maharaj Ki Jay.* South Fallsburg, N.Y.: SYDA Foundation, 1979.

———. *Satsang with Baba,* vol. 4. South Fallsburg, N.Y.: SYDA Foundation, 1978.

Yogananda, Paramahansa. *Autobiography of a Yogi.* Los Angeles: Self-Realization Fellowship, 1977.

English Translations of Eastern Scriptures and Yogic Texts

Buck, William. *The Ramayana.* Berkeley and Los Angeles: University of California Press, 1976.

Burtt, E. A. *The Teachings of the Compassionate Buddha.* New York: Mentor Books, 1955.

Dyczkowski, Mark S. *The Aphorisms of Shiva.* Albany, N.Y.: State University of New York Press, 1992.

Feng, Gia-Fu, and Jane English. *The Tao Te Ching.* New York: Vintage Books, 1989.

Hariharananda, Aranya Swami. *Yoga Philosophy of Patanjali.* Albany, N.Y.: State University of New York Press, 1981.

Johari, Harish. *Breath, Mind, and Consciousness.* Rochester, Vt.: Destiny Books, 1989.

Mair, Victor H. *The Tao Te Ching.* New York: Bantam Books, 1990.

Mascaro, Juan. *The Dhammapada.* New York: Penguin Books, 1973.

Muller-Ortega, Paul. *The Triadic Heart of Siva.* Albany, N.Y.: State University of New York Press, 1989.

Prabhavananda, Swami, and Christopher Isherwood. *Bhagavad-Gita: The Song of God.* New York: Mentor Books, 1961.

———. *The Crest-Jewel of Discrimination: Viveka-Chudamani.* Hollywood, Calif.: Vedanta Press, 1978.

Prabhavananda, Swami, and Fredrick Manchester. *The Upanishads: Breath of the Eternal.* New York: Mentor Books, 1964.

Singh, Jaideva. *The Doctrine of Recognition: Pratyabhijnahrdyam.* Albany, N.Y.: State University of New York Press, 1990.

————. *Shiva Sutras: The Yoga of Supreme Identity.* Delhi: Motilal Benarsidass Publishers, 1990.

————. *Spanda Karikas: The Divine Creative Pulsation.* Delhi: Motilal
Benarsidass Publishers, 1980.

Subramanium, Kamala. *The Mahabharata.* Bombay: Bharatiya Vidya Bha-
van, 1983.

*Zen Buddhism: An Introduction to Zen with Stories, Parables and Koan Rid-
dles.* White Plains, N.Y.: Peter Pauper Press, 1959.

ACKNOWLEDGMENTS

I WOULD LIKE TO EXTEND MY SPECIAL THANKS to Paramahansa Yogananda and the Self-Realization Fellowship. All of the quotes from Swami Yogananda that appear in this book were taken from two of his books, *Autobiography of a Yogi* and *Man's Eternal Quest,* both published by the Self-Realization Fellowship. Yogananda's books provide many fascinating glimpses and illuminating insights into the nature of spiritual reality, as well as some remarkable first-hand descriptions of living in a permanent state of oneness with God.

I would also like to thank Jane Huang and Michael Wurmbrand, authors of *The Primordial Breath*: *An Ancient Chinese Way of Prolonging Life through Breath Control,* published by Original Books, Inc. Most of the Taoist quotes I use in this book come from these two insightful and helpful translations of ancient Chinese treatises on Taoist methods of breath control.

I would also like to extend special thanks to the SYDA Foundation, publishers of *Darshan Magazine. Darsham Magazine* is a virtual treasure house of inspiring stories and teachings from the lives of great saints and enlightened beings of all cultures and religious traditions. It also contains a wealth of practical information concerning the nature of spiritual evolution and the inner processes we undergo during our development as spiritual beings. Although it is now out of print, back issues of *Darsham* can be obtained by contacting the SYDA Foundation, South Fallsburg, NY, 12779.

I'd like to give special thanks to Georgia Hughes, editorial director of New World Library. Georgia's many insightful suggestions helped greatly, to clarify and simplify the materials contained in this book.

INDEX

Page references in italics refer to illustrations.

A

accidents, 50–51
acupuncture, 52, 146
Adam, 12
adrenaline, 74–75
AIDS, 48
alcoholism, 185
allergies, 43–44, 48–49, 165–66
aloha (may God be with you), 8
alveoli, 100–101
Anal-Haqq mantra (I am that), 278
anger, 182, 184–87, 204, 212–13
angina, 89
angina pectoris, 77
animals healed by pranic energy, 215–18
Ann (a client), 50–51, 149
antibiotics, 48
anu (human soul), 5
anxiety
    angina pectoris, 77
    during asthma attacks, 100, 103
    attacks of, 61
    blocking, 97–98, 105

    from blocks in breathing, 43, 52–53, 83, 181
    controlling, 179–80
    drugs for, 179
    vs. excitement, 199–200
    vs. fear, 76–78, 118, 119–20 (*see also* fear)
    from over-releasing, 22
    sobbing during release of, 67–68
    Sufi parable about, 170–71
    Tarzan technique for dispelling, 60
    See also emotional healing
apathy, 98, 106
arrhythmia (irregular heartbeat), 22, 89
asthma, 42, 43–44, 66, 99–100, 103, 171–76
astral body, 137
athletes, 79, 92, 200
audiotapes on breathing techniques, xvii
Augustine, Saint, 227, 264
auras, 137, 144

Autobiography of a Yogi (Yogananda), 81, 226
autoimmunity, 49–50
Ayurveda, 146

B

Baba, Ghanda, 226
balancing techniques, 97–114
  and breathing disorders, 99–102, 103
  correcting the pause, 104–9
  and emotional roller coasters, 98–99
  gentling the in-breath, 103–4, 174
  over-releasing counteracted by, 22
  overview/benefits of, 19–20, 97–98, 102–3, 114
  perfecting balance of tensions, 113–14
  strengthening the out-breath, 109–14, 174–75
balancing the stick, 246–49, 252
bastrikha. See gentle rapid breathing
Becker, Robert, 144–45
Bell's palsy, 44, 212–13
Bergson, Henri, 12–13
Bernard, Claude, 47
Betty (a client), 213–14
bhandas (locks), 245
big bang, 257
biochemistry, 178–80
bioelectrics, 145–46
biomagnetic energy fields, 143–45
bipolar disorder, 98
bliss, 234–35, 255
blocks in breathing, 16–17, 18
blocks in breathing, and illness, 41–54
  allergies/autoimmunity, 48–50
  breath as key to healing, 51–54
  and fear, 43–44
  and medical thinking, xviii
  meditation for healing, 52–53

  overview, 41–43
  pranic energy healing, 44–46
  self-conflict and accidents/injuries, 50–51
  self-conflict and infectious diseases, 46–48
  and the Tarzan technique, 62, 64
  Yogananda on, 42
Bodhidharma, 224
body
  astral, 137
  causal, 138, *139*
  chemistry of, 178–80
  emotional, 138, *139*
  etheric (*see* invisible man)
  mental, 138, *139*
  physical (natural), 136, 138
  subtle (spiritual), 136–38, *139*, 179
Brahman (Godhead), 222
  See also Godhead
Brahmin priests, 8
brain vs. mind, 147–48
breath control. *See* science of breath control
breathing disorders, 61, 85, 99–102, 103
  See also specific disorders
breathing techniques,
  studying/practicing approaches, xvi–xvii
breathless state. *See* samadhi
breath of Creation, 221–29
Breath of Life (spiritual life-force; Breath of God), xii, 3–14
  as a Divine ray, 4
  elan vital, 12–13
  New Testament references, 11–12
  Old Testament references, 9–11
  overview, xi–xiii
  vs. physical breath, 4, 6–9, 13
  pneuma, 6–7, 9, 11–13
  ruah Yahweh, 9–11, 12–13

Western conceptions, 12–14
    See also *Prana*
Brett (a psychiatrist and client),
    68–69
bronchial dilators, 161, 172
Buddha
    arrow story, 190–91
    in concentration pose, 31
    meditating on his breathing,
        13–14
    on mindfulness of breathing,
        xiii, 63
    miraculous powers of, 223–24
    silent teaching of, 284
Burr, Harold, 143–44

C

calmness, 64, 65, 67, 69
candida, 48
canoe analogy (staying balanced),
    34–36
cardiac problems, 61, 89, 92, 95
Carol (a client), 180
causal body, 138, 139
CDs on breathing techniques, xvii
chakras (part of the etheric body),
    140, *141*
Chi (spiritual life-force), xii, 6, 42, 52
    See also pranic energy healing
Chi Kung, 240
chin mudra (hand position), 31, *31*
Christian tradition, 11–12
chronic fatigue syndrome, 47
chronic obstructive pulmonary dis-
    order (COPD), 43–44, 103
Churchill, Winston, 255
cigarette smoking, 43–44, 100
communion with God, 232–34,
    282–83, 285
concentration pose, *30*, 30–31
congestion, 165–66
conspirator/conspiracy, 208
control of the breath. *See* science of
    breath control
COPD (chronic obstructive pul-

monary disorder), 43–44, 103
courage, 60, 64, 78–81
Crazy Horse, 75
Creation, breath of, 221–29
Creation, gateway to, 257–67
    Om, 258
    opening of the eye of God, 259
    overview, 257–58, 259–62
    and samadhi, 264–67
    and Swedenborg, 265–67
    twilight zone of consciousness,
        262–63, 264, 267
curanderos (folk healers), 209

D

Damon (a client), 210
Dan (a client), 143
danger consciousness, 74–76
death, fear of, 79, 80–81
decongestants, 161, 172
depression, 42, 43, 47, 98, 105–6, 179
detachment, 115–27, 276
    and fear vs. anxiety, 118, 119–20
    Janus technique, 120–22, 127,
        203
    and the lion and the monkey,
        126–27
    overview/benefits, 115–16, 127
    slaying the Medusa, 118–19
    and tides of fear, 116–17
    Tippy technique, 119–20,
        122–27, 176, 203
determination, 60, 64
Diane (a client), 101–2
discouragement, 98
diseases, 46–48
    See also blocks in breathing,
        and illness; healing
dismay, 98
Divine communion, 232–34, 282–83,
    285
Divine Consciousness, 4, 5–6,
    222–23, 232, 240, 258, 284
dizziness, 22
Delores (a client), 186–87

Don Juan, 137
Dumo (Buddhist breath control), 16, 224–25
Dune (Herbert), 73–74, 78

E

Eckhart, Meister, 222, 233
ecstasy, 234–35
Egyptians, 8–9
elan vital (spirit in breath), 12–13
electricities, spiritual, 140, *141*, 142
Elisha, 11
Elizabeth (a client), 158
Embryonic Breathing, 15–16
　　See also science of breath control
emotional body, 138, *139*
emotional healing, 189–205
　　anxiety vs. excitement, 199–200
　　breaking free of unruly thoughts, 201–5
　　calming a troubled mind, 193–95
　　healing disturbed emotions, 197–99
　　making friends with troubled feelings, 195–97
　　overview, 189–90
　　recalling/reenacting past experiences, 191–93
emotional roller coasters, 98–99
emotions, 177–87
　　anger, 182, 184–87
　　and body chemistry, 178–80
　　mistrust of, 183–84
　　negativity, neurosis, and evil, 183–85
　　overview, 177–78
　　primary vs. secondary, 183
　　and the subconscious mind, 180–82
　　See also anxiety; emotional healing; fear
emphysema, 43–44, 99–102, 103
The Empire Strikes Back, 81

energy fields, biomagnetic, 143–45
enlightenment, 238–39, 284–85
entrainment, 207–8
environmental illness, 49
environmental pollutants, 43–44, 48–49, 100
etheric double/body. *See* invisible man
evil, 184
excitement vs. anxiety, 199–200
exercises
　　balancing the stick, 246–49, 252
　　breaking free of unruly thoughts, 201–5
　　calming a troubled mind, 193–95
　　correcting the pause, 104–9
　　gentle rapid breathing *(bastrikha)*, 23, 57, 61, 63–69, 86, 111–12, 157, 173
　　gentling the in-breath, 103–4, 174
　　Ham Sah mantra meditation, 278–80
　　healing disturbed emotions, 197–99
　　healing triangle, 153–57, 161–65, 175, 197–99
　　"I am" consciousness, 277–78
　　Janus technique, 120–22, 127, 203
　　meditation on the breath, 31–33, 35–36
　　meditation on the heartbeat, 89–91
　　posture, 29–30, 30
　　prolonging the space of God, 246, 252–55
　　relaxing the throat, 168–70, 174
　　solidifying technique, 84–89, 166–68, 172, 202
　　solidifying the breath, 246, 249–52
　　staying balanced (canoe analogy), 35–36
　　strengthening the heart, 92–95

strengthening the out-breath, 109–14, 174–75
Tarzan technique, 57–63, 64, 68–69, 86, 111–12, 173
Tippy technique, 119–20, 122–27, 127, 176, 203
witness consciousness, 18, 52, 272–77
exhalations/inhalations, 91, 97
See also balancing techniques
expire (breathe out; die), 7–8

F

fatigue, 47
fear, 73–82
vs. anxiety, 76–78, 118, 119–20 (*see also* anxiety)
and blocks/illness, 43–44
as danger consciousness, 74–76
of death, 79, 80–81
and emotional healing (*see* emotional healing)
and greatness of spirit, 79–81
in heros/heroines, 77
mastering via the breath's powers, 23
overview, 73–74
as a primary emotion, 183
repressed, 97–98, 102, 142–43, 182–83 (*see also* balancing techniques)
self-mastery over, 81–82, 117
and strength/courage, 78–81
subconscious, 148–49
of suffocation, 159, 165, 176
tides of, 116–17
See also emotions
feelings. *See* emotional healing; emotions
field of human consciousness, 137
See also invisible man
folk healers, 209
fountain of love, 158
Fred (a client), 214–15
Freud, Sigmund, 180–81

frogs, 144–45
frustration, 183, 204

G

Gandhi, Mahatma, 80
gastrointestinal disorders, 42
gazing techniques, 120
Genesis (Bible), 9–10, 12, 259, 269–70
gentle rapid breathing *(bastrikha)*, 23, 57, 61, 63–69, 86, 111–12, 157, 173
gentling the in-breath, 103–4, 174
Gerber, Richard, 145
Ghanda Baba, 226
God, 233
breathing with God's own breath, 283–84
meditation on the space of, 239–43
prolonging the space of, 246, 252–55
See also Divine Consciousness; sacredness of the breath
"God bless you!", 8
Godhead, 221–23, 232, 240, 258, 284
See also Creation, gateway to
God-realization, 238–39, 284–85
gorillas, 57–58, 60
Gospels (Bible), 11
grace, 255
Great Depression, 73, 77–78, 184
greatness of spirit, 79–81
See also courage
grief, 196–99
grounding/strengthening techniques, 83–95
meditation on the heartbeat, 89–91
overview/benefits of, 19, 83–84
solidifying technique, 84–89, 166–68, 172, 202
strengthening the heart, 92–95
guilt, 185

H

Ha (God; breath), 8
habits, 205
Hagios Pneuma (Holy Spirit; Holy
  Ghost), 11–12
hallucinations, 106
halos, 137, 138
Ham Sah mantra (I am that),
  277–80
hand positions, 30–31, *30–31,* 84
  See also solidifying technique
hatha yoga, 240
Hawaiian greeting ritual, 8
healing
    basic/advanced techniques,
      generally, 24–25
    breath as key to, 51–54
    gentle rapid breathing, 64 (*see
      also* gentle rapid breathing)
    the healing triangle, 151–58, 153,
      161–65, 175, 197–99
    meditation for, 27–28, 52–53
    miraculous powers of, 227–29
    overview, 23–24
    pranic energy, 44–46
    ragas for, 146
    via samadhi, 238–39
    shamanic, 146
    Tarzan technique, 60–61 (*see
      also* Tarzan technique)
    and transformation, 238–39
    vibrational, 145–46
    See also emotional healing;
      pranic energy healing; respi-
      ratory disorders, healing
heart attacks, 92
heartbeat meditation, 89–91
heart problems. *See* cardiac problems
heart strengthening, 92–95
helplessness, 98
Herbert, Frank
    Dune, 73–74, 78
heroism and fear, 77
Hesychasm, 270

Hildegarde von Bingen, 269, 270
Hindus. *See Prana*
Hitler, Adolf, 184
HIV, 48
Holy Spirit/Ghost, xii, 11–12, 82
hostility, 184
Hsuen, T'ung, 228
human energy field, 137
    See also invisible man
hypertension, 61
hyperventilation, 22

I

"I am" consciousness, 277–78
illness. *See* blocks in breathing, and
    illness; healing; *specific disorders*
immortality, 282, 283
inadequacy, 60, 185
infectious diseases, 46–48
injuries, 50–51
inner vs. outer breath, 6
in-/out-breaths (inhalations/exhala-
    tions), 91, 97
    See also balancing techniques
insomnia, 105
invisibility, 225, 226
invisible demon, 170–71
invisible man, 135–49
    biomagnetic energy fields,
      143–45
    causal body, 138, *139*
    emotional body, 138, *139*
    etheric double/body, 137–38,
      139
    mental body, 138, *139*
    mind vs. matter/brain, 147–48
    overview, 135–37
    phantom limbs, 142–43
    physical (natural) body, 136, 138
    spiritual electricities, 140, *141,*
      142
    subconscious fear in, 148–49
    subtle (spiritual) body, 136–38,
      139, 179
    vibrational healing, 145–46

J

Janus technique, 120–22, 127, 203
jealousy, 201–2
Jesus, 11–12, 137, 218, 277–78, 284
Jewish tradition, 9–11
Job (Bible), 11
John (Bible), 11–12
joy, 183

K

Kabir, 5
kapalabhati, 23
Karen (a client), 45–46, 148, 210
Kono Mama mantra (I am that), 278
koshas (sheaths), 137, *139*
kumbhak (pauses at the end of the breath), 240

L

Lao Tzu
    on conquering oneself, 73
    on creation, 257, 264
    on keeping breath soft and gentle, 82
    on Tao, 221
    Tao Te Ching, 6, 264, 270
League of Nations, 184
lethargy, 98, 106
letting go, 22
levitation, 225, 226–27
Lindsay (a client), 260–62
lions vs. monkeys, 126–27
Lotte (a client), 98–99
love, 182, 183
LSD, 239
lupus, 49–50

M

magnetic-field therapy, 145
Maharishi Mahesh Yogi, 225
manic/depressive behavior, 98

manifesting breath (out-breath), 109
    See also balancing techniques
Man's Eternal Quest (Yogananda), 237–38, 263
mantras, 28
Master Great Nothing of Sung Shan, 151
medical treatment, xviii
meditation on the breath, 27–39
    Buddha on, 13–14
    with closed/open eyes, 39
    distractions, 34–36, 39
    healing via, 52–53
    importance, 18–19
    instructions, 31–33, 35–36
    meditative consciousness, 33–36, 157, 192–93 (*see also* samadhi)
    Muktananda on, 27, 28
    overview/benefits of, 27–28, 33, 37–39, 83
    posture/hand positions, 29–31, *30–31*
    practice schedule, 37–39, 61, 66–68
    respiratory disorders healed using, 160–61
    See also exercises
meditation on the heartbeat, 89–91
meditation on the space of God, 239–43
Medusa, 118–19, 276
menstrual periods, 47
mental body, 138, *139*
Michael (a client), 212
microorganisms, 47
mind, 147–48, 180–82
mindfulness of breathing, xiii, 63
miraculous powers, 223–29
mood-altering drugs, 179
Moses, 10, 277
Mother Nature, 41, 51–52
    See also Prana
mudra (yogic hand position), 84
    See also solidifying technique

Muktananda, Swami, 27, 28, 177
muscle spasms, 22
muscle tension, 84

N

nadis (part of the etheric body), 140
Nazis, 184
neuromuscular problems, 211–14
neurosis, 183–84
    See also anxiety
neurotic thoughts, 201–5
New Testament, 11–12
Nikophoros the Solitary, 270
nimilena samadhi (introvertive
    samadhi), 235–36
nirvikalpa samadhi (thought-free
    samadhi), 236
nirvythana samadhi (extrovertive
    samadhi), 236–37

O

obsessive-compulsive behavior/feel-
    ings, 43, 185, 201–2
Old Testament, 9–11
Om, 258
one hand clapping, sound of,
    233–34
organ transplants, 142
Original Breathing, 15–16
    See also science of breath
        control
Orpheus, 119–20
Orr, Bobby, 200
out-/in-breaths (exhalations/inhala-
    tions), 91, 97
    See also balancing techniques
over-releasing, 22

P

pain
    chronic, healed by pranic
        energy, 209–11
    repressed, 97–98, 142–43

panic attacks, 61, 89, 105
panicky feelings, 22, 78
panting, 65
    See also gentle rapid breathing
Paramahansa Yogananda, 42, 135–36,
    242
paranoia, 43, 184, 201–2
passivity, 97–98
Pasteur, Louis, 47
Patanjali, 233
    Yoga Sutras, 225–26
path of the breath, 281–86
Paul, Saint, 232
pausing at the end of the out-
    breath, 104–9
peace of God, 232, 233, 255
    See also samadhi
Pepe (an animal client), 216–18
perfected masters, 239
Perseus, 118–19, 276
peyote, 239
phantom leaf effect, 144
phantom limbs, 142–43
physical activity, 204
physical (natural) body, 136, 138
pneuma (life-force), 6–7, 9, 11–13
Poe, Edgar Allen, 272
pollutants, 43–44, 48–49, 100
post-traumatic stress disorder, 204
posture/hand positions, 29–31,
    30–31, 84
    See also exercises; solidifying
        technique
power of suggestion, 215–18
Pradipika, Hatha Yoga, 189
Prana (spiritual life-force)
    and Egyptian beliefs, 8–9
    healing power of, 51–52
    Hindu tradition, xii, 4–6
    and illness, 42
    Prana Yoga, 15
    and samadhi, 20–21
    See also pranic energy healing
pranic energy healing, 44–46,
    207–18

of animals, 215–18
of chronic pain, 209–11
entrainment, 207–8
of neuromuscular problems,
    211–14
overview/benefits of, 207–9
as the power of suggestion,
    215–18
Primordial Breathing, 15–16
    See also science of breath
    control
prolonging the space of God, 246,
    252–55
psilocybin, 239
psychosis, 42, 48, 179, 185–87
psychosomatic illnesses, 211–12
pulse reading, 146

R

ragas, 146
Reich, Wilhelm, 52
relaxing the throat, 168–70, 174
release techniques, 55–69
    blocks dispersed by, 22, 54
    gentle rapid breathing *(bas-
        trikha)*, 23, 57, 61, 63–69, 86,
        111–12, 157, 173
    over-releasing, 22
    overview/benefits of, 19, 55–57, 83
    Tarzan technique, 57–63, 64,
        68–69, 86, 111–12, 173
religions, 281–82
    See also specific religions
resentment, 183
resources, xvii
respiratory disorders. *See* breathing
    disorders
respiratory disorders, healing,
    159–76
    asthma, 171–76
    the healing triangle, 161–65, 175
    and the invisible demon, 170–71
    medications, 161, 172
    meditation, 160–61
    overview, 159–60

relaxing the throat, 168–70, 174
sinus congestion, 165–66
solidifying technique, 166–68,
    172
respiratory technique, 52
respire (breathe), 7
Resurrection, 12
retention techniques
    balancing the stick, 246–49, 252
    overview/benefits of, 20–21,
        245–46
    prolonging the space of God,
        246, 252–55
    and samadhi, 20–21, 34, 245
    solidifying the breath, 246,
        249–52
retreats on breathing techniques,
    xvii
Roman Catholic Church, 11–12
Roosevelt, Franklin D., 73, 77–78
ruah (spirit; breath; wind), 9
ruah Yahweh (spirit of God; breath
    of God; wind of God), 9–11, 12–13
Russell, Bertrand, 147

S

sacredness of the breath, 269–80
    contemplations on, 271–72
    Ham Sah mantra meditation,
        278–80
    "I am" consciousness, 277–78
    overview, 269–70
    witness consciousness, 18, 52,
        272–77
sadness, 182, 183, 196–97
sahaja samadhi (the great samadhi),
    237–38
saints, 79, 82, 113, 137
salamanders, 144–45
samadhi (the breathless state), 231–43
    bliss of, 234–35
    Divine communion, 232–34
    four stages of, 235–38
    and the gateway to Creation,
        264–67

samadhi *(continued)*,
  healing/transformation, 238–39
  meditation on the space of
    God, 239–43
  overview, 231–32
  and retention techniques,
    20–21, 34, 245
Samson and Delilah, 273
schizophrenia, 185–87, 214
science of breath control, 15–26
  Eastern vs. Western, 21
  five stages of perfecting breath,
    18–21 (*see also* balancing
    techniques; grounding/
    strengthening techniques;
    meditation on the breath;
    release techniques; retention
    techniques)
  fully developed sciences, 21–23
  healing, 23–26
  health of body/breath, 16–17
  and over-releasing, 22
  overview/benefits, 15–17
screaming, 204
Second Council of Constantinople
  (553 A.D.), 12
second wind, 79, 92
self-acceptance, 211
self-confidence, 60, 64
self-conflict
  and accidents/injuries, 50–51
  getting a grip on oneself, 77
  and infectious diseases, 46–48
self-criticism, 185
self-mastery over fear, 81–82, 117
self-pity, 185
shamanic healing, 146
The Shiva Sutras, 223
shortness of breath, 22, 85, 89, 103,
  160, 165
shyness, 60
sinus congestion, 165–66
The Six Yogas of Naropa, 224–25
sleep apnea, 43–44, 99–100, 103
sleeping vs. meditation, 33–34

slow-motion perception, 75–76
smoking, 43–44, 100
sneezing, 8
sobbing effect, 67–68
  See also gentle rapid breathing
Socrates, 79–80
solidifying technique, 84–89,
  166–68, 172, 202
  See also grounding/strengthen-
    ing techniques
solidifying the breath, 246, 249–52
sound of one hand clapping, 233–34
The Spanda Karikas, 262–63
spirit, greatness of, 79–81
  See also courage
spiritual electricities, 140, *141,* 142
spiritual masters, 113
spiritual practices, 226–27, 238–39
spiritus (spirit), 7, 9
Spiritus Sanctus (Holy Spirit), 11–12
Stalin, Josef, 255
stillness, 232, 234, 284
  See also samadhi
strength, 57–58, 64, 78–79
  See also grounding/strengthen-
    ing techniques
strengthening the heart, 92–95
strengthening the out-breath,
  109–14, 174–75
stress, 43, 48, 60, 64
subconscious mind, 180–82
subtle (spiritual) body, 136–38, *139,*
  179
suffocation, fear of, 159, 165, 176
suggestion, power of, 215–18
sumyama (a Hindu technique), 152,
  225–26
Sunyata (Godhead), 222
  See also Godhead
supernatural powers, 223–29
sushumna (part of the etheric
  body), 140, *141,* 235
Swedenborg, Emanuel, 265–67

T

Tai Chi, 240
Tao (Godhead), 221, 222
    See also Godhead
Taoists
    on balancing inhalations/exhalations, 97, 113
    on Chi, 6, 83, 84–85, 91
    on diseases rid by breath energy, 55, 159
    on exercising the breath, 60
    on the healing triangle, 156
    on illness caused by breathing blocks, 42
    on immortality, 282
    on the powers of healing, 227–28
    on restraining the breath, 249
    on science of breath, 15–16, 17
    on teaching healing techniques, 24
Tao Te Ching (Lao Tzu), 6, 264, 270
Tarzan technique, 57–63, 64, 68–69, 86, 111–12, 173
tension, 43
Teresa (a client), 46, 149
Teresa of Avila, Saint, 80–81, 226–27, 234–35
thoughts, unruly, breaking free of, 201–5
"A thousand-mile journey begins with the first step," 26
throat relaxation, 168–70, 174
Tibetan Buddhists, 209, 224
Tippy technique, 119–20, 122–27, 127, 176, 203
Tolstoy, Leo, 3–4
transcendental state of consciousness, 263
transformation, 238–39
trigeminal neuralgia, 44, 212–13
trusting your breath, 129–32
T'ung Hsuen, 228
Twain, Mark, 205

twilight zone of consciousness, 262–63, 264, 267

U

Ueshiba, Morihei, 75–76, 84–85
ultrasound therapy, 145
unity consciousness, 237
The Utmost Secrets of the Methods of Breathing, 6, 227–28

V

vibrational healing, 145–46
The Vijnana Bhairava, 245
vision quests, 232
vitality, 60, 64
the void, 222

W

warriors, 78–79
website for breathing techniques, xvii
Whitehead, Alfred North, 265
wisdom of the breath, 130–32, 157
witness consciousness, 18, 52, 272–77
World War II, 184
worry, 43
worthlessness, 185

Y

Yahweh (God of Israel), 9
yeast infections, 47
yoga, 281–82
Yogananda, Paramahansa, 42, 135–36, 242
    Autobiography of a Yogi, 81, 226
    Man's Eternal Quest, 237–38, 263
Yoga Sutras (Patanjali), 225–26
The Yoga Vashishtha, 193, 231
Yogi, Maharishi Mahesh, 225

Z

Zen Buddhism, 224, 233–34

ABOUT
the
AUTHOR

UNTIL THE EARLY 1970s, Andy Caponigro was a well-known concert guitarist and a faculty member at Boston's
prestigious Berklee College of Music.
Today he is internationally known as a
uniquely gifted healer and as a "master
of breath" who teaches people how to
heal themselves with their breath.

Andy's transition from the world of music into the realms
of healing first began when he realized that his most inspired
musical performances were manifestations of the higher states
of consciousness described by the Eastern spiritual masters. In
search of those higher states, he began to study various kinds of
yogic practices and spiritual disciplines prescribed by the Eastern masters — especially meditation on the breath.

When Andy began working with breathing techniques to
improve his playing, he also taught them to his students to help

them overcome two of their most difficult problems — performance stress and anxiety. To his great surprise, not only did his students begin playing with greater ease and confidence, but also many of their chronic aches and pains rapidly disappeared.

When his students told their friends and families about their healing experiences with Andy, people began calling him for help with a wide range of mental and physical problems. As time went by he became so immersed in his healing work that in 1978 he left his career as a professional musician.

Andy possesses a rare ability to use his breath for healing both himself and others. He also has the more rare ability to awaken the same powers of healing in other people. Andy currently has a private practice and conducts workshops throughout the United States. His workshops and private lessons have provided remarkably effective help for hundreds of people suffering from chronic illnesses and deep-rooted psychological problems that conventional approaches have failed to help.